ROOTS OF CONFRONTATION IN SOUTH ASIA

ROOTS
OF
CONFRONTATION
IN
SOUTH ASIA

Afghanistan, Pakistan, India, and the Superpowers

Stanley Wolpert

New York   Oxford
OXFORD UNIVERSITY PRESS
1982

Copyright © 1982 by Oxford University Press, Inc.

Library of Congress Cataloging in Publication Data

Wolpert, Stanley A., 1927–
Roots of confrontation in South Asia.

Bibliography: p.
Includes index.
1. South Asia—History.   2. South Asia—Foreign
relations.   I. Title.
DS340.W64   954   81-9454
ISBN 0-19-502994-1   AACR2

Printing (last digit): 9 8 7 6 5 4 3 2 1

Printed in the United States of America

092850

for my son
DANIEL
who helped,
with love and admiration

Preface

When I first steamed into Bombay harbor thirty-four years ago, I don't think I had ever heard of Afghanistan or Pakistan. I knew that "millions of children were starving in India," because my mother had often told me that when I failed to finish my food, but I understood little more about the world's second most populous nation. This meant, perhaps, that I was as "well-informed" about South Asia as most Americans. The ensuing three decades, television, two India-Pakistan wars over Kashmir, the birth of Bangladesh, and most recently the Russian invasion of Afghanistan have taught all of us in the United States a great deal more about South Asia than the average American knew in 1948. However, the basic facts of South Asian geo-political, as well as cultural, reality appear to remain almost as remote from modern American consciousness as the vast subcontinent itself.

In this book I have tried to diminish what is perhaps the most dangerous continuing gap in our understanding of our interdependent world by viewing the current superpower confrontation over Afghanistan in the light of South Asia's history. I have few illusions about the impact of history on official policy but persist in believing in the powers of education and truth, and hope that their influence and wider diffusion may help in formulating a peaceful solution to what has become one of our most potentially incendiary global problems.

This work began with a lecture I gave at UCLA one rainy evening in February 1980, on "Afghanistan, Pakistan, India, and the Superpowers.'' It was the eve of my departure for Pakistan to do research on my forthcoming *Life* of that nation's founding father, Mr. Jinnah. Many friends braved the storm to hear what I had to say, and several urged me to develop in written form the story I had outlined of the ''Great Game'' played by Britain and Russia on Afghanistan's high plateau, and how it affected India, and now Pakistan, and ourselves, and the entire world. That ''Game'' continues. We have taken Britain's place in it. Pakistan and India inch closer to atomic arsenals. The stakes grow higher, the risks and dangers magnified accordingly.

I am indebted to so many friends and students for stimulating questions and encouraging remarks that helped to inspire this book that I could not possibly name each of them, but I must mention a few. First let me thank my good editor, Nancy Lane, for having become so excited about the idea of this book and for helping to name it. For my understanding of Afghanistan I am indebted primarily to two old friends and colleagues, who together embrace all of Afghan history and culture, Professors Vartan Gregorian and Ludwig Adamec. By standing on the sturdy scholarly shoulders of these two historians of modern Afghanistan, I have been able to see more clearly the tortuously winding trails of that sad and rugged land beyond the Khyber. I thank you, Vartan and Ludwig, for all you have taught me but absolve you both of any responsibility for this book's conclusions and analysis, which are mine alone.

I can never thank my dear wife, Dorothy, enough for all that she does to help me, but I hope by now that she knows how much I appreciate her labors of love. To our dear sons, Daniel and Adam, and to their generation of young Americans, who must learn to understand and live with South Asia's one-fourth of humankind in this fast-shrinking world of ours, I am truly indebted for the inspiration to write a book that just might help to make this troubled planet of ours a happier place on which to plan for the future.

Los Angeles   S.W.
September 1981

Contents

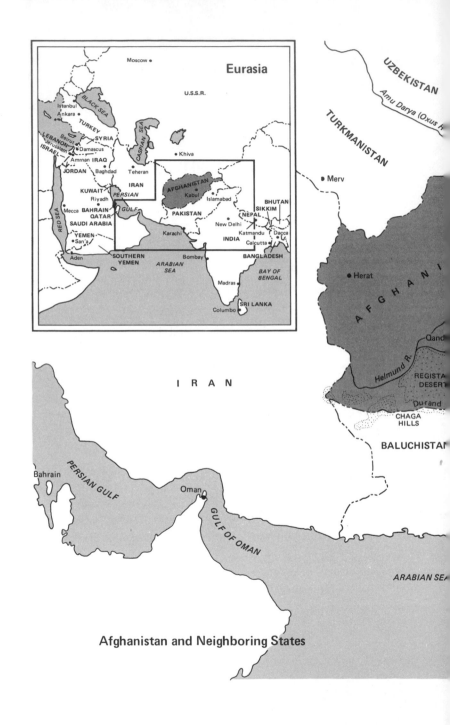

Afghanistan and Neighboring States

ROOTS OF CONFRONTATION IN SOUTH ASIA

ONE

Introduction

Russia's invasion of Afghanistan in December 1979 proved almost as rude a shock in New York and Washington as it did in Kabul and Islamabad. Even casual acquaintance with the map of Asia, if not of its recent history, however, should have helped prepare the West for that most recent advance of the southern glacial edge of Russia's vast empire. For more than a century, Imperial Russia, first in its tsarist, now in its Soviet incarnation has moved with irreversible force farther and farther from its Petersburg-Moscow center of power onto the turbulent frontier sands of predominantly Muslim Central Asia. First the Kazakhs and Kirgiz, next the Turkmens, Tadzhiks, and Uzbeks were each "pacified" and then absorbed into the Union of Soviet Socialist Republics, the latter three sharing a common border of more than 1000 rugged miles with Afghanistan.

Though Afghanistan ("Land of the Afghans")[1] is roughly the size of Texas, its quarter-million square miles of barren, mostly dry terrain barely supports its population of some 18 million on its own meager resources of food. Most Afghans are Pashtu-speaking, orthodox Muslim Pathans,[2] hardy and resourceful tribals, many of whom continue to live as pastoral nomads, guarding their herds of fat-tailed sheep and karakul with rifles they have become adept at using. Land-locked between Russia, Iran, and Pakistan, with a narrow mountainous fuse of land pointed east to China, Afghanistan lies like a timebomb on the rugged plateau overlooking South Asia, which has for more than 3500 years served as a historic springboard for invading hordes.

3

The earliest inhabitants of Afghanistan were, in fact, Indo-Aryan nomads, who wandered from their original homeland in Southern Russia to settle on the Afghan plateau about 1800 B.C. Some of those Aryan tribes were the first known invading conquerors of India several centuries later. They came on horseback and wielded weapons superior to those of the more "civilized" peoples they subdued. Will Russian tanks and gunships follow the same route taken by their ancient ancestors, several years, decades, or centuries from now? Or was this "invasion" really nothing more than mere protection by Russian arms of their "legitimate sphere of interest,"[3] as Soviet leaders have come to think of Afghanistan, especially since the Kabul coup of April 1978 brought the first of a series of pro-Communist regimes to power in Afghanistan's mile-high mesa capital.

The 1978 coup replaced the monarchic "Republic" administration of President Mohammad Daoud (1913–78) with a government led by People's Democratic Party President-Prime Minister Nur Mohammad Taraki (1919–79), whose *Khalq* ("Masses") faction of the PDP was staunchly pro-Moscow. Taraki himself had earlier served as cultural attache in Afghanistan's Washington Embassy and worked for the U.S. Agency for International Development (AID) mission in Kabul.[4] Taraki's two deputy prime ministers in 1978 were Hafizullah Amin (1925–79) and Babrak Karmal (b. 1928), the latter soon sent to Czechoslovakia as ambassador and arrested in Kabul after returning there from Moscow a few months later. In September 1979, Prime Minister Amin, a graduate of Columbia University, seized Kabul's presidency after his guard assassinated Taraki, who was accused of working for the Central Intelligence Agency (CIA). Three months later, Amin, accused of working for the same agency, was also shot dead in his Kabul palace, this time by the guard that hailed Afghanistan's new savior, Babrak Karmal, who rode home on Boxing Day escorted by Russian MIGs, tanks, and helicopter gunships. Leader of his PDP's smaller *Parcham* ("Flag") faction, Prime Minister Karmal insists he invited Soviet troops to Kabul to save his country from imminent collapse in the face of increasingly militant and victorious Muslim *Mujaheedin* ("Freedom Fighter") forces, who were preparing a massive assault on Kabul with "CIA support" on the eve of the Soviet interdiction.

Whether it is termed "aggressive invasion" or "protective interdiction," however, the reality of the Soviet presence is not altered. Some 80,000 troops of the regular Soviet Army, roughly "ten division equivalents: seven motorized rifle divisions, two composite airborne divisions, and four independent motorized rifle regiments,"[5] have moved south of the Oxus (Amu Darya) River to establish themselves firmly, apparently permanently, in Afghanistan. It is a formidable new reality, indeed, one that has cost the Russians an estimated 1500 mortal casualties in their first year of occupation alone, and the less well-armed and organized Muslim *Mujaheedin* doggedly pitted against them, at least twice as many dead or seriously wounded. By 1981, more than 60 of Russia's rocket armed MIG-19s and MIG-23s were, moreover, based at Afghanistan's Qandahar airport, "poised only 650 miles from Persian Gulf shipping lanes."[6]

In response to Russia's lightning advance toward the West's oil lifelines from the Persian Gulf and across the Indian Ocean, the United States has moved, less dramatically but with almost equal martial muscle, into a region that has hitherto received a surprisingly low priority of interest or attention from either State Department, Pentagon, or White House planners. Within six months of Russia's invasion of Afghanistan, however, the U.S. naval presence in the Persian Gulf-Indian Ocean area had increased from one seaplane tender and a rotating half-dozen other small units to a nuclear-missile-armed fleet of some thirty-five ships of the line, including two giant aircraft carriers. The atoll Diego Garcia, leased by Washington from Great Britain for fifty years, has, moreover, become the entire U.S. fleet's supercarrier service-and-communications base in the middle of the Indian Ocean, more than a thousand miles south of the southern tip of India. Several hundred million dollars have been spent in a top-priority Pentagon program to expand port facilities as well as jet runways on that island, now equipped with the world's most sophisticated radar and electronic monitoring devices. The Joint Chiefs have also authorized creation and training of a 100,000-man Rapid Deployment Force of U.S. soldiers, paratroopers, and marines, who could be based within easy striking range of the Gulf and moved swiftly enough to check any possible Russian drive toward Arab oilfields.

Washington recognized, of course, that a continuing Russian presence in Afghanistan not only posed a potential threat to Persian Gulf oil and shipping, but presented the chilling prospect of further Soviet advances to the south and east. Afghanistan's immediate neighbor in both those vital directions is Pakistan ("Land of the Pure"), another Muslim nation, 310,000 square miles in size, but far more fecund and easily capable of supporting its population of some 80 million, mostly Punjabis and Sindhis, though over six million are Pashtu-speaking Pathans and almost a million Baluchis. Naïvely, the White House tried in February 1980 to purchase Pakistan's promise to stand firm against any tidal wave of Red power that might flood the Khyber and Bolan passes to drown the Indus Valley plain, in return for $400 million worth of military and economic assistance spread over a two-year period. General Zia ul-Haq (b. 1924), Pakistan's president, responded by rejecting such "peanuts," for his Islamabad office was but a day's ride from the Afghan border. Less than two weeks after that offer was made, Soviet MIGs circled for hours with brash impunity well within Pakistan's airspace, immune from the "challenge" posed by outmoded Pakistani F-86 Sabre jets that scrambled to ward off this provocative intrusion. Moscow's message rang loud and clear in the ears of those Pakistanis who watched in helpless apprehension as the refugee tide of Afghans seeking food and shelter across Pakistan's border rose well beyond the million mark and reports of Russian ruthlessness continued to echo on the chill winds that blew across the Khyber.

To the east of Pakistan is India, named for the River Indus, whose waters, ironically, mostly fructify Pakistani soil today. Until 1947 India and Pakistan were both part of the British Indian Empire, a historic anachronism whose faded glory is often recalled with nostalgia by those who remember how forcefully Great Britain used to play the "Great Game" that kept Russia's chessmen north of the Oxus at all times. New Delhi, unlike Islamabad, did not initially view the Russian invasion of Kabul as a threat or menace to its vital interests or ultimate security. In 1971, Prime Minister Indira Gandhi (b. 1917), who was returned to power in January 1980, had concluded a twenty-year Treaty of Peace, Friendship, and Cooperation with the Soviet Union, just prior to engaging Pakistan in the war that brought independent nationhood to its eastern wing, Bangladesh ("Bengali Nation"). During the previous quarter-century, India and Pakistan had fought two bitter undeclared wars over Kashmir, and the residue of Hindu-Muslim conflict that tore the South Asian subcontinent apart with the birth of two nations in 1947 continued to fester, draining the energies and resources, undermining the mutual good will and faith of both peoples.

Is there any policy the United States can pursue, in the critical years and decades ahead, to help secure this vital region against further Soviet aggression without increasing the internal conflicts, fears, and hatreds that have already shattered its integrity and stability? As the world grows technologically smaller and weapons systems become not only more expensive and destructive but too swift, once armed and triggered, to recall or contain, the imperative of increased early-warning awareness of both the policy options still enjoyed and their possible potential implications grows more urgent.

If the past is in fact prologue, any study of future policy options in South Asia must begin with some consideration of that subcontinent's history. Since the history of India[7] alone can be traced back more than 4000 years, no attempt will be made in this short work to explore that vast subject in any comprehensive way, but merely to unearth those important roots of its ancient yet enduring forest of complex culture that help to clarify the dominant ideas, attitudes, fears, and aspirations of its modern heirs. Though Pakistan first emerged as a national entity in 1947, ideologically born out of the relatively recent religious brotherhood inspired by Islam, its geographic roots are as deep as any in all of Indian history. Afghan culture is similarly indebted to that same remarkable mainstream of Arabic thought and faith that has spread throughout the world, as is that of Bangladesh. Afghanistan did not attain independent national identity until the mid-eighteenth century, however, and Bangladesh was born in 1971. An examination of India's cultural roots should therefore be followed by a consideration of Islam's Universal Brotherhood before the more recent history of South Asia's conquest and transformation by the West can be explored as background to the Great Game between Imperial Russia and Britain. The present confrontation in the Indian Ocean is but the most modern and perilous version of that game.

TWO

India's Cultural Roots

Ninety percent of India's approximately 700 million people are Hindus. Hinduism, the world's oldest enduring religion, reflects every major facet of India's 4000-year-old historic tradition. Like the Indian Ocean itself, it has been fed, enriched, fructified, and polluted by countless streams of thought and rivers of customary behavior evolved within the 1.5 million square miles of the South Asian subcontinent, whose littoral extends into the Arabian Sea on the west and the Bay of Bengal on the east.

While non-Hindus usually think of Hinduism as a uniquely integrated way of life most closely connected with a strict social hierarchy called the caste system, Mahatma Gandhi (1869–1948), Hinduism's most famous and saintly practitioner of recent times, defined it as "Cow-worship, neither more nor less." The sacrosanctity of the cow dates back at least 3000 years, and the most ancient scripture of the Hindus, sacred hymnals known as *Vedas* ("Books of Knowledge"), refer to these gentle, lowing creatures as units of currency among the nomadic Aryan tribals, who brought their invaluable herds with them when they invaded and conquered the urban dwellers of the Indus Valley around 1500 B.C. Though Indians have not been the only people to worship their "money," they may well have been the first and have since maintained tender reverence toward the cow and all of its by-products. Devout Hindus not only abjure beef and cow's fat, wear or touch no leather, and drink no cow's milk or curds, but think of cows as dear former relatives and especially on sacred festival days will bring or buy gifts of food to give the sacred cows much in evidence at Hindu temples. One of the continuing causes of Hindu-Muslim conflict and mistrust is rooted in Hindu cow-worship on the one hand and Muslim cow-sacrifice on the other.

Though cows are not the only objects of Hindu worship, their sacrosanctity underscores the central Hindu belief in cycles of human-animal-divine and, indeed, even vegetative-insect continuity in a cosmic scheme that reflects underlying religious law or order called *Dharma*. Moreover, each individual Hindu has his own *dharma,* something of a spark from the cosmic mother-lode, which varies and changes over time, and differs for every "soul," depending on one's birth (*jati*) or class (*varna*). The Portuguese word "caste" really applies to the former more than the latter, but will, for simplicity's sake, be used here in reference to both social stratifications, though there are thousands of Hindu *jati* in modern India and still only four *varna*.

The greatest difference between Hindu beliefs and all Western religious systems is connected to the cyclical transmigration of souls over time (*samsara*) and appears to be one of South Asia's most ancient indigenous concepts, bubbling out of its subtropical jungle soil, so to speak, though it first emerges in the literature of pre-Hindu doctrine in Upanishadic Vedantic texts that date back only to about 800 B.C. What made ancient Indians believe that one life on earth was hardly enough for them? Was it their solution to the universal search for immortality? Or did they feel that some people and certain deeds were so evil as to merit more than a single lifetime of punishment? Whatever the cause, the idea of rebirth and redeath in a cyclical chain extending both backward and forward in time over eons (*kalpas*) became axiomatic to Hinduism, and is intimately associated with other basic Hindu doctrines.

The first of these doctrines, more familiar to Western thought, is the immortality of Soul. Hindu Souls (*Atman*) are viewed as perfect in their pure and "unsnared" pristine immortal condition, but as soon as they are trapped by impure and degrading matter of whatever sort, they must enter life's fray, whether as insects, animals, humans, or gods. What determines each Soul's status and how long it will take for the ultimate goal of "release" from ensnarement (*Moksha*) is each individual's every deed or action (*karma*). The Law of Karma is inextricably associated with that of *Samsara*. When a Hindu body is cremated, its *Atman* is said to rise with the flames that liberate it from the "ensnaring shell" of human form to be reborn either higher or lower on the cosmic ladder of existence, depending on the still unused balance of deeds or actions that must bear fruit in future and similar deeds and actions over as many lifetimes as it takes to use up the entire karmic account.

The ideal goal of a Hindu is, thus, total release or escape from the snares, delusions, pains, suffering, illusions, fears, and ignorance that are thought to be inextricably connected to human name and form. Like all ideal goals, of course, Hinduism's is so elusive that only the rarest of souls will escape the traumas of rebirth in this or a thousand future lives to experience that indefinable *Moksha*, which is most often described as "Not this, not that." That that release rather than Paradise, Immortality, or Happiness is Hinduism's ultimate goal, however, further differentiates it from the Islamic as well as Judeo-Christian traditions of the West. For centuries Western travelers to India have recorded their frustrations at finding Hindus "passive," "slothful," "indifferent," or simply "lacking in action-mindedness," but for a good Hindu *nothing* is more important than to diminish one's karma to the point of ultimate extinction.

Good karma was early perceived to be little better than bad karma by Hindu holy-men and saints, variously called *yogis, sadhus, rishis,* or simply *Brahmans,* the latter also being the name of the highest Hindu caste, whose members were born to preach or teach by chanting the Sacred Utterances of the Vedas. Since every action results in a similar future action, all the reward good behavior can bring to the best of souls is rebirth in the same high caste one enjoyed in this lifetime. Which means more work, the cosmic punishment of having another fifty years or so in which to perform deeds of goodness, consideration, and kindness to the suffering beings with whom one is inevitably thrown into contact in this *maya* world of ignorance and illusion.

Whether such thinking is considered realism, as Hindu philosophers call it, or pessimism, as Western critics believe it to be, the passivity of mind it induces often drives adherents of more self-assertive systems to outrage or exasperation in daily dealings with Hindus. To the West's Faustian Man, always aspiring onward and upward, ready to sell his soul to achieve and amass more of everything material and pleasurable, the yogic withdrawal from life and yearning for that equanimity of mind Hindus call *Shanta-rasa* ("Mode of Peace") is all but incomprehensible. Transcendental Meditation has, of course, become very popular in the West of late, but those few moments of organized *mantra*-contemplation prove so salubrious precisely because they are exceptions to a routine ruled by Rush, Run, Accumulate, and Spend. The "better" the Hindu the less he will value material possessions of any kind, which is why revered *yogis* and *sadhus* sit naked and try to diminish their input of food to nothing, just as they seek to stop breathing and to slow the rate of their pulse, attempting to burn up all residual karma in the divine heat (*tapas*) of their single-pointed concentration.

There is, however, another way of diminishing karma, or at least not accumulating more, which does not require ascetic withdrawal from every sensory outpost of one's body and mind. Indeed, since the dawn of the Christian era, when the *Bhagavad Gita* ("Song of the Blessed One") was completed and inserted into the vast Hindu epic *Mahabharata,* an alternative method of eluding karma was devised, which has since permitted masterful Hindus to enjoy all the activities of this workaday world without fear of suffering prolonged future existence. The *Gita's* method is *Karma-Yoga,* literally the "Discipline of Action," and requires indifference or non-attachment in performing any deed, abstracting ego and emotion from one's behavior at all times, acting only from a sense of duty rather than for personal gratification or aggrandisement or out of passion of any variety. If the doer has no yearning for the "fruit" of his deeds, they will not "cling" to him, and no additional karmic bank-balance accrues for repayment in some future life. One to whom "clods, stones, and gold are one," one who is steadfast in yoga, abandons attachment, and is "even-minded in success and failure," he is a true *Karma-Yogin,* a Hindu fully capable of functioning in the modern world but never entrapped by its seductive lures and delusive snares. This sort of behavior pattern is naturally much closer to Western modes of thought, but seems, nonetheless, cold-blooded, subtle, or, as early British travelers in South Asia often wrote of Hindus they encountered, "serpentine."

The unique longevity of Indian history and the size of its arena have conspired to make Indian society the world's most complex human tapestry. The caste system has contributed more than any other single Indian institution to Hinduism's durability, for it has literally organized and established generally accepted rules for the relatively peaceful coexistence of seemingly incompatible groups of people. Caste has thus proved to be Hindu India's most important asset, but remains one of its greatest liabilities as well, at once weakening, even undermining, the structure it holds together. Throughout its long history, India has been vulnerable to invasions and conquests that might well have been warded off by a more tautly integrated or homogeneous society. To think of Indian history evolving without a caste system, however, is as self-contradictory as to speak of either element without Hinduism.

Perhaps closest to the root cause of the emergence of a social network as hierarchically stratified as India's caste system was small-group fear of extinction, known by the dawn of the Christian era. Indigenous peoples, clans, tribes, greatly extended families throughout South Asia appear very early to have decided that to protect themselves from the twin threats to their survival posed by "pollution" and assimilation from neighboring indigenes or invaders, they had to withdraw behind walls of social isolation. To retain and protect the purity of their blood or traditional beliefs-held-sacred, they resolved never to marry outside the fixed limits of their group, howsoever defined, perhaps because bitter experience had taught them that foreign brides either purposely poisoned or inadvertently "polluted" their husbands with strange foods. Taboos against marriage and eating outside one's group thus emerged as the most powerful and enduring restrictions in the caste system.

There were also work-related taboos. Most castes came to be associated with unique jobs, though these are by no means universally practiced or observed, especially in modern times, when Brahmans often work beside low-caste *Shudras* or Untouchables (now ex-"Untouchables") in factories and offices. Traditionally, of course, Brahmans were expected to chant the sacred mantras and officiate at the many rituals that should fill a Hindu's life from pre-conception to postcremation. *Kshatriyas* ("Warriors"), the second-highest caste class, were expected to fight. Hence, the "Blessed One's Song," Krishna's message to the mighty warrior Arjuna, who loses heart on the eve of his greatest battle when confronting the visages of his cousins and aged teacher in the front ranks of the enemy. A Kshatriya *must* fight, for that is his Duty (*Dharma*) by virtue of birth!

Clearly the most debilitating, at times insidious, aspect of caste is the impersonal way it hierarchically categorizes all Hindus from birth to cremation. Social inequality is the system's most basic premise, and individual talent, genius, ambition, or idiocy really make no difference in the status or personal prospects of individuals who accept the system's fundamental rationale. Since the birth of independent India's Union in 1950 as a secular, democratic republic, all citizens have been promised "social justice" and "equality of status and opportunity" by their constitution, and "Untouchability" has been abolished by law. Social habits, especially those ingrained by religious teaching and generally accepted for millennia, are, however, hard to change by mere edict, slow to be altered in actual practice. Brahmans, therefore, usually continue to behave as "Gods on earth," as they are called in Hindu Legal Text, and if they no longer walk six inches above the common dust of polluting soil, as some ancient texts would have us believe they used to do, they nonetheless receive much of the deference due to their awesome *Atmans* by virtue of the good karma they enjoyed in countless past lives.

Karma's unwritten but pervasively powerful law offers the ultimate

rationalization for a system that might seem monstrously unfair to anyone who had no knowledge of or faith in it. If one accepts the cosmic
justice of Karma's impartial decisions, after all, a person has no one
to blame but himself—or more accurately his past selves—for his current condition. We are what we deserve to be, thanks to the sum total
and balance of all we have done in all of our past lives! The good and
virtuous, the wealthy and wise only enjoy the ripe fruit of their wisdom, virtue, and past generosity. The mean and lowly, the poor, sick,
and lame have ruined themselves, and their only escape from greater
punishment in future lives is to accept, to abide by their karmic fate,
and do their Duty without hesitation or complaint. For one who per-
forms his caste obligations in the uncomplaining spirit of a True One
(*Sati*), even if his lot in life is to sweep dust all day from paths trod
by those born to enjoy higher status, will be rewarded in his next
round of existence by rebirth into a higher caste. Resentment, bitter
feelings, violent behavior, cursing, or rebellion against one's natural
lot might, on the other hand, lead to rebirth as a mosquito!

Hindus are sometimes spoken of as the world's most tolerant people, and such tolerance perhaps is a product of the ideal goal of *Moksha,* with the passivity of mind it helps induce, and of the caste system's dampening impact on jealousies and personal aspirations. There
are, of course, glaring exceptions to these generalizations, as any attempt to sketch a profile for hundreds of millions of human beings will
obviously bring to mind. Still, it seems appropriate to say that by
virtue of their faith in reincarnation, the caste system, the goal of
Moksha, and the Law of Karma, Hindus as a rule are more accepting
of suffering, inequity, hardship, and social injustice than most peoples
the world over. Obliged as they have been to suffer so many climatic,
natural, social, and political ills for so long a time, the "Great Tradition" that evolved in ancient India might almost be viewed as a Brah-
manic religio-philosophic superstructure designed to make many vir-
tues of necessity. Indic civilization grew over too great a span of time,
however, drawing upon too many local traditions for its source material, to be attributed to any single source. And like India's down-
growing banyan trees, its very branches have struck roots in fresh soil,

and those once-tender roots have in turn achieved the girth of mighty trunks long after the earliest trunks of inspiration disintegrated.

Many great heterodox thinkers emerged from ancient India's soil to challenge the less palatable axioms of Brahman supremacy and caste inequality. The most famous and important of these ingenious Indians was Siddhartha Gautama (563–483 B.C.), revered the world over as the *Buddha* ("Enlightened One"). His four Noble Truths and Noble Eightfold Path won tens of thousands of devout disciples to his monastic Order (*Sangha*) during his lifetime in North India, and since his attainment of *Nirvana* (Buddhist *Moksha,* literally the "blowing out," as of a candle's flame), Buddhism has enjoyed many reincarnations in different forms and has been carried from India first to Southeast Asia and Sri Lanka, then to China, Korea, and Japan, and by now to the rest of the world.

Like his contemporary Brahmans, the Buddha viewed life as filled first and foremost, from birth until death, with pain and sorrow. "Suffering" was the first of his noble Truths. To escape suffering, he taught the middle path of celibate restraint, non-possession—making a virtue of poverty—and non-violence (*ahimsa*). The Buddha also taught the "transient" and "soulless" nature of reality, in his latter doctrine departing most radically from orthodox Brahmanism. Later Buddhist schools of the Greater Vehicle (*Mahayana*) introduce cosmic heavens filled with a rich variety of Buddhist gods, but in the earliest records of the Buddha's original teachings he never speculated about what might happen "hereafter," confining his lessons and preaching to the here and now. Born a Kshatriya prince, he rejected Brahman pretentions to primacy of place merely by virtue of birth, arguing that "Only those who behave like Brahmans should be treated as Brahmans!" His Order was free of caste restraints, and before his death, though he was initially reluctant to do so, the Buddha admitted nuns as well as monks to his fold, keeping the sexes strictly separate however. Buddhism denied the sacrosanctity of the Vedas, but treated cows, as it did all sentient life, as too sacred to be harmed in any way. Because of the emphasis placed on *ahimsa* by Buddhism and Jainism, another contemporary heterodox school of North Indian thought, the idea of non-violence has remained a potent theme in Indian history, and an oft-alluded-to aspiration of many Indian leaders from Emperor Ashoka (''Sorrowless''), the greatest of the Mauryans who ruled India in the third century B.C., to Prime Minister Jawaharlal Nehru (1889–1964).

Hinduism's ocean managed neatly to absorb Buddhism, much as it did every other heterodox school of thought in ancient South Asia, adding the Buddha to the tenfold list of Lord Vishnu's "earthly emanations" (*avataras*) sometime early in the Christian era. There are no less than thirty-three gods named in the Vedas, and supposedly 330 million Hindu gods in all. Jainism, in several ways more extreme than Buddhist doctrine, was also to become a Hindu-alternate way of life, and its emphasis on the virtue of fasting unto death, as its founder was said to have done, was revived in recent Indian history by Mahatma Gandhi as one of his most powerful political weapons against British rule. Hindu moderation and tolerance for difference of opinion and the seemingly innate Hindu gentleness of heart and aversion to violence of any sort owe much to the Buddhist-Jain traditions that started in opposition to Brahmanism but have been brought into the Hindu mainstream. Ancient India's first great imperial unification was, in fact, achieved under a Buddhist-Jain dynasty founded by Chandragupta Maurya (reigned 325–301 B.C.), who was said to have joined a Jain monastic order toward the end of his life, and whose remarkable grandson, Ashoka, certainly long believed in and propagated the Buddha's ideas if he did not actually join his *Sangha*. In seeming paradox the great Mauryan dynasty, which ruled most of South Asia for about 140 years (roughly as long as the British would some two millennia later), defending India's frontiers, and securing its borders and shores better than they had been for centuries, was ruled by emperors who believed in non-violence and exalted the "Law of Love" as their highest religion.

Mauryan unification was, however, more the historic offspring of Alexander the Great's (356–23 B.C.) catalytic invasion of India in 326 B.C. than the paradoxical by-product of non-violent Buddhist-Jain thought. Like most of South Asia's subsequent conquerors, Alexander

followed the river Kabul east to its juncture with the Indus, over the
Khyber Pass just north of north latitude 34°. Landi Kotal, headquarters
of the British Empire's famed Khyber Rifles, with its mighty stone
fortress that still stands guard beside this classic gateway to India and
modern Pakistan, was not, of course, erected as yet when Aristotle's
greatest pupil led his 30,000 Macedonian cavalry and Asiatic Greek
foot soldiers down toward the plains of the Punjab ("Land of Five
Rivers"). Neither was Peshawar there, capital of the North-West
Frontier Province, an army city bristling today with soldiers and Pathan tribesmen. Nor was the single-lane suspension bridge of steel that
currently crosses the river Indus at Attock, where the river narrows
after bending sharply and near where Alexander led his army onto
Indian soil, even imagined at that time. Or the crenellated medieval
fortress, manned now by Pakistani troops, whose fire would defend
the Punjab from any future invading force. Once the Indus was
crossed, the plain presented no obstacles for the next fifty miles to the
gates of Taxila, whose Aryan ruler, Ambhi, never thought of attempting to defend his capital against the clearly superior invading force.

What was perhaps more surprising than Ambhi's instant capitula-
tion, however, was his failure to fall back to join forces with his more
powerful neighbor across the river Jhelum to the east, to offer a united
front of Aryan resistance to foreign invasion. Clearly, there was no
unified sentiment, no sense of political brotherhood or national cohe-
sion that inspired the various Aryan tribes, who lived in hostile proximity across the Punjab and never thought of the soil they inhabited as
worthy of waging a common struggle to defend. Indian society at this
time was not only divided into castes but also into competing, conflicting tribes, much as the more remote frontier regions of South Asia
and Afghanistan remain to the present.

Though Raja Ambhi's small army offered no resistance to Alexander's superpower, there were several naked yogis "practicing en-
durance," Alexander was told, outside Ambhi's city wall, oblivious
to its martial conquest. The general sent one of his officers, a disciple
of Diogenes named Onescritus to interview these yogis and learn their
secrets. Strabo reported that first confrontation between East and

West, between Onescritus and the yogis he found seated stark naked on rocks too hot for Greek soldiers to stand upon with bare feet. One of the yogis informed Alexander's lieutenant that no one in heavy armor, bearing weapons of any kind, could learn his wisdom. Another explained that to try to teach his discipline through three interpreters would be like trying to make water flow clear through heavy mud. A third yogi was optimistic enough to try and went back to Taxila with Onescritus.

> This was Calanus, who had insisted that Onescritus should listen naked to his discourses. Calanus returned with the Macedonian army into Persia, where, at Susa, he fell ill . . . mounted the pyre chanting hymns of praise to the Indian gods, and ordered the torch to be applied. As the flames rose around the motionless ascetic Alexander commanded the trumpets to sound and the soldiers to shout their battle-cries in honour of a courage that came not from physical prowess but from spiritual strength.[1]

Raja Puru did muster his elephants and chariots and a vast army of foot soldiers to confront Alexander's undefeated force along the east bank of the river Jhelum in what is now Pakistan's Punjab province. Puru was a mightier and braver king than Ambhi and relied on India's traditional military advantage: a front line of martial elephants, positioned like tanks, with arrow-firing marksmen seated in their lofty howdahs. Puru's infantry, unfortunately for them, were stationed in standard position behind the elephants, who served as natural walls of defense. Alexander, however, was a brilliant adversary and ordered his men to use the one weapon most effective against elephants, fire. Flaming arrows aimed at the elephants' eyes made them turn in terror, stampeding their own army. Alexander's cavalry rounded the flanks to finish off what was left of Puru's crushed and swiftly defeated force. Puru's own life was spared by the wise general, who knew that his humbled opponent would loyally serve him best in effectively governing his own people.

Alexander's army marched on, defeating each of the Aryan rulers who separately sought to resist his advance. The only force that proved mighty enough to stop Alexander's eastern march across South Asia was his own mutinous army. Near the city of Gurdaspur, on the banks of the Beas, the fifth river they reached in what is now India's Punjab, Alexander's soldiers lay down their weapons and struck. They were homesick and as weary of winning as of wandering. After three days of isolated reflection in his tent, Alexander surrendered to the one army capable of defeating him and reluctantly gave the order to turn back and head for home. While waiting on the banks of the Beas he reportedly met a young stripling from farther east, named Sandracottas (since identified as Chandragupta Maurya) who seemed to have caught Alexander's ambition to unify the world. Chandragupta, at any rate, learned the great secret that no Indian raja had appreciated before him, namely that a unified India was impervious to invasion or conquest, but as long as political divisions remained, each of the petty tribes would fall.

Before his death, Chandragupta united all of North India, from his capital home base of Magadha (modern Bihar) in the east to the Khyber, concluding a treaty with Alexander's Bactrian heir, Selucus Nikator, in 305 B.C., which established the Khyber Pass and the Hindu Kush's eastern mountain wall as Mauryan India's western border. Greco-Bactrian rulers remained in command of the Afghan plateau for the next few centuries, until Central Asian invaders deposed them. South Asia's first imperial unification, embracing what is now India, Pakistan, and Bangladesh under Chandragupta's Mauryan successors, continued firm for 140 years. Mauryan emperors claimed their royal share of approximately one-fourth of all crops grown on the subcontinent, and this land revenue, which has always remained South Asia's most important tax, sumptuously supported the royal family and paid for the vast bureaucracy of collectors and clerks as well as the standing army of half a million foot soldiers, some 30,000 cavalry, 9000 war elephants, and several thousand chariots. South Asia's resources were thus used most efficiently to buy the maximum defense capability the subcontinent could muster, which proved more than adequate in maintaining its integrity.

Mauryan rulers were, moreover, shrewdly advised and trained in methods of *realpolitik,* embodied from this era on in classics of Hindu polity, the most famous of which is *Arthashastra ("Science of Material Gain"*). That textbook for princes advises all who aspire to power over others first to conquer the six enemies within themselves: lust, anger, greed, vanity, haughtiness, and exuberance. Indian monarchs were also advised always to employ many spies, indispensable news-gatherers in history's pre-modern-media age, to keep themselves informed of the "joy or distress," "loyalty or treachery" of queens, ministers, soldiers, and common subjects. A fascinating general theory of international relations is expounded in this ancient text, which antedates Machiavelli's *The Prince* by about 1800 years. The *Mandala* ("Circle") theory sets the Mauryan emperor at the center of the innermost of twelve concentric circles. The ruler of the circle closest to the central one is identified as the Enemy, while the monarch in the next circle is called the Friend. In the next circle is the Enemy's Friend, while the prince beyond is called the Friend's Friend, etc. Remoteness imparts special status, however, for the rulers of the two outermost rings are called respectively, the Intermediate King and the Neutral King.

Unfortunately for South Asia, interludes of imperial unification, like the Mauryan, were few and relatively brief exceptions to prolonged eras of internal fragmentation and quasi-feudal conflict that have plagued almost numberless dynasties of princely states, petty or powerful. The lessons taught by Alexander to Chandragupta Maurya were soon forgotten, and caste or tribal differences, regional jealousies, linguistic barriers to communication, and racial fears and hatreds conspired to weaken and divide a subcontinent whose size, wealth, and vast population alone should have ensured its security against external attack from any quarter. Instead, as the Mauryan monarchy weakened and covetously competing royal claimants subverted the authority of the court, pitting jealous rival factions against one another, pretentious bickering spread to the provinces and left frontier defenses to rust and tarnish. Local governors and generals squabbled amongst themselves, while merchants and peasants stopped paying their shares of wealth to the greedy agents of competing claimants, most of whom lacked the authority or power to enforce their exorbitant demands. There were, of course, always "barbarians" waiting at the high and barren passes, lured by the lush wealth of the civilized plains, eager to take advantage of every moment of weakness.

Greco-Bactrians were first to march as the ramparts of Mauryan might crumbled. Once the Punjab was taken, it was not to be restored to indigenous Indian control for more than five centuries. Their armies were followed by Pahlava Persians, who had heard tales of India's fabled "golden sands," first reported by Herodotus, who had written of "giant gold-digging ants" racing back and forth across the Punjab, filling their sacks with the precious metal! From Central Asia came the Shakas (Scythians), followed by even fiercer Kushanas. Wave after wave of these wild men, with no visible eyes and little neck to separate their heads from broad shoulders, cut through the Indus plains as fast as their tough horses could gallop, while the rest of South Asia withdrew behind regional, caste, and local linguistic walls that turned the once-united subcontinent back into a mottled patchwork of fearful remote feudatories.

Ancient India's second imperial unification was not effected until A.D. 320, when Chandra Gupta I reunited the North and established a line of mighty Hindu Kshatriyas strong and wise enough to keep the subcontinent together for a century. The Guptan Dynasty nominally survived another century and a half, until the full force of Central Asia's Hunas (Huns) dealt it a death blow. For South Asia, the fourth century of classical Hindu India's Golden Age of unification more than amply attested to the rewards and value of unity, proving indeed the most prosperous and artistically creative era as well as the strongest and most stable since the peak of Mauryan glory six centuries earlier. The court of Chandra Gupta II (reigned 375–415) was immortalized by poet-playwright Kalidasa, author of the matchless *Shakuntala* (*"Birds"*), whose few surviving classical Sanskrit works offer, like the glorious fragments of fresco glimpsed on the cave walls and ceilings of Ajanta, such magnificent and beautiful insights into the age of Guptan glory that it is easy to understand why so many barbaric hordes were tempted to hurl themselves at its glittering gates—until they were torn down by the forces of Toramana and Mihiragula in the sixth century. It marked the end not only of Guptan glory but of Hindu India's final unification as an independent civilization. Never again would the "White Umbrella" of a single Hindu or Buddhist Universal Emperor (*Chakravartin*) stretch its protective fabric over the kite-shaped four corners of South Asia's subcontinent.

THREE

Islam's Universal Brotherhood

Islam, which means "Submission" to the will of Allah, was born with the flight (*hijrat*) of the Prophet Muhammad (580–632) from his home in Arabia's Mecca to Medina in A.D. 622. In less than a century Islam spread with inspired militant ferocity westward, across all of North Africa and into Spain, and to the east as far as India, where its first beachhead was established in what is now Pakistan's southern province of Sind in A.D. 711. Never before, nor since, has any religious faith moved with such dazzling speed to capture the nominal allegiance, if not the hearts and minds, of so many millions of diverse peoples. There are now no less than 800 million Muslims in the world and at least 37 nation-states that adhere to a major form of Islam.

Islam, like Hinduism, is far more than a religion. Its unique historic spread and continuing impact can only be understood in light of its multifaceted, all-pervasive appeal, social, political, economic as well as ideological. The sacred *Qur'an* (*"Recitations"*), embodying the "Revealed Words" of God as heard by the Prophet when conveyed to him by the archangel Gabriel, is but part of the comprehensive faith that guides, inspires, dictates, and controls every path of action, every course of behavior, every major aspiration and ultimate goal of a true Muslim—one who adheres to and lives by the code of Islam.

Muhammad's own behavior provides precept to all Muslims who, by adhering to the traditions (*Hadith*) of everything he said and did,

literally seek to follow his "trodden path" (*Sunnah*), for such is the
path of righteous action in submission to God's will. Orthodox Muslims should, therefore, walk "energetically" and with "a purposeful
goal" in mind when they set out on a journey, for such was the
Prophet's mode of walking. They should never laugh "overmuch,"
for too much laughter "kills the mind," or such was the Prophet's
belief. The central tenet, the Credo of Islam, is the sincere affirmation
that "There is but one God, Allah, and Muhammad is His Prophet."
That alone suffices to make one a Muslim, part of the Brotherhood,
the Universal Community (*Umma*), joined in awesome submission to
"The One God," a Transcendent Being whose nine and ninety "most
beautiful" names include The Compassionate One, Creator, Lord of
Judgment, The Merciful, Keeper, Hearer, Seer, Pardoner, Guide.

Contrast this simplicity, this unity, this universality of God and
human brotherhood at the heart and core of Islam with the pantheon,
pluralistic divisiveness, and hierarchic relativity inherent in Hinduism.
The centrality and undeviating insistence upon the all-pervasive mon-
otheistic power of God in Islam is what gave the Muslim nation its
cohesive vitality and social strength. Not that Islam was to remain
totally orthodox, for a deep and enduring schism soon cut into the
heart of the *Umma*, luring a large minority of Muslims to the path of
Shi'ite heterodoxy as faithful followers of the murdered fourth Caliph
Ali (*c*.600–661), Muhammad's son-in-law, and his martyred heirs.
Since the sixteenth century, moreover, Iran has adopted Shi'ism as its
national faith, and between 10 and 20 percent of South Asia's Muslim
population belongs to one or another Shi'ite sect.

Sunni orthodoxy was, however, to remain the cutting edge of the
sword of Islam. Its first pillar is the Credo (*Shahada*) noted above,
whose Qur'anic elaboration of Islam warns that "Whosoever denieth
God and His Angels and His Books and His Aspostles and the Day of
Judgment hath strayed far from the Truth." There are four more pillars as well. Muslims should pray no less than five times daily, starting before dawn, ending after dark. They must prostrate themselves
facing Mecca, reciting or listening to their *Imam* (leader) recite the
sacred verses of *Qur'an*, never losing sight of the inspired source of

their life's faith, its Arabic roots. On Fridays at noon prayer, the entire congregation joins together, coming to the open courtyard of a mosque (*masjid*) where the faithful bow as one man, worshipping as an army would march, trained in prayer to move, speak, think in unison, magnifying their strength by the number of their community, always facing the Arabian source of their Prophet's inspiration.

No orthodox Afghan, Pakistani, Indian, or Bangladeshi Muslim can thus forget for one day the external origins of his faith, its Western wellsprings in the oil-rich sands. At least once in his lifetime, moreover, a good Muslim should travel to Mecca, ideally performing the pilgrimage (*hajj*) every year if he can afford to, visiting the sacred *Ka'aba* and kissing the Black Stone during the last month of Islam's lunar year. He must also give a generous portion of his wealth as alms (*zakat*) for his poorer brethren, a gift made for "the love of Allah" that reinforces in practical terms the theoretical equality of all members of the *Umma,* the socialist theory at the root of Islam's economic doctrine. One-twelfth of each year, throughout the ninth month (*Ramadan*) of the Islamic calendar, orthodox Muslims should eat no food and drink no liquids between sunup and sundown. Though fasting is quite common in Hindu tradition, Ramadan is the holiest month for Muslims, since it was supposedly during this interlude that the *Qur'an* was revealed to the Prophet. The month of prayer and abstention ends with a festive day (*Id al-Fitr*) that includes the sacrifice of many animals to God, usually cows in India. Another festival day of sacrifice, celebrated throughout the orthodox Islamic world, is the final day of the *hajj,* called *Id al-Adha,* when sheep or camels are generally sacrificed.

Muslim civilization is a cultural entity, self-contained, self-sufficient, so self-confident that it cares little to comprehend or interact with civilizations other than its own. Islam requires community and conformity from all individuals who consider themselves Muslim. There is, in fact, no dichotomy between a Muslim's personal faith and his responsibilities to the *Umma* or his membership in an Islamic state. History is viewed as the process of enacting God's revelation in this world, and the closer each Muslim comes to helping achieve that

Qur'anic goal of fulfillment, the better off all will be on the Day of Judgment, when every being must rise from his grave to stand before the Almighty and hear his eternal sentence. Satan is always seeking to seduce true believers and lure them from the "trodden path" of righteousness that leads to the "watering place," a paradise of perpetual bliss and joy, of fountains and dancing girls and all the heart of man could ever desire. Satan's fires are always lit and ready to consume those whose sinful pride makes them think they know better than the revealed Word of God; or that they are wiser than the Prophet was and dare, therefore, to ignore his precept in their own behavior; or that they know more than the Community, whose consensus can make and even change laws. God's Community as a whole is never wrong, while individuals all too often are deluded, misguided, deceived. An orthodox Muslim cannot truly live as a Muslim unless he inhabits a Muslim land, nation, state, *Dar-ul-Islam* ("Land of Submission"). If he is living in a *Dar-ul-harb* ("Land at War"), then he should wage Holy War (*Jihad*) against the ruler, whose lack of righteousness makes him unworthy of kingship, or else he should leave the impious land to join his brethren elsewhere. Islam is a strict and unyielding faith, as harsh and unforgiving as the swords of steel so many of its adherents wielded with deadly aim when carrying its banners aloft across continents.

Islam first established itself on South Asian soil in Sind early in the eighth century. The Ummayid *Caliph* ("Deputy" of the Prophet of God), who sent his expeditionary force of some 50,000 Arab troops to conquer those 48,000 square miles of the lower Indus, was concerned primarily with securing the Arabian Sea against pirates rather than with enlarging his already vast tracts of desert land. Sind was not, therefore, the first stage in a master Muslim plan to take over the subcontinent. To Syrian Arab eyes, however, Hindus of Sind were *kafirs* ("infidels"), whose only options were Islam or death. Many at once submitted to conversion. Sind thus early became and was to remain a predominantly Muslim province, its major port of Karachi destined to be Pakistan's first capital and greatest metropolis in modern times.

When the center of Islamic power moved east to Baghdad after 750, the vigorous new Abbasid Caliphs (who exalted themselves as "Deputies of God") did launch a number of martial probes as far north as Kashmir, using Sind as their point of departure. Expeditions of Muslims were also sent by sea from the mouths of the Indus to Gujarat's Kathiawar peninsula up the Gulf of Cambay, extending Iraqi power farther into the Indian Ocean. The Abbasid Caliphate prospered on the world trade it virtually monopolized wherever its fleets were sent, and the Persianized Caliph grew in despotic power and pretentions until he came to be known as the "Shadow of God on Earth." Muslim armies were ruthless in their early conquests of Sind: we read of a general massacre at Debal that lasted "three whole days," and of another at Nairun, where idols were broken and *kafir* worshippers "cut in two" by the sword. To the strictly iconoclastic eyes of devout Muslims, every Hindu idol or image in every Hindu temple, cave, or home was viewed as an offensive abomination to God, something to be smashed, broken at least to the symbolic extent of having its nose cut off.

Once Muslim *amirs* ("governors") were firmly established in Sind, however, and found themselves obliged to raise local taxes to support their own troops, they had to rely on Brahman collectors and other Hindu collaborators to administer that "strange and sullen" province. A third, more moderate option, was, therefore, extended to Hindus who refused to convert to Islam but who were more useful alive than dead. They could remain Hindus, provided they paid a special head tax (*jizya*), which had initially been reserved under Islamic law for Jewish and Christian "Peoples of the Book" (*Dhimmis*), whose prophets were partially inspired by God, precursors to Muhammad's Prophetic "Seal." The *jizya* averaged about 6 percent of a Hindu's total wealth, and all who were obliged to pay it bitterly resented finding themselves discriminated against and exploited in their own homeland. Considering the alternatives, however, most twice-born Hindus (Brahmans, Kshatriyas, and Vaishyas) at least availed themselves of this special status, while lower-caste Shudras and Untouchables often converted to Islam.

One of the strongest arguments against the creation of Pakistan, often voiced by Mahatma Gandhi, Nehru, and others, was that most modern Muslims in South Asia were originally Hindus, converted either forcibly or opportunistically to the faith of their conquerors. The ethnic similarity in appearance of peasant Sindhis and Bengali Muslims to their Hindu counterparts is, in fact, quite apparent, and Muslim Sindhi truck and bus drivers in modern Pakistan continue to this day lovingly to adorn their vehicles with as much ornate silver foil, multicolored decor paint, and flowers just as any Hindu peasant bedecks his bullock cart and the horns of the beasts that draw it.

By the ninth century four great schools of orthodox Islamic Law, (*Shari'ah*), named for the Muslim scholars (*alims*) who arranged them, were generally followed as the correct path leading to the "watering place" in different parts of the Islamic world. The Shariat School, which was to become dominant in Central and South Asia and is looked to at present as most authoritative by most Afghans, Pakistanis, and Bangladeshis, is the Hanafi School, founded in the eighth century by Abu Hanifa (699–767). All four Sunni Shariat schools are based on Qur'anic scripture and Prophetic *Hadith,* but each differs somewhat in its laws of inheritance, property, contract, and other such matters of jurisprudence where local custom generally prevails over any universal standard on which all Muslims, from West Africa to Southeast Asia, can reach agreement. To the orthodox Muslim however, nothing is more important than strict acceptance of the Law, thereby conforming to the will of God, preparing oneself for the Day of Judgment by never acting in such a way as to require adverse judgment to be passed.

Certain actions, e.g., the five pillars, are obligatory for all Muslims, others are only recommended as desirable in the Shariat, while many others are found to be objectionable and some prohibited. The latter class are subject to punishment of the most severe sort, including amputation for theft, whipping for drinking any intoxicating beverage or usury, and stoning to death for adultery and rape. Hindu converts to Islam were often hard-pressed to live by the letter of the Law they came under after they did convert, and many of the harshest punishments under strict enforcement of the Islamic Code in Indian history appear to have been imposed upon such individuals. The prevalence of prohibition in modern India is perhaps the clearest example of the cultural impact of Islam, for from at least Vedic times Hindus have lavished libations upon every fire sacrifice offered to their gods, one of the most popular of whom was the "intoxicating" divinity, Soma.

The Muslim invasions destined to bring all of South Asia under the iron rule of Islam flowed over the Khyber Pass from the Afghan fortress of Ghazni, starting in A.D. 997. *Sultan* ("King") Mahmud of Ghazni, third in the dynasty of Turkish slaves that toppled Persian Samanid power from Afghanistan in the latter half of the tenth century, led his "Friends of God" on a bloody series of annual raids into the Indus Valley. Mahmud, a devout Muslim warrior, who was hailed by his court historians as the "Sword of Islam," is said to have razed no less than 10,000 Hindu temples during the last two decades of his life, which he devoted to attempting systematically to transfer all the wealth and much of the population of what is now Pakistan and Gujarat over the Hindu Kush ("Killer of Hindus") to Ghazni. Though the actual number of temples credited to Mahmud's sword may have been somewhat smaller, his tenth raid alone supposedly yielded him 100,000 Hindu slave girls, and the most terrifying of all his raids, launched against fabled Somnath in 1025, reaped 50,000 Hindu lives in a single day and millions of dinars' worth of gold and precious stones.

With the army of slaves and wealth he brought back to Afghanistan from his yearly hunt, Mahmud was able to turn Ghazni into a city that rivaled Baghdad for its scholarly brilliance and affluent power in the eleventh century. The Persian poetic genius Firdawsi, and the great Arab historian al-Biruni imparted cultural warmth and luster to Mahmud's cold and lofty capital. Al-Biruni's *History of India* (*Kitab-ul-Hind*) offers some insight into how it was that Mahmud's raids, year after year, were never warded off by the vast populace of the plains, who seemed paralyzed, waiting like insects caught in a spider's web for the inevitable destruction that they must have known would come with winter's first thaw.

"Hindus believe that there is no country but theirs," wrote al-Biruni, "no nation like theirs, no kings like theirs, no religion like theirs, no science like theirs. They are haughty, foolishly vain, self-conceited, and stolid. They are by nature niggardly in communicating that which they know, and they take the greatest possible care to withhold it from men of another caste among their own people, still much more, of course, from any foreigner."[1]

After A.D. 1020, Mahmud brought the Punjab into his Ghazni Empire, leaving a Turko-Afghan governor to rule from Lahore, which has since that time served as provincial capital. Kashmir was also raided. Thus, almost a millennium ago, all of what is Pakistan today had come under the martial control of a king whose center of imperial power was less than 100 miles south of modern Kabul. Instead of uniting to resist this foreign conquest, many Hindus of Lahore and elsewhere in the Punjab joined forces with the Ghaznis, some even serving in their army.

In Delhi, however, 225 unobstructed miles southeast of Lahore, Hindu rajas not only remained enthroned until A.D. 1193, but at least one of them, Raja Mahipal, tried in the mid-eleventh century to recapture Lahore. The Hindu resurgence failed, however. The only power capable of ousting Ghaznis from India were their western Afghan neighbors, the Ghurs. By the mid-twelfth century, in fact, Ghur power had stripped the Ghaznis of everything but their Punjab province, reducing the wealthy, once-beautiful Ghazni to rubble, ignoring the first tenet of Islam that "Muslims must never harm fellow Muslims" and proving that Turko-Afghan tribal hatreds and rivalries were far more deeply entrenched in the hearts of Ghaznis and Ghurs than their relatively new faith of Islam. As the first bearers of Islamic culture to the Punjab, the Ghaznis and Ghurs left Pakistan the skeleton of Lahore and its administrative entity as well as a share of Central Asia's fierce genetic lode that was to be reinforced during the ensuing half-millennium with continuing waves of Islamic invaders from the region now partly Russian, partly Chinese, the then nomadic borderland wastes of Central Asia.

The South Asian subcontinent first became *Dar-ul-Islam* with the founding of the Delhi Sultanate in 1206. Qutb-ud-din Aibak, born a slave of the Ghurs, had risen to amir of Delhi under his mighty master Muhammad Ghuri. The latter was assassinated on his journey back to Afghanistan, and Aibak proclaimed himself sultan as soon as he learned the news, founding a line of Muslim monarchs in India that was to continue across five successive dynasties and number thirty-five sultans over the next three and a quarter centuries. By fastening Muslim rule at the geostrategic center of South Asia, athwart the Indus and Gangetic plains where India's major clusters of population are centered, a new era of Hindu-Muslim conflict and obligatory accommodation was begun. The mounting cultural tensions inherent in the vastly differing systems of Islam and Hinduism now led to many violent confrontations on North Indian battlefields, whose soil was saturated with the blood of tens of thousands of Hindu Rajputs and Jats vainly seeking to ward off invaders who proved themselves tougher, more unified, more determined fighters because inspired by their conviction that death in battle on behalf of Islam would ensure them eternal Paradise after the Day of Judgment.

New mystic forms of Islam emerged at this time, the Sufi thread of religio-philosophic faith, whose *pirs* ("preceptors"), also called *shaikhs* and *khwajas,* undertook the task of seeking to convert India's masses to Islam through mystic illumination, poetry, and love, rather than by militant force or fear. Walking with bared heads and feet, clad in nothing but the simplest of garb, these Muslim "saints" strongly resembled Hindu mystic *gurus* (also "preceptors") of contemporary devotional (*Bhakti*) sects, the popularity of which had spread north from Southern India, especially taking root in Bengal. The latter province was to become the most successful field for Sufi conversions, and virtually the entire population of modern Bangladesh is descended from Hindu and Buddhist converts to Islam made during the thirteenth through sixteenth centuries. Sufi asceticism, poverty, practice of breath control, and similar characteristics reminded Hindus of the yogis and sadhus they had long known. As far as Sunni Muslims were concerned, however, the behavior of Sufi saints was certainly much closer to the model of Prophetic abstinence and sober hardship than that of the Abbasid or Persian courts, or indeed, even the court of Delhi, where prohibited wine usually flowed whenever dancing girls of the harem came before the sultan. More traditional Islamic *alims,* whose leading luminaries came to be called as a group, *Ulama,* acknowledged the validity of Sufism, since the Prophet himself had gone into total isolation and trance when he heard the *Qur'an,* much the way these "God-intoxicated saints" often behaved. As long as the pirs and shaikhs remained loyal to the sultan, as most of them did, he had no cause to complain of their labors of love, which only helped swell the ranks of Islam in a land that remained mostly Hindu and hostile to the *Umma.*

The administrative reunification imposed by the Delhi Sultanate over North India, harsh and painful though it proved to many Hindus, soon served as something of a shield for South Asia's subcontinent against the historic hurricane unleashed by Ghengiz Khan's Mongol horde across Afghanistan, Persia, Iraq, and Turkey. Would the Mongol nomadic superpower, which made the world tremble, have carried its dance of death deeper than it did into India's heartland had there been no Muslim armies braced to resist such assaults behind India's gates? The full power of the Abbasid Caliphate certainly proved insufficient to withstand that irresistible assault. Afghanistan and Persia were flattened, totally defeated, crushed by the rapacious ferocity of that untamed Central Asian human whirlwind. Even India felt its force throughout the last decade of the thirteenth century, until in 1303 the Mongol army that plundered Lahore withdrew of its own volition. Yet there is no denying that the Sultanate had more martial muscle at its command with which to resist and punish, if not defeat, Mongol invaders than any pre-Sultanate Indian army or combination of armies could have mustered. Many of those who swelled the ranks of the sultan's cavalry, moreover, were Turks and Afghans, Tajiks, Khaljis, and Pathans, who had left their upland homes in anticipation of the Mongol storm to join the gathering remnant of Muslim warriors from near and far that rallied round Delhi's fort. In the wake of the Mongol terror, the Sultanate did enjoy almost a century without invasion, during which it extended its power the full length and breadth of South

Asia under the Tughluqs. The weft of Islam was now woven, inextricably, through the warp of Hinduism, the seemingly incompatible fibers meshed to form a fabric often coarse and ugly in its patterns of pain, yet also merging in beautifully new syncretic patterns of thought and art.

Sikhism, the faith born of Hindu-Muslim thought, founded by Guru Nanak (1469–1538) in the Punjab, is the most famous of a number of syncretic schools that emerged in North India out of the prolonged coexistence of two great civilizations. Nanak was Hindu by birth but had studied Islam under his closest friend, a Muslim, and had found himself so attracted to its undeviating monotheism and rejection of caste in favor of Universal Brotherhood that he was inspired to teach a new religion to his disciples (*Sikhs*), exalting Truth (*Sat*) as God and welcoming all its adherents, male and female of whatever caste, class, or original faith, into what was to evolve as a community of the true faith, and later an "Army of the Pure" (*Khalsa*). Nanak and the nine gurus who succeeded him are now worshipped by Sikhs as Divine Beings. Muslim persecution led to the most bitter battles between Sikhs and Muslims, from the seventeenth century until the subcontinent's partition in 1947. Much like Buddhists and Jains, Sikhs have now returned to their Hindu Mother as something of a unique caste, the martial fist of modern India, virtually inheriting military service as their *Jati*'s occupation. These sturdy, bearded and turbaned sons of partitioned Punjab are a sobering reminder of the magnificent possibilities that intercourse between Islam and Hinduism offered to South Asia, and of the tragic pitfalls that have faced the offspring of that historic union.

The final phase in Islam's prolonged conquest of South Asia was inaugurated by Babur ("Tiger") (1483–1530), descended from both Ghengiz Khan and Delhi's 1398 plunderer Timur the Lame (Tamerlane), founder of the great Mughal Dynasty. Babur was a Barlas Turko-Mongol Muslim, who was forced in his youth by family rivals to flee his Samarqand home in what is now Russian Uzbekistan. A brilliant strategist, whose martial genius rivaled that of Alexander the Great, Babur first carved a new domain for himself out of Afghanistan's rugged mile-high plateau around Kabul, then used it as his springboard for the conquest of India. He had no tanks or gunships but brought foreign (*feringhi*) cannon with him from Central Asia and used the new weapons most effectively in scattering the walls of elephants and charging lines of cavalry he confronted on India's hard-fought plains. He followed the classic highroad of assault over the Khyber through Peshawar to Attock, pausing to take and consolidate his grip over Lahore, then on to Delhi, where North India's fate was decided on the field of Panipat in April 1526.

Babur wrote in his *Memoirs* that from 1505, when he first seized Kabul, he "never ceased to think of the conquest of Hindustan."[2] It took him five successive assaults. In the last, "by the munificence and liberality of God," Delhi's gates were flung open to him after the bloated army of Sultan Ibrahim Lodi was left scattered over Panipat's plain. Babur did not pause to worry that the Lodis were also Muslim, but moved southeast along the river Yamuna (Jumna) to capture what was to become the major capital of the Mughals, Agra. He defeated Rajput Hindus and Afghans in a series of stunning battles that proved him the mightiest warrior in the world at this time, and that was a further sobering reminder of the subcontinent's vulnerability to attack when politically fragmented.

The last century of the Sultanate had, indeed, proved a time of both economic and administrative weakness. On the eve of Babur's conquest, regional armies were vying with one another, draining the total resources of a land whose wealth had been wasted in almost constant warfare. Plundered and looted, its people were dispirited and without hope or any sense of commitment to the dying regime that selfishly retained power, feeding its elephant corps while peasants starved and famine spread across the land. Ironically, Babur himself, Islam's first South Asian emperor (*padishah*), whose dynasty would last longer than any in all of Indian history, felt no strong attachment to India or its people. He wrote:

> They have no idea of the charms of friendly society or familiar intercourse. They have no genius, no comprehension of mind, no politeness of manner, . . . no ingenuity or mechanical in-

vention . . . no horses, no good flesh, no grapes or musk-
mellons . . . no ice or cold water, no good food or bread in
their bazaars, no baths . . . no candlestick. . . . The chief
excellency of Hindustan is that it is a large country and has
abundance of gold and silver.

The Mughals reunited India and ruled not only over South Asia
but brought Afghanistan within their imperial orbit for more than half
a century as well. Though the dynasty remained Sunni Muslim
throughout its more than two centuries in actual power (nominally surviving until 1858), its greatest monarch, Akbar (literally "Great"),
sought for much of his fifty-year reign (1556–1605) to introduce a
national element of unity into his administration. Akbar was the first
Muslim monarch to abolish the hated *jizya* on Hindus, winning far
more popular support and loyalty by that act alone than he could have
purchased in lost revenue. He also followed a conscious policy of
attaching powerful Rajput families to his court through marriage, and
his descendants were all part-Hindu by birth if not religious predilection.

The lavish, sumptuous elegance of the great Mughal court and harem, replete with its silks, jewels, music, poetry, wine, and opium,
resembled Shi'ite Persian, Hindu Rajput, and South Indian court life
far more than the austere sobriety of early Islam. Akbar's Sufi eclec-
ticism and originality of mind finally led to his founding a syncretic
Divine Faith (*Din-i-Ilahi*) at his court, whose ambiguous salutation
"Allah-u-Akbar" can with equal accuracy be translated "God is
Great" or "Akbar is God." Some orthodox mullahs and pirs now
proclaimed the emperor as heretic, lured from the path of Islam by
Satan, and led a number of local *Jihads* against the padishah who
boldly tried to reconcile Hinduism and Islam in a state of enduring
friendly coexistence.

None of Akbar's successors sought to follow his path, reverting
instead with increasing care and caution to accepted Shariat Law. By
the reign of Akbar's great grandson Alamgir (1658–1707), the *jizya*
was reimposed, wine and music were banished from court, and "In-
spectors of Muslim Morals" were sent throughout the land to check

on provincial governors and judges to be sure they were enforcing the Islamic Code. Popular rebellion erupted north and south, Sikhs and Jats, Marathas and Rajputs rising in desperation against the harshness of Alamgir's administration. The more the Hindus revolted, however, the clearer it seemed to the emperor's *Ulama* that his orthodoxy was, indeed, unique enough to warrant the title of *Khalifa* (Caliph) they bestowed upon him, the only South Asian monarch ever to be proclaimed "Deputy of God."

Mughal power at its peak was maintained by a military administration with a standing army of close to half a million foot soldiers and more than 100,000 cavalry. All of South Asia's surplus was required to sustain the elephantine burden of that huge machine, whose force was most wastefully expended against internal revolts rather than threats beyond its borders. By the death of Alamgir, however, a vigorous new force was well established at three tiny toeholds on the peninsula's littoral, quietly trading and busily learning the complex secrets of the great empire, whose provincial fringes now started to break free of the center's crumbling authority. The *Khalifa* himself was sewn into a simple shroud of jute, buried with the *Qur'an* he personally copied, in the least pretentious mausoleum of all his ancestors, in the parched soil of Central India that proved receptive to Muslims only after they died.

FOUR

South Asia's Conquest and Transformation by the West

Pepper and cloves, vital for keeping European meat palatable in the pre-refrigeration era of history, were the spurs that drove Vasco da Gama and his tiny fleet of cannon-bearing Portuguese caravellas round the Cape of Good Hope to India's Malabar Coast in 1498. It was the dawn of a new age, for the enormous profits reaped from that trip stimulated the building and launching of thousands of India-bound sailing vessels, not only in Lisbon but in Amsterdam, Rotterdam, London, Greenwich, and Liverpool. The West's first great scramble for India and the Indies had moved into high gear by the end of the sixteenth century, when Iberian Catholic power lost its monopoly on the Eastern seas and Protestant Dutch and British merchant seamen hauled sail for warmer waters. The "Honourable" British East India Company of London merchants, founded by Elizabeth I in 1600, started its lucrative mercantile career (which was to culminate in the establishment of the mightiest empire in modern times) by pirating the spicy cargo of Portuguese vessels captured near the Straits of Sumatra. British merchant empire-builders took more than valuable cargoes from the Portuguese, however, borrowing strategic techniques for controlling Indian Ocean sea lanes and methods of securing coastal South Asian toeholds as well.

The key to tiny Portugal's retention of a virtual monopoly of the Indian Ocean spice trade for almost a century was not simply the mounted cannon that gave their swift ships an advantage over all previous vessels to sail in the region, but their early conquest of subsidiary allies, like the shaikh of Ormuz at the mouth of the Persian Gulf. Aden on the Red Sea, Colombo in Sri Lanka (Ceylon), Malacca in the Eastern Straits were similarly secured by Lisbon's ingenius viceroy, whose central base of insular power was Goa, midway along India's western peninsular coast. A Portuguese subsidiary ally retained his throne as long as he agreed to a Portuguese agent residing in his palace and turned over enough of his land to support a garrison of Portuguese troops barracked outside the palace wall. Since the king knew that the resident agent could call in his troops whenever he wished, he simply accepted the agent's advice in all matters of policy. Yet he appeared independent of foreign control to his own people. In this way, a country of only one million subjects could control the trade of three continents half a world away with just a few hundred ships and a few thousand soldiers and sailors.

Portuguese power puppeteers kept a firm grip on every major bottleneck into and out of the Indian Ocean, until tougher and stronger British and Dutch buccaneers blasted them out of the water. The Dutch, who had more ships and national support than London's chartered East India (John) Company initially received, took the Banda and Molucca spice islands for themselves. The British were reluctantly obliged to fall back on what seemed the second-best pickings of India's trade. British merchants and ambassadors who first wended their weary way to the court of the "Great Mogor" at Agra were chagrined to find that India had no need for European produce and Mughal officials little time or interest to talk of treaties with powers, of whom they'd never heard. "This is the dullest, basest place that ever I saw," wrote King James's first ambassador from Agra. His advice to his mercantile countrymen, after years of frustration at trying to negotiate a treaty with India, was that "If you will profit seek it at sea and in quiet trade."[1] It would take British merchants almost two centuries from the humble dawn of their intimate association with India and its rulers to reach paramountcy over South Asia.

That lengthy process was not a simple uphill journey but a series of jerky, often devastating fits and starts, with as many failures and pitfalls as small victories and happy hours. The toll of lives lost, robbed by disease or debauchery, and years wasted will never be known, though cemeteries throughout India, many of whose stone tablets are barely legible today, attest to part of the price paid by long-forgotten Englishmen for Great Britain's acquisition of the "brightest jewel" in her Imperial crown. For some, however, expecially those owning most of the East India Company's stock, the enterprise proved so profitable that other merchants of London soon viewed the Company's monopoly with covetous eyes. British tenacity and persistence overcame the darkest hours of despair, but while the Mughal court was ruled by mighty emperors like Akbar and Alamgir, there was really no opportunity for European traders to transmute themselves into imperial rulers of South Asia. Company directors like Sir Josia Child had dreamed, indeed, before the end of the seventeenth century of establishing "a large, well-grounded, sure English Dominion in India for all time to come,"[2] one whose motto sounded like the name of an English pub, "Just and Stout." It was more bravado and bluff than prescient realism at the time. Half a century later, however, Mughal tremors gave Western factors residing in their bustling, young port cities new reason for hope and the sudden prospect of winning unimagined power.

The metamorphosis of a small peaceful company of British merchants, residing primarily in the port cities of Bombay, Madras, and Calcutta that they had created on the littoral wilderness, into the rulers of South Asia's subcontinent is one of the most extraordinary events of recent history. Most amazing perhaps is the speed with which it was accomplished, for the essential process took less than fifty years. Yet this brief period at the end of the eighteenth century transformed not only Indian but world history. It introduced a major new factor into the subcontinent's balance of political power, which initially destabilized but ultimately reunified South Asia.

This remarkable process was triggered by the War of the Austrian Succession in 1740, giving French and British merchants in South India the excuse they sought to seize one another's port capitals of Madras and Pondicherry with their loot of spices, bullion, and cotton goods stored in crowded warehouses. The almost incidental by-product of that rather trivial conflict between two greedy bands of Europeans on the Coromandel Coast was that it exposed the relative martial weakness of South Indian provincial governors (*nawabs*), until then considered mighty potentates, to two extraordinary men, a brilliant French governor named Joseph François Dupleix (1697–1764) and a bluff British bully named Robert Clive (1725–74).

Dupleix was the mastermind, who understood the Mughal Empire and its weak points better than any South Asian of the time and was light-years ahead of his European contemporaries in his appreciation and knowledge of South Indian regional politics. He understood that what the Portuguese had done at Ormuz and Aden in the sixteenth century could be achieved over all of South India, in much the same way in the eighteenth century, and at no greater cost in bullion or French blood. He had learned a vital secret at the Battle of St. Thome in 1746 when, with a handful of French officers, who had trained a few hundred Indian soldiers (*sepoys*) in close-order drill and musket fire, he had defeated the local nawab's undisciplined army of 100,000 men, who had come to "claim" British Fort St. George that the French had just captured from the sea.

Dupleix had the wisdom, moreover, to refrain from openly taking the nawab's throne at Arcot that awaited him, installing instead a puppet claimant, whose loyalty he'd purchased in advance. He then did the same with the throne of the *subedar* ("viceroy") of the Deccan, an even higher Mughal magnate, who had broken free of Delhi and established his own hereditary kingdom of Hyderabad, a domain also controlled for some time by Dupleix and his lieutenants. Dupleix could have done more, but his company's directorate lost faith in him, listening instead to a jealous rival who claimed Dupleix was simply carving out his own kingdom in India. So Versailles recalled the only Frenchman who could have ruled India, leaving his British rival to pick up the ripe mangoes of provincial power that now lay waiting for any one strong and ruthless enough to grab them.

Clive had gone to Madras as a young writer in John Company's employ. The tedious hours in the countinghouse factory copying lists of lading induced such ennui in his unstable mind that one afternoon he put his pistol to his head and pulled the trigger. But it was too damp a day; the shot never fired and Clive became his company's most daring, dauntless soldier. He had been in Madras when it was seized by Dupleix's army, but was saved by European diplomacy, thanks to the Treaty of Aix-la-Chapelle, which turned back Fort St. George and its garrison of prisoners to the British in exchange for the Louisiana Territory in America. Captain Clive learned as he earned, fighting the French all along the Coromandal Coast, and was bright enough to appreciate the wisdom of Dupleix's "Nabob (British for *nawab*) Game." The second phase of the Anglo-French Austrian succession struggle, which broke out a decade later as the Seven Years War, gave Clive an opportunity to put what he'd learned in Madras in the 1740s to the test in Bengal, farther north.

The nawab of Bengal, who had died in 1756, had been a shrewd old Mughal, passively tolerating British traders in his province as long as they paid him an agreed-upon share of all they bought and sold within his realm. British Company headquarters in Bengal was at Fort William in Calcutta, the port city they had founded on the east bank of the river Hughli. It was several hundred miles north from Calcutta to the nawab's capital, Murshidabad, and as long as the chests of silver and gold came up from time to time there was little contact between these centers of British and native power. The new nawab was, however, much younger, more arrogant and impatient than his great-uncle. Soon after he took the throne, he dispatched many demands to Fort William. But he was so displeased with the replies he received that he mounted his elephant and marched south with an army of over 50,000 to take control of the fort for himself. It was a usual sultry, sweltering June in Calcutta in 1756. Half of the small British garrison was on "sick leave," and all but two of the cannonballs were too wet to fire, as was most of the powder. As word of the nawab's advancing army reached Fort William, the British governor led an undignified race for the river boats, beating women and children, whose ample skirts and shorter legs proved no match for men inspired by fear. Less than 150 Englishmen remained to face the nawab's army, and their seniormost, J. Z. Holwell, surrendered the fort to Nawab Siraj-ud-daula, whose name would be engraved in the minds of unborn generations of English public school boys together with the "Black Hole" lockup in which that wretched band of British brothers spent what for most of them would be their last anguished night.

The blood of these "martyrs" cried out for vengeance, and Colonel Clive led the force from Madras to recapture Calcutta. He did much more, of course. He toppled the nawab from his throne and took Bengal—but not without help, and not for himself. He remembered well the lessons taught by Dupleix. He took full advantage of Indian pluralism and the treachery inspired by hunger for power. Calcutta was easy to recapture, for the nawab himself had abandoned it, preferring his palace in the north. Once Clive and his force were back inside Fort William, the general called in the richest Hindu bankers from the bazaar and convinced them to pay for the training and arming of more sepoys. Then he used his spies to contact the nawab's bitter uncle Mir Jafar, who felt *he* should have inherited his brother's throne. Mir Jafar led Siraj's cavalry, a crack force of 15,000 that could have trampled Clive's entire smaller army at Plassey the following June had the Mir but raised his arm to order the charge. Withholding his force instead, he won the throne of Murshidabad, but was controlled by Clive from Calcutta.

Clive's personal payoff after Plassey was half the treasure of Bengal and the rents from almost a hundred thousand square miles, more gold and jewels than he could carry home in half a dozen ships' chests. At thirty-five, Clive returned to London rich enough to buy a controlling share of his company's stock, several rotten-borough seats in Parliament, and more country homes, carriages, and servants than he could count. He was the first of the "Nabobs," reviled and envied, admired and despised in his homeland, but clearly a "King of the Indies," inspiring all who lusted for wealth, power, fame, and fortune to sail east, following his rapacious example.

The British were thus securing their first major territorial base in Mughal India in its eastern province on the Bay of Bengal. The tottering emperor in Delhi and Agra was so preoccupied with attacks from the northwest and southwest that he was unable to confront the British with his once-mighty imperial legions until it was too late. Nadir Shah of Persia had captured Qandahar in 1738, moved north to take Kabul, then west to Delhi the following year. Shi'ites since 1502, the Persian Muslims did not hesitate to attack the bastions of Sunni power to their east. Nadir's army of over 80,000 troops shattered Mughal frontier defenses, driving their sword to the heart of Delhi. Not since Timur's raid of 1398 had Delhi suffered such violent humiliation. No less than 20,000 people were "put to the sword within the city of Delhi itself" by Nadir's ferocious plunderers.[3] Fabled jewels and furniture, including the *Koh-i-nur* ("Mountain of Light") diamond and Peacock Throne, were dragged back over the mountain passes after the Persian horde had finally sated itself on Delhi's women, blood, and wealth. Persia retained control of the Punjab and Sind as well as Afghanistan until Nadir Shah's assassination in 1747—a year which proved an important turning point for Afghanistan.

Ahmad Shah Abdali (*c.* 1720–73), chief of the Sadozai clan of the great Durrani ("Pearl") tribe, liberated Qandahar and Kabul from Persian rule in 1747, rallying sufficient support from other Afghan chiefs to proclaim Afghanistan an independent kingdom for the first time in its long and troubled history. A fierce warrior and shrewd diplomat, Ahmad Shah bolstered his country's western defenses against divided Persian power and was soon sufficiently secure on his plateau perch to launch a series of devastating raids against Persian garrisons of the Punjab and Sind. As a Sunni Muslim, Ahmad Shah believed it his mission in life to clear his domain of all heretics, and in the quarter-century of his vigorous reign he won Lahore and Kashmir as well as Sind, marching against Delhi itself. Though intially defeated outside Delhi by a Mughal army over five times the size of his Afghan force, Ahmad Shah returned several times to that capital and was finally "invited" back in 1759 to help defend Delhi and Muslim rule in India by Shah Wali Allah (1703–62), the greatest *alim* at the Mughal court.

Wali Allah, credited with leading the Muslim modernist revival in South Asia, realized that without Afghan military support, weakened Mughal power would be destroyed by the growing might of a Hindu

Maratha pentarchy. The Maratha forces had proved powerful enough to seize Lahore in 1758 and march west to Attock itself. They deposed one Mughal puppet in favor of their own, galloped to the very suburbs of Calcutta in the east, and controlled virtually all of central India and the southern peninsula from the Deccan headquarters of the Brahman *peshwa* ("prime minister") at Poona. Maratha power was the sharp dagger of Hindu revival aimed at the soft underbelly of a flaccid and debauched Mughal court, but the Afghan army of Ahmad Shah poured over the passes in 1759, recapturing Lahore and moving its Muslim sword and shield into position at Panipat for what was to be a Hindu-Muslim war of mutual destruction in South Asia in 1761. Some 50,000 dispirited Maratha troops were slaughtered by over 60,000 of Ahmad Shah's tougher Durrani fighters, several thousand of whom also died in that battle. The Afghan king moved into Delhi's palace in the aftermath of his victory for Islam, but Durrani and his Mughal brothers started fighting among themselves soon after having disposed of their common Hindu enemy. Had he lived longer, Ahmad Shah would have been startled to learn he had saved India for a Christian, British company he had never heard of rather than for a Mughal or Afghan Muslim dynasty.

The combined armies of the Mughal emperor and the nawabs of Oudh and Bengal were beaten by a small but disciplined force of British soldiers and sepoys on the south bank of the river Ganga at Buxar in 1764. It was a more important battle than Plassey, for three huge Mughal armies were scattered by well-coordinated musket fire and carefully placed cannon. The following year, by the Treaty of Allahabad, John Company was formally brought within the bureaucratic structure of the Mughal Empire as revenue collector (*diwan*) for all of Bengal province in return for the promise of a small annual tribute to be paid to the padishah. In reality, however, the emperor was but a stipendiary of the foreign company that had usurped his richest province's revenues. The sham was to continue for almost another century: silk-robed and bejewelled old Mughals sulking around their harems, puffing their opium, painting their miniatures, riding atop beautifully caparisoned elephants to wave at cheering bazaar crowds on festival holidays. They played their part in the Nabob Game with hardly a whimper or treacherous shout, for the "Great Company" had its ears everywhere and paid well for early warnings of discontent or treason.

To the Hindu majority of India's population, moreover, the "New Raj" was in many ways preferable to the old, and many of the brightest lads of Bengal flocked to its service, civil and military. To most British eyes, natives all looked the same, dark and sinister, dirty, untrustworthy, shifty-eyed, dim-witted. It made little difference to young "Tom Raw," fresh from London's fair port and clime when he disembarked at Calcutta's steaming, fetid, noisy wharf whether the "boy" (usually twice his age) who eagerly hefted his bag and steamer trunk onto a naked shoulder was Hindu, Muslim, or atavist. India's new super-Brahman "caste" of White *sahibs* (masters or lords) had no difficulty in treating all natives alike, without favor, fear, or prejudice. Thanks to these "Heaven-sent Sahibs," Hindus found themselves overnight out from under the sword of Muslim tyranny, no longer obliged to pay any *jizya,* and even able to earn better wages than they had ever dreamed of, if they only worked hard and loyally served these odd, new, pink-cheeked "gods."

Hindu mythology often portrays gods as children. Lord Krishna's most endearing form is *"Bal-Krishna"* ("Baby-Krishna"), the ideal pudgy darling of Hindu motherhood. Brahma, another great god of the Hindu pantheon, was said to have planned a return to earth as a "fair-haired child." And here were young giants with golden curls and blue eyes and skin white as the ash sadhus smeared on their faces to protect themselves from evil coming from boats whose tall masts seemed to scour the sky. Of course they were gods! How else could they possibly be so fearless and strong as to conquer a land they knew nothing about—not its languages, customs, climate, or culture?

As warmly as Hindus initially welcomed their liberation under the Company Raj, Muslims reacted with cold, aloof withdrawal, if not openly violent opposition. Muslims knew enough about Christians to understand that, like Hindus, they were *Dhimmis,* no better than second-class subjects of the Great Mughal. Their continued arrogant revolt against official authority damned these deluded *feringhis,* "sons of Satan,'' as mullahs across North India were soon to shout, calling upon congregations in a thousand mosques to wage *Jihad* in defense of religion (*din*).

Once the British had established their Bengal beachhead, however, they were not easily displaced or put down. Their assets included the corporate immortality of the Company and its seemingly limitless fund of stock, which allowed it to replenish any loss: ships blown off course or sunk; warehouses robbed or their stock of woollens turned to green mold by a monsoon climate that corroded leather, rusted metal, and disintegrated weaker fabrics; or coffers of silver and gold looted by robbers, who were usually trusted servants. The servants themselves were continuously replaced: the pirates by less rapacious, shrewder minds, Bob Clive by Warren Hastings (1732–1818), a scholar and power-politician rather than a naked plunderer. Hastings understood enough Persian, Bengali, and Hindustani to know which of his lieutenants and Indian allies were troublemakers, dealing with women as swiftly and as harshly as men. He even extorted money from widows such as the famous *Begums* of Oudh, whose plaints could be heard in Westminster Hall itself during Hastings's impeachment trial.

Hastings deserves at least as much credit as Clive for founding the British Indian Empire, for he pulled up the two lesser presidencies of Bombay and Madras to toe the mark set by his headquarters in Bengal, helping with troops timely sent from Fort William to save those outposts against rampaging Maratha Hindu and Mysore Muslim forces. Hastings was more thorough in managing his own men, moreover, careful to keep them from robbing too much from the company they were supposed to serve, though his contemporaries could not understand why he suddenly wanted to change the rules of the game Clive had taught every red-blooded Englishman to play—"Shake the Pagoda Tree" it was called, named for the gold pagoda coin of South India. The company servants usually behaved as though they believed the coins grew on India's trees, ripe and ready to be shaken loose for easy pickings. But Hastings was a good company man and a clever raja at the same time. He never forgot that profits were of primary significance to the "Old Men of Leadenhall Street," the directors in London's East End whom he served, and that whenever their ledger's bottom line was written in red, it meant some one's blood would flow in the field.

The House of Commons had launched its first major investigation of the Company shortly before Hastings was appointed its governor-general. Commons was looking into the state of affairs in Bengal that had allowed so many "nabobs" to return home with sacks full of gold and diamonds yet had left the Company to plead poverty when it came to paying a promised annual stipend to Great Britain's Home government. Lord North's Regulating Act of 1773, the first of many official acts, resulted. It pruned Company dividends, opened the Company books and dispatches to Commons's perusal, and gave His Majesty's government a say in appointing several councillors who advised the governor-general. It was the beginning of dual government by Company and Crown, a highly ambivalent marriage that in eighty-five years was to lead to the total devouring of the former by the latter.

Hastings was so outraged by Pitt's India Act in 1784, Commons's next predatory bite out of the Company's long-standing privileges, that he resigned rather than continue to serve under so ignominious a statute. The most liberal members of Parliament, like Edmund Burke, were, however, shocked by what they learned of the wretched state of poor, famine-depleted, produce-looted Bengal. Burke rose trembling with rage in Parliament to declaim against his fellow countrymen in India, "animated with all the avarice of age and all the impetuosity of youth" who rolled "wave after wave" onto Bengal's beaches, until their dark sands were "whitened" with the bones of natives " picked clean" by such "standard-bearers" of "higher" civilization.[4]

The aftermath of Hastings's native-Company Raj was white Christian British rule with a vengeance, under no less righteous a Whig lord than General Cornwallis, who left Bengal in 1793 with a new code of rules and regulations designed to convert British India from a land of native and Company lassitude and corruption into a haven protected by Anglo-Saxon law, enjoying British order, guided by Christian conscience. Cornwallis's most important contribution to India's modernization was his introduction of the common law of private property to Bengal. Mughal tax collectors (*zamindars*), who had hitherto gathered the Imperial share of a region's harvest only for the duration of their emperor's pleasure, were transformed overnight into little Whig landlords, provided they paid British Company collectors a fixed annual sum, which was settled permanently in 1793. These *zamindars* each received deeded titles to their property, which could be retained in perpetuity by their heirs, or sold whenever they wished. It was a revolutionary concept for India, something neither Hindu nor Muslim legal codes had earlier evolved. All land in South Asia had hitherto belonged to the king or emperor, who owned it as part of his sovereign right, in return for which he protected his subjects, each of whom enjoyed some share in his ruler's total annual bounty of crops. Intermediaries of all sorts, called *zamindars, taluqdars, jagirdars,* or *in-amdars,* participated in every harvest, reaping a share based on service to a maharaja or padishah, usually connected with valor in war or court favor of another sort.

Now, all one had to do was to be born into the right family to inherit great wealth and constantly accruing fortune, for though the annual rent paid to the Company remained the same, the actual value of Bengal's land, with its increasingly intensified cultivation, conspired to turn all its *zamindar* families into wealthy barons by the mid-nineteenth century, deeply indebted to British rule and its principles. Initially, however, many of the original Mughal *zamindars,* especially after a year of drought, had such difficulty paying the agreed-upon tax to government that they went to Hindu moneylenders in Calcutta to borrow the sum, leaving their title deeds as collateral. Interest rates were so high and Mughal grandees so lavish in their expenditure, especially if they had daughters to marry off, that much of Bengal's property changed hands within a quarter-century, passing to absentee Hindu banker-moneylenders in Calcutta. British justice enforced contracts and their specific demands with the same impartiality British civil servants showed toward all natives, yet once again it was Hindus, whose religious codes never prohibited taking usurious interest, as does the *Qur'an,* who benefited far more than Muslims from the introduction of British rule.

History tends to reinforce trends, once established, in South Asia as elsewhere. By the end of the eighteenth century and throughout the early nineteenth that meant the expansion and consolidation of British rule by twin processes of direct conquest and indirect absorption through subsidiary princely-state alliances. It also meant the education and enrichment of many Hindus, especially in British port cities, who took early advantage of British legal codes and Britain's need for indigenous collaborators, and the relative deterioration in the economic as well as political status of most Muslims. Each vector of change, however, introduced limiting factors that tended to inhibit continued development. As the power of the Company Raj expanded and parliamentary supervision increased, British Christian conscience and evangelism, free-trade competition, and Benthamite concerns over "the greatest good for the greatest number" all diluted the earlier profit-and-power motives of Company merchant-soldiers of fortune. Ideas as distracting as salvation for native souls and as subversive as universal humanitarian egalitarianism became commonplace in learned circles of Calcutta and Bombay.

By the first decade of the nineteenth century, the Company was ready to pay no less than £10,000 annually simply to educate native youths of intelligence and promise, while some of its British servants were learning Sanskrit and translating India's classics into English. Missionaries also learned Indian languages in order to bring the Bible to natives who knew no English. As for the Hindus, who acquired new fortunes and pride with their English and labor in the East India Company's employ, the most brilliant and sensitive among them learned that theirs were the wages of servitude and subjugation in a land that had once proudly belonged to their ancestors. They soon started to assert their appreciation of the greatness of their own cultural heritage, despising the "slaves" of the British sahibs, those who aped everything Western and condemned as worthless all things Hindu-Indian. Contrarily, individual Muslims of courage and foresight began to awaken to the reality of their minority community's true status, urging their brethren to do something positive about improving it rather than sulking in their tents of Perso-Arabic despair.

By 1818 British arms finally crushed Maratha power in the west, bringing vast tracts of South Asian real estate under the Company's direct and now paramount rule. The process of British martial, administrative, and economic integration and consolidation that continued for the rest of the nineteenth century was basically aimed at the pacification of native resistance, or what British historians liked to call the imposition of *"Pax Britannica"* and "civilization" over a strife-torn subcontinent previously ruled by petty-pilfering "heathen" princes. Evangelical missionaries, Utilitarian Positivists, and later Liberals insisted that British motives were altruistic and gloriously idealistic—as some in fact proved to be. The primary, underlying motive that continued, however, to fund and defend as great an investment and enterprise as the British Indian Empire remained profit tempered by glory for individual merchants and Company servants and vast wealth for the British nation as a whole. If anyone has ever doubted the reality of the latter, he need but look at Great Britain, its economy, and sadly diminished status in the world since losing India's insatiable market for its unemployed young graduates, Manchester-manufactured cotton goods, and Midland steel produce. The wealth of India's resources, raw materials, manpower, and military, sustained a gigantic British bureaucracy and army for 140 years, paying off a mounting debt of "Home charges" and pensions for thousands of British subjects, who enjoyed modest but secure retirement back home after completing their Indian careers.

Much of the luster, glory, lavish wealth, and power of the Victorian and Edwardian eras resulted from Indian contributions to London, Manchester, Leeds, Liverpool, Birmingham, and Edinburgh. India gave more than the brightest jewels in the crowns and scepters locked in the Tower of London, more than the indigo, saltpeter, opium, cotton, silks, spices, tea, coffee, ivory, and jewels that flowed in such bountiful rivers of trade to Britain's shores and other Imperial dependencies. It gave "Little England" that lovely, ineffable sense of supremacy and power that the conquest of an untamed heart alone could bring. To generations of British recruits, first of the Company and after 1858 of the Crown, India was virgin country, theirs to explore, control, educate, convert, transform—to modernize.

The process of Westernization first set in motion in the port cities of British India radiated toward the hinterland along Industrial Revolution-bred telegraph, penny post, and railroad lines of modernized change. It was brought to the remotest *mofussil* ("hinterland") by missionaries with their King James versions of the Bible and spread with silver by Manchester merchants seeking raw cotton for Lancashire mills that could spin and weave more in an hour than an entire Indian village in a year. It was hammered, injected, insinuated into, scattered and broadcast over the soil of South Asia. Its seeds were blown away by strong winds in some regions, took root in others, where plants blossomed but soon died, were strangled by weeds or left too long without water or flourished and continued to nurture infrastructures or institutions, like India's rail net or post and telegraph system, that grew more vital and important with time, outlasting the Raj that had introduced them and continuing to thrive in a subcontinent that has made them its very own.

FIVE

The Great Game

Because the British founded their empire as they did on the eastern wing of North India, they were slow to reach the Indus Valley or worry about the frontier. The first British governor-general to show any concern with the lands beyond South Asia's western borders was Richard Colley Wellesley (1760–1842), who sent envoys to Persia's Shah and Afghanistan's Amir to ward off any possible threat to British India posed by French machinations at both courts. It was the beginning of the "Great Game" that would dominate European diplomacy in its dealings with Asia throughout the nineteenth century.

Napoleon Bonaparte (1769–1821) launched his "Army of the Nile" on the first lap of what was to have been its victorious march to India in 1798. Admiral Nelson's fleet soon scuttled that dream of glory in the Mediterranean. But Napoleon tried once again to orchestrate an invasion of India, this time a joint Franco-Russian venture set to begin in 1801. Tsar Paul I (1754–1801) promised to match Napoleon's 35,000 French troops with an equal number of Cossacks. The two armies were to join forces at Astrakhan and from there move, with Persian assistance, to Afghanistan's Herat, on to Qandahar and over the Bolan Pass to the Indus. Tsar Paul died, however, before his troops crossed the Volga, aborting the twin-pronged plan. Napoleon was soon too preoccupied with more urgent problems in Iberia to give further thought to India.

The Great Game,[1] of course, outlived Bonaparte. Russia's push to

53

the south had, in fact, begun during the reign of Peter the Great (1682–1725), who viewed expansion into Asia as his country's destiny, and the absorption of Turkish and Persian Khanates on his border as Russia's "civilizing mission." After the British became paramount in India, however, further Russian expansion in that direction was viewed by London's Whitehall as a threat to Great Britain that could no longer be passively tolerated. In 1828 when Persia opened Teheran to a Russian presence for the first time, British Indian strategists felt that the glacis of their newly acquired empire was under assault. In London, the destiny of Asia Minor was feared to be at the mercy of the unsheathed claws of the Bear. With Russians south of the Arras River line, the British saw no defensible fortress to fall back upon short of Herat in western Afghanistan. There the Bear must be stopped, for east of Herat was no bastion before Qandahar, some 250 miles east and south on the opposite side of Afghanistan. A joint Russo-Persian drive against Afghanistan suddenly loomed not only as a possibility, therefore, but as a terrifying one with the potential to jeopardize all that half a century of British nabobism had won.

To British strategists in London and Calcutta, the solution appeared to lie in trying the familiar nabob formula again, this time in Afghanistan. Intratribal rivalry had driven the Sadozai monarch, Shah Shuja, from Kabul's throne in 1812. The leader of the Barakzai clan, Dost Muhammad Khan, emerged seven years later as the new amir (or shah) of Afghanistan, a position he would enjoy, with only three years' interruption, for four decades, until his death in 1863. Dost Muhammad was quite willing to enter into friendly relations with the British and, in fact, naïvely wrote in his first letter to Governor-General Lord Auckland, "I hope Your Lordship will consider me and my country as your own." His Lordship made the mistake of literally doing just that.

Shah Shuja had been living as a British pensioner in Ludhiana since 1818, and Auckland's ambitious young advisers urged the governor-general to use the deposed shah as a passport to Kabul power, allying British arms with him and the Sikh kingdom that ruled the Punjab between the river Sutlej and the Khyber, under the "one-eyed Lion'' of that land, Maharaja Ranjit Singh (1780–1839). Ranjit's army of Sikh "Lions" (*Singhs*) had wrested Peshawar from Barakzai Afghan control in 1818 and took Kashmir the following year. Since his coronation as "Maharaja of the Punjab," Ranjit had worked not only to unite his Sikh nation into a mighty fighting Community (*Khalsa*) determined to liberate the entire Punjab from Muslim rule of any sort, but also to maintain friendly relations with his British neighbor. Ranjit had managed to convince British officials of his friendship after signing his first treaty with the Company in 1806. On the eve of his death in 1839, the Sikh maharaja signed another treaty, joining into a triple alliance with the British and Shah Shuja to liberate Afghanistan from Barakzai rule and restore Shuja to Kabul's throne.

The "Eastern Question" had by now become of primary concern to Lord Palmerston (1784–1865), Britain's foreign minister, who insisted in 1837, "We have long declined to meddle with the Afghans and have purposely left them independent, but if the Russians try to make them Russian, we must take care they become British."[2] When Persia moved toward Herat, all the expert players at Whitehall and in Calcutta therefore viewed that advance as a Russian saber aimed at British India. The only cautionary advice voiced by an old India hand came from Sir Henry Durand (1812–71), father of the man for whom the Indo-Afghan Durand Line would be named. Sir Henry cautioned against "exaggerated fears of Russian power and intrigue" and argued that Herat was not of "vital importance" to British India, insisting that to speak of it as such "was a hyperbole so insulting to common sense as scarcely to need refutation."[3] He was ignored. The government of India launched a naval attack from Bombay, landing a force on the Island of Karrack (Kharag) in the Persian Gulf, which frightened the Persians away from Herat early in 1838. But that was only the beginning.

A glorious "Army of the Indus" was mobilized at Karnal by the British, and Auckland issued his Simla "Declaration of War" on October 1, 1838, charging Dost Muhammad with having "made a sudden and unprovoked attack" on Britain's "ancient ally, Maharajah Ranjit Singh."[4] The Dost was also charged with intrigues with Persia.

Auckland concluded "we could never hope that tranquility of our neighbourhood would be secured, or that the interests of our Indian Empire would be preserved inviolate" as long as that Barakzai amir remained in power in Kabul. Pious, wishful, hollow words. Off marched the best and brightest of British India's soldiers, 16,500 strong. Old ally Ranjit, whose claims to Peshawar and to honor were being defended, refused at the final hour to send any troops of his own, even denying the British army passage across his Punjab kingdom. In vain, the Duke of Wellington warned that crossing the Indus once to change governments in Kabul would be the start of a perennial march into that wretched land. Shah Shuja had to be restored, and all the governor-general's men promised that the bazaars of Afghanistan would be filled with the ex-shah's cheering supporters. But no one came out to cheer as the British army marched long-exiled Shuja back into Kabul. No one stepped forward when the former amir sat again on his throne. The political climate of Kabul only grew colder. British India's liberation guard became an army of occupation, obliged to remain at the hated amir's side to protect him from the fury of his own people, who despised this puppet pensioner of foreigners for bringing so many *Angrezi* ("English") *feringhi* onto Afghan soil.

For three costly, wretched, harassed years the British army remained in occupation of Kabul and Qandahar. In 1840 Dost Muhammad, who had fled north at first sight of the British force in 1839, surrendered himself to British custody and was taken to India. London's Court of Directors, appalled at the expense of "Auckland's folly," ordered the governor-general either to increase British strength in Afghanistan as a whole, directly annexing it, or to pull back the troops sitting idle around hostile palaces. Auckland, however, foolishly attempted to trim his expenses by cutting the bribes of silver and gold that the British paid border Pathan chiefs to use their passes unmolested. As soon as the subsidies stopped, the assassinations of British officers and Indian soldiers began. Silent contempt shifted to violent resistance. By the winter of 1841, the British decided it might be best to go home. Too late. The passes were closed by Pathan marksmen, who picked off rear echelons as the dispirited army headed east.

One man out of the original 16,500 galloped, half dead, into Jalalabad to report to the British outpost waiting there, "I am the Army of the Indus!"

The Signal Catastrophe,[5] as General Sir John Keane was to call the retreat from Kabul, was the worst blow British Indian arms and pride ever suffered, from Plassey to the end of the Raj in 1947. Over 15,000 troops were dead, more than £20 million wasted, and for what? Shah Shuja was cut to ribbons shortly after British guards left his side. Dost Muhammad was permitted by the Company to return to his Bala Hissar throne and was quietly subsidized there by Calcutta for the next twenty years. As a national hero, the Dost was soon able to reunite his fragmented, war-ravaged land. For the immediate future at least, the British had learned that there were limits to imperial power, including their own, and loyalties that arms alone could not sever or destroy.

The British also decided that it would be cheaper and much easier to conquer Sind and the Punjab before venturing back over Afghan passes. Sind proved no problem at all. Charles Napier, who trampled over its low-lying delta and desert with ferocious ease, wired his famous one-word Latin cable to Calcutta, *Peccavi*—"I have sinned"— a doubly accurate message. Sikhs were tougher customers, but after Ranjit's death his lieutenants had fought among themselves, weakening their hold on the Punjab. Nonetheless, it took the British army two rounds to defeat those hardy defenders of their homeland. The first Anglo-Sikh War of 1846 gave British India a leg across the Sutlej and a new subsidiary ally, the Hindu Dogra Rajput Maharaja of Kashmir, who had abandoned his Sikh "friends" for a basket full of British silver. The beautiful 85,000 square miles of Kashmir state, set like a glittering jewel atop South Asia's subcontinent, was to remain under that same Dogra Rajput dynasty until after the British withdrawal, leaving independent India and Pakistan to fight bitterly over its strategic, economically precious real estate. The second Anglo-Sikh War of 1848–49 brought the British Company Raj west to Peshawar and the Khyber, planting the Union Jack on territories of the Pathan North-West Frontier, still claimed by Kabul as its sovereign domain. John

Lawrence, Britain's first chief commissioner of the Punjab, favored pulling back British forces to the east bank of the Indus, which he felt was much easier to defend than the turbulent North-West Frontier. Lawrence's motion found no second, however, in either Whitehall or Calcutta councils, where masterly inactivity might be tolerated but retreat was condemned as un-English.

British concerns over Herat rose to fever pitch again in 1854, when Persia's shah moved troops toward that Afghan outpost on the west. Persia's revived belicosity drove Dost Muhammad into Simla's waiting arms, and a treaty of friendship was actually signed between British India and the Dost in 1855 in Peshawar. Each power solemnly engaged to respect all territories of the other, and Afghanistan promised "to be the friend of the friends and the enemy of the enemies of the Honourable East India Company."[6] This diplomatic landmark in Indo-Afghan relations proved fortuitously advantageous to both parties. The following year, when Persia captured Herat, Britain did in fact declare war in the Crimea. After three months of bloodletting on Persian soil, the shah felt obliged to withdraw from Herat, which was then formally returned by the Treaty of Paris to Kabul's control in March 1857. Throughout the Crimean War, moreover, Dost Muhammad was most handsomely paid 100,000 silver rupees a month to bolster his army.

For the British, Afghan friendship and the Dost's loyalty could not have been purchased at a more opportune time. In May 1857 the so-called "Sepoy Mutiny" erupted, a fierce North Indian war and revolt that all but drove the British Raj from South Asia a century early. Grease on new Enfield cartridges issued to Bengal Army sepoys was only the spark that ignited a tinder mountain of Hindu discontent and Muslim frustrations, rallying tens of thousands of both faiths round the tattered standards of an octogenarian Mughal emperor and an adopted ex-peshwa of Poona. Had Dost Muhammad and his Afghans joined that "Great Mutiny"[7] it might well have tipped the balance enough to convert British India's hard-won and protracted victory into a more ignominious defeat than that sustained in 1842. A word from the Dost would have sufficed to send waves of Pathan tribals over the Khyber, tying down Lawrence's Punjab army and keeping its force west of the Indus instead of releasing it to recapture Delhi and Lucknow. After that war, direct Crown rule replaced the Company and its armies.

Indo-Afghan friendship and mutual non-intervention remained the keystone of Lord Lawrence's foreign policy during his half-decade as viceroy of India from 1864–69. Lawrence's lifetime of experience in the Punjab and among frontier Pathans had taught him to respect their strong sense of independence, zealous religious faith, and fierce pride. The inactivity with which Lawrence's name would be linked in denigration by younger, more restless advocates of the Forward School of British Indian diplomacy gave Delhi and Kabul a much-needed interval of peace. Though Dost Muhammad's death in 1863 left his sixteen sons at daggers point with one another for more than half a decade, the wise Scot who ruled India refused to intervene in any of Kabul's succession disputes. His policy was based on knowledge and sensitivity to Afghan mores, not timidity nor a willingness to surrender India, as some critics charged. Lawrence urged his secretary of state, in fact, to press Britain's Cabinet to try to reach some "understanding and even an engagement with Russia" delimiting "spheres of influence of the two great Empires in Central Asia." "Failing that," he added, "we might give that power to understand that an advance towards India beyond a certain point would entail war in all parts of the world with England."[8] His policy would not be tested, however, until 1907.

The year before Lawrence left India, Sir Henry Rawlinson (1810–95), an old India hand then serving on the Secretary of State's Council in Whitehall, wrote his influential "Memorandum on Central Asia" that was to become the theoretical standard of Forward School gamesmen for the next half-century. Russia "entrenched upon the Oxus," argued Sir Henry in 1868, would prove "so pernicious an influence" for Afghanistan as a whole that it was "a duty which we owe our subjects in the Punjab" for British influence to move directly to Kabul. "Anarchy is contagious," Rawlinson warned. He therefore concluded, "In the interests of peace, in the interests of commerce, in the interests of moral and material improvement . . . interference in Afghanistan has now become a duty."[9]

On Petersburg's side of the Great Game, Prince Gorchakov, the tsar's chancellor, had used much the same rhetoric as Rawlinson in his earlier "Memorandum" of 1864.

> The position of Russia in Central Asia is that of all civilised states which come into contact with half-savage, wandering tribes possessing no fixed social organisation. It invariably happens in such cases that the interests of security on the frontier, and of commercial relations, compel the more civilised state to exercise a certain ascendancy over neighbours whose turbulence and nomad instincts render them difficult to live with. . . . If we content ourselves with chastising the freebooters and then retire, the lesson is soon forgotten. Retreat is ascribed to weakness, for Asiatics respect only visible and palpable force; that arising from the exercise of reason and a regard for the interests of civilisation has as yet no hold on them. . . . Such has been the lot of all countries placed in the same conditions. The United States in America, France in Algiers, Holland in her colonies, England in India,—all have been inevitably drawn into a course wherein ambition plays a smaller part than imperious necessity, and where the greatest difficulty is in knowing where to stop.[10]

The following year the Russians took Tashkent, and a year later Russian troops marched along the north shore of the river Oxus.

Sher Ali, Dost Muhammad's elder son, emerged in Kabul as amir at this time, receiving British arms and money to help retain his throne for precisely one decade. Like his father, Sher Ali enjoyed popular support by keeping British troops out of his land, but he also went personally to India to meet Lawrence's successor, Lord Mayo, who supplied him lavishly with guns and ammunition. Mayo viewed Afghanistan as part of British India's "sphere of influence," and promised to protect Sher Ali from any foreign invasion. Lord Mayo was, however, the only viceroy of British India to be assassinated, falling victim to a Pathan prisoner's knife during his visit to the empire's

Andaman Island detention camp early in 1872. The following year Russian troops advanced to take Khiva and seemed once again to be moving with Imperial lust toward Afghanistan itself. Sher Ali looked to Simla for greater support, but Mayo's successor, Lord Northbrook, who was most anxious to cut taxes and keep Indian expenditure low, found Lawrence's policy of non-intervention more attractive than any leap westward.

The Forward School was by now reinforced, however, by the voice and pen of Sir Henry Bartle Frere (1815–84), governor of Bombay, who argued in favor of a "well-defined scientific frontier" for the British Indian Empire that should include all of eastern Afghanistan to the Kabul, Ghazni, Qandahar line. Gladstone's "Little England" Liberal government was displaced in Westminister and Whitehall in 1876 by a Tory government led by Benjamin Disraeli, a strong advocate of Forward School imperialism. "Dizzy's" choice for Viceroy of India, Lord Lytton, was equally addicted to the Great Game and was, like Disraeli, a romantic poet. Soon after reaching India, Lytton assured Lord Salisbury, then secretary of state, that "it will not be difficult to put the screw on Sher Ali." [11] To Rawlinson he wrote that there was no longer "an Afghan question," arguing "these are only departments of the great Russian question, and should be treated accordingly." Lytton's prior experience in government service had been exclusively European. He found the "prospect of a war with Russia immensely exciting" and proposed in November 1876 that British India "should at once take the offensive in Central Asia, where Russia is really very weak. . . . So far as India is concerned, no event could be so fortunate as a war with Russia next Spring." In June 1877, Disraeli wrote Queen Victoria, after having convinced her that year to add the title "Empress of India" to her regalia, that if Russia dared move toward Constantinople, the Bear should be "attacked from Asia . . . Troops should be sent to the Persian Gulf . . . the Empress of India should order her armies to clear Central Asia of the Muscovites and drive them into the Caspian." [12]

Lytton imperiously informed Sher Ali that he was sending a British mission to Kabul and asked the amir where he preferred to receive such distinguished guests. The viceroy had characterized Afghanistan as "an earthen pipkin between two iron pots," but the pipkin now stubbornly refused to welcome British officers back to Kabul or Qandahar. Sher Ali's reportedly warm reception of a Russian mission, led by Major-General Stolietoff, who arrived in Kabul in the summer of 1878, is usually noted as the major historic provocation for the second Afghan War. Lytton's mission, led by Neville Chamberlain who was assisted by Peshawar's commissioner, Major Louis Cavagnari, was firmly turned back at the Khyber by the Afghan commander of the pass. But the British advance into Quetta a year earlier, fortified by Sir Robert Sandeman, its first Resident, had provoked Sher Ali "to play with the Russians,"[13] since that new British Baluchi outpost beyond the Bolan Pass was not only in easy range of Qandahar but had long been considered part of Afghanistan's sovereign domain. Sandeman, a clever, vigorous Forward gamesman, had purchased Quetta from the khan of Kalat, its local prince, whose combined rents from the rest of his 280,000 square mile state, hardly equaled the annual sum the British now paid him for Quetta, the Bolan Pass, and permission to build a broad-gauge railroad across his land to allow swift fortification of this most forward post of the British Empire. Sher Ali feared such aggressive British action enough to invite the Russian mission from Central Asia. Although General Stolietoff left Kabul within a month of his arrival there, Lord Lytton could see "no honourable alternative" for British India but war.

Lytton launched the second Afghan War in November 1878, ordering an Indian army of over 20,000 troops to "restore British honour in Kabul." Three columns moved west over the Khyber, Bolan, and Peiwar passes, dragging seventy heavy artillery pieces across those mountain walls, smashing every fortress they confronted. Sher Ali fled north in terror, but found no Russian army advancing across the Oxus to his aid. He died of a heart attack in flight near Balkh. Kabul and Qandahar fell once again to superior British arms. Major Cavagnari, Lytton's political agent, dictated the terms of a most humiliating subsidiary alliance treaty to the new young amir, Yakub Khan, in May 1879. The amir granted the Khyber Pass and Kurram

Valley in the northern Frontier region and Pishin, Sibi, and Bori around Quetta to the British Raj.

On July 24, Cavagnari and his guard moved into Kabul's Bala Hissar, the final step in teaching the Afghans a proper lesson in good manners. Thanks to a newly strung telegraph that linked Bala Hissar to Peshawar, and thence to Simla and Calcutta, Cavagnari kept in daily touch with the viceroy. On September 2, 1879, he cabled Lytton "All Well." The next day he and every Englishman in Kabul were murdered by an angry mob of tribals, within sight of the amir's private apartments in the palace. Simla sent a fresh army to teach Kabul another lesson. But Afghans were slow to learn and proved just as treacherous the following year in Qandahar. The year 1880 was, in fact, almost as costly and tragic a year for British martial fortunes as 1842. London's electorate now refused to pay for any further Afghan adventures, ousting Disraeli and bringing Gladstone back to power.

A new amir, Abdur Rahman Khan, Sher Ali's nephew, who was reared in Russian-Central Asian exile after his father lost the struggle for Kabul's throne, returned home to start an uninterrupted reign of twenty-one years. Lord Ripon, Gladstone's Liberal viceroy of India from 1880 to 1884, granted immediate recognition and aid to his western neighbor, despite Abdur Rahman's Russian apprenticeship. Probably the shrewedest of a line of clever Barakzai monarchs, Abdur Rahman quickly learned to make the most of the Great Game raging beyond his borders. He was supported lavishly by annual British stipends in silver and guns, yet surrendered no internal autonomy to his mighty eastern neighbor, promising only to abstain from relations with any other foreign power. By thus accepting British suzerainty over his realm, Abdur Rahman bought invaluable time, strengthening his grip on his relatives and rivals. He was not, however, able to persuade his new benefactors in Simla to withdraw their troops from any of the Afghan districts wrested from Kabul's control during the second Afghan War. The road beyond the Khyber, in the hard-to-defend Kurram Valley, remained with Britain's expanded North-West Frontier Agency. Pishin, Sibi, Quetta, and the Bolan Pass were integrated into a British Baluchistan. Kabul thus came within fifty miles of British

India's new tribal buffer zone, and Pathans who guarded the passes, especially the Afridis and Mohmands, were paid off each year by British agents to "keep the peace."

Russia responded to Britain's new moves by advancing to Khiva in 1881 and annexing Merv in 1884. The latter started an epidemic of "Mervousness" in London, impelling Gladstone's government to propose to Petersburg the immediate creation of International Boundary commissions to define Afghanistan's borders. Before those deliberative bodies could meet, however, Cossacks overran Panjdeh in 1885, advancing the Russian front to within 100 miles of Herat. Gladstone rose in the House of Commons solemnly to warn Russia that a march against Herat would mean war with Great Britain. Two corps of the Indian Army were fully mobilized, and the Liberal prime minister requested immediate authorization of his peers in Parliament to raise a loan of eleven million pounds sterling to "protect our vital national interest" in western Afghanistan. But the party of "Little England" did not survive the next general election in the face of that Russian advance.

A Tory victory at the polls brought Lord Salisbury, Disraeli's heir, to the head of a new administration as the bitter, frustrating negotiations to delineate the northwestern boundary of Afghanistan continued. Russian border guards probed every undefended inch of Afghanistan, grabbing as much territory as they could, even as the Boundary Protocol was being drafted. Salisbury reiterated Gladstone's weighty warning, and the Bear drew in its claws.

While Britain kept Russia out of Herat, Abdur Rahman consolidated his internal power and emerged as the "Iron Amir," reorganizing and tightening his administration. He divided Afghanistan into seven districts and four provinces, established new boards of trade and treasury, and even introduced a skeleton of constitutional government to Kabul. By magnifying his monarchic powers at the expense of local tribal chiefs and mullahs, Abdur Rahman helped Afghanistan unite without modernizing the country any faster than suited his interests. He was, for example, careful to exclude railroad construction, industrial development, and Western education from his reforms, seeming to sense that rapid change would topple him along with other out-moded Afghan institutions. The one institution significantly modern-ized by the Iron Amir was his army, which was reorganized along British Indian lines, equipped with new Enfield rifles and artillery, and kept over 50,000 strong. The absolutism of Abdur Rahman's rule was, however, in the mainstream of Islamic tradition, and before his death, he was hailed as "Light of the Nation and Religion" (*Ziya al-Millat wa Din*) by his *Ulama*.

After 1893, even Abdur Rahman could not defer British demands to agree upon a border between his nation and India. Sir Mortimer Durand, India's foreign secretary, went to Kabul and negotiated the line that immortalized his name. Actual demarcation of the Durand Line was not completed until 1895. It has since proved "politically, geographically, and strategically untenable,"[14] for not only did it cut through the center of major Pathan tribal areas, but it brought remote and hardly defensible rugged bulges of Afghanistan under the umbrella of the British Raj, which subsequently wasted much of its wealth and manpower in seeking, over and over again, to "civilize" the natives. Abdur Rahman accepted the line only because Durand almost doubled his annual payoff in money and guns, but the reluctant amir was not fooled for a moment by his rapacious, greedy, piously pretentious British ally-protectors. As he noted after Durand left Kabul, "Though England does not want any piece of Afghanistan, still she never loses a chance of getting one—and this friend has taken more than Russia has."[15]

To Great Britain, however, drawing the line seemed crucial, for two reasons. First, it served to legitimize British India's additions to its Baluchistan and North-West Frontier tribal zones since the second Afghan War. Second, it solved the international dispute with Russia's Imperial force, for now Afghanistan was at last a geographically de-fined national entity—for the first time. There was finally a map to open and point at when facing the Russians and warning, "The State within these lines must remain inviolate!" Afghanistan had become, albeit foolishly and imperfectly, a verifiably delineated international buffer state between the world's two largest empires. To the neat and legalistically clean minds of statesmen in Whitehall and Calcutta, that was an important achievement.

To Mohmand Pathans and the Darwesh Khel, to Waziris and Afridis, to Hazaras and Ahmadzais the Durand Line was ridiculous, an insult and an absurdity, a thing so foreign to their nomadic, penuriously independent life-style of wandering in search of food, shelter, family, tribal friends, or "game" to plunder or shoot that drawing it only served to set the border ablaze for the closing years of the century. A mini-Game was started, much like the original Great Game, only this time British India's new border tribal zones were the coveted prize, and Afghanistan and British India the opposing players. The amir had never reconciled himself to the loss of that tribal domain on the North-West Frontier or even in Baluchistan. Why should he? Because the Englishmen he hated had told him to? Because he was paid well for that rocky land? Abdur Rahman was a practical fellow. He knew his limitations and the source of his army's arms and monthly salaries. But he was also a king and, above all, a Pathan. His language and blood were the same as those of the border tribes. Could he ever truly, inwardly accept new "British" status?

British agents posted along the new border accused Abdur Rahman of "intriguing with the tribes," calling him "duplicitous," "faithless," and using every harsh word in the lexicon of empire-builders to denounce this Afghan ally for stirring up trouble against his neighboring Raj. They had good reason to feel bitter, for wherever they went, tribal response was the same. The Shiranis turned the slopes of the Sulaiman Range into shooting galleries where the British served as targets, as did the Orakzai of the Samana Range, the Isazai tribes of the dread and hated Black Mountain, and the chiefs of Hunza and Nagar. The Hazara border was in perpetual ferment, and the Khyber was watched day and night by Zakka Khels and Mohmands, who waited for the isolated horseman, the undermanned patrol, or the unguarded caravan heading west. More than once in the latter half of the 1890s Simla was ready to retaliate by launching another march on Kabul, but longer memories and cooler heads in London ordered restraint.

Abdur Rahman had openly warned Lord Lansdowne, the Forward School viceroy who had sent Durand to Kabul, what would happen "If you should cut them [his tribal territories taken within the British Frontier] out of my dominions." The amir understood his proud people better than any Englishman and was a wiser diplomat than most of his contemporaries.

They will neither be of any use to you nor to me. You will always be engaged in fighting or other trouble with them, and they will always go on plundering. As long as your government is strong and in peace, you will be able to keep them quiet by a strong hand, but if at any time a foreign enemy appears on the borders of India, these frontier tribes will be your worst enemies. . . . In your cutting away from me these frontier tribes, who are people of my nationality and my religion, you will injure my prestige in the eyes of my subjects, and will make me weak, and my weakness is injurious for your government. [16]

Once the line had been drawn, however, there was no turning back for the Raj. Every inch would be probed, every pocket of isolation unveiled, no matter how remote. Even Chitral,[17] remote fastness of the Hindu Kush, 150 miles north of Peshawar, had to be opened to British agency. No sooner had British troops moved into that wild, high region than a strong anti-English party emerged there. In 1895 *Jihad* was proclaimed against the British Raj throughout the wilds of neighboring Dir, Bajaur, Swat, and Chitral itself, where a beseiged British garrison was totally cut off and forced to remain inside its fort for forty-one days. "Fanaticism" was the term most commonly used by the British to describe those tribal acts of self-defense, desperately designed to preserve cherished independence along civilization's latest frontier.

By 1899, when Lord Curzon arrived in Calcutta to take up his burden as viceroy, there were no less than 10,000 regular troops of the British Indian Army garrisoned permanently in the wilds of the North-West Frontier. The cost was inordinate, and for most of the year several of those remote garrisons were totally isolated by snow, guarding nothing but their own sanity and dwindling supplies. Though Curzon was one of Britain's most ardent Forward imperialists, he had the intelligence to realize that regular British troops were not only much too expensive to waste in such isolated regions, but that their mere presence provoked the unrest they had been sent to quell.

The militia scheme he introduced along the North-West Frontier tribal belt, therefore, first called for immediate withdrawal of all British Army regulars to cantonments in the settled districts to the east and south of the tribal zone. Tribal militia—chosen tribesmen with rifles—were thereafter paid regularly by the British to "keep the peace" in their designated zones. These tribal levies were not only much cheaper than regular soldiers, but proved far less provocative to neighbors. Indeed, many Pathans, once bitter opponents of British expansion, soon became heroic Khyber Rifles or Samana Rifles, chosen defenders of the passes and rugged lands they loved. Curzon never intended to bribe all the tribes, however, and some therefore remained fiercely opposed to the Raj and to the "turncoat" tribals who became its defenders after 1900.

Curzon's scheme depended on two other major factors: fast-moving columns of regular British troops strategically located to the rear but within fairly close range of remote tribal zones, and new railway lines that could "fly" those columns to the front whenever a border blaze flared. Peshawar thus became the base for the Khyber flying column that would relieve Landi Kotal, if called, and Kohat served the same supportive function for the Orakzai country and Fort Sandeman. Quetta had earlier been designated for much the same duty in Baluchistan. In most respects Curzon's militia scheme was just an elaboration of the prior Sandeman system that since the late 1880s had worked well in the land of the Baluchi and Brahui tribals of the southern sector of the Frontier.

Curzon's Frontier reforms were completed in 1901 by full administrative integration of the regularly settled districts of Hazara, Peshawar, Kohat, Bannu, and Dera Ismail Khan and the new tribal tracts between them and the Durand Line into a single province of British India—the North-West Frontier Province. This new trans-Indus province was initially run by a series of military chief-commissioners directly under the viceroy's command, who helped to expedite its support or defense in time of tribal unrest or international tension. The traditional Pathan code of honor (*Pakhtunwali*), under which blood-feud was a man's sacred duty, was permitted within tribal zones but not inside any of the settled districts. The problem of keeping culprits from one legal system out of the contiguous zone where a different code applied became a major administrative headache for British officers. The democratic ethos of Pathan tribes also required convening councils (*jirgas*) to try more serious cases of murder or mayhem, and at times these *jirgas* seemed to include every adult male of a tribe. Understaffed young British officers had their hands full. Administrative costs rose alarmingly. Nor did all this new expense and trouble bring peace and contentment to the Frontier. Quite the contrary. In Waziristan, the "barbarous" Mahsud were perpetually up and fighting. No amount of money or punishment seemed to satisfy those "criminals." They stubbornly continued to assassinate every British officer they found within their wild domain. For two years, 1900–1902, total blockade was tried, but even that failed to chasten the "wolfish Mahsud," who were the only Pathan militiamen to murder their own officers. Finally, in disgrace, they had to be disarmed in 1905 and disbanded. There was no gratitude, no sense of responsibility, in such people.

Abdur Rahman died in 1901, as Victoria did, just as the twentieth century began. The Iron Amir, toward the end of his life, came to think of his little country as a goat on which a lion and a bear kept constant watch.[18] He wrote of Afghanistan and its serene isolation as a swan, who stayed in the middle of her lake because a Russian wolf pack was snarling on its north shore, while an old British tigress lay dozing on the south.

Abdur Rahman's son Habibullah succeeded in taking his father's throne without challenge. He was young and wanted to modernize his hermit kingdom, so he accepted an invitation from Curzon's successor, Lord Minto, to visit India in 1906. The new amir was completely fascinated by motorcars and generally taken with Western technology.

Warmly convivial by temperament, he was considered a dreadful boor by British officialdom, especially his viceregal host. "He is a fat little man," Minto wrote to Secretary of State John Morley about Habibullah. "When he intended to be witty he prefaces his remarks with 'Now I make joke.' "[19] Minto and his staff were much relieved to see Habibullah head home, though before leaving for Kabul the amir requested "a railway expert; a geologist, a man to lay out racecourses . . . a man to can fruits, a landscape gardener, a motor mechanic and a metallurgist." The British viceroy sent none of those experts, however, for the last thing Britain wanted to do was to convert Kabul into another Simla, Peshawar, or Delhi. Afghanistan today remains virtually the only nation in the modern world that has no railroad, a remarkable distinction considering the size of British India's rail net, which was more than 25,000 miles long by the turn of the century.

To best serve the British Empire as a true buffer, however, Afghanistan had to be kept as difficult to cross and as technologically backward as possible, for improved communications would only facilitate a possible Russian advance, and modernization would inevitably increase trade and contacts with the north. Habibullah had, unfortunately, been foolish enough to believe the British rhetoric he read and heard. His youthful enthusiasms made him *want* to believe, of course, that the British were not simply paying him off to keep out the Russians. He actually thought they liked him, those Mintos, Ibbetsons, and Hares. He imagined they wanted to help him and his nation grow and prosper. He was more naïve than his father.

No sooner did Habibullah return to Kabul in 1907 than he learned the true nature of his relationship with Great Britain. He was informed that London and Petersburg had concluded a new "convention" concerning Afghanistan, of which he had never been told a word prior to its signing and about which he had learned nothing in all his lengthy talks, meetings, dinners, and balls in British India. The Anglo-Russian Convention was Great Britain's last attempt at detente with Imperial Russia, a diplomatic try for a comprehensive settlement of the Eastern Question. It was Morley's brainchild in great measure and seemed at the time a sensible Liberal alternative to the increasingly noisy bellicosity of Forward hard-liners. The convention, like Campbell-Bannerman's Liberal party victory of 1905, was first a product of British popular disenchantment with the inflated price of protecting and constantly defending British Imperial outposts the world over, especially since the Boer War. Persia, Afghanistan, and Tibet all were viewed as posing the same potentially disastrous traps to outflanked or beleaguered garrisons of an empire that had simply grown too fast, too large, and cost far too much to man and secure. In 1905, after most of the Imperial Russian navy had fought its way to the bottom of the Sea of Japan, the tsar's government felt much the same way. It was a unique opportunity for peace—the world's two Goliaths each having met his own David on different continents. The Bear and the Lion were ready to sit down amicably to divide the goats of Central Asia between them. How could an idealistic young amir appreciate such *realpolitik?* Best leave him out of such delicate diplomatic negotiations, which were sufficiently difficult with only two parties to satisfy. So Whitehall concluded at least. Was it due to the thoughtlessness of power? Ignorance of Afghan, Pathan, youthful, and royal pride? Or merely the nature of the beasts and their feast?

The Anglo-Russian Convention divided Persia into northern and southeastern "spheres of influences," Russians retaining the former, British the latter. Tibet went to China. Great Britain got Afghanistan, the British winning full control over Kabul's foreign policy. Russia would, however, hereafter enjoy "equal commercial opportunities" within Afghanistan, and could send its own commercial agents to Kabul. Morley and Britain's Cabinet were convinced that because of the convention, the threat of a Russian attack on India had been ruled out of practical politics, since Russians now understood that Great Britain viewed the frontiers of India and Afghanistan as identical. The Liberal Cabinet hoped that the convention would make possible an immediate and substantial reduction in the cost of India's martial establishment, but they reckoned without Minto or Lord Kitchener, Minto's military commander-in-chief, who really ruled India at this time. To reduce martial budgets would only encourage unrest they warned, "endangering the lives of British civilians." No home government could risk such a thing. Not a British colonel or a subaltern was fired from the Indian Army in the wake of what many Londoners considered the diplomatic conclusion of the Great Game.

Habibullah refused to sign the convention, and after 1907, "secret" border reports began to reach British India of a brisk trade in new arms and ammunition pouring into Afghanistan from the Persian Gulf. The volume of that trade could be measured in part by the drastic reduction in the price of a Martini rifle, which had sold for 500 rupees along the Frontier in 1906 but was down to 130 rupees by 1908. The following year, 40,000 rifles were imported to Kabul from sources other than the British as were 16,500 rifles, 352 pistols, and over a million rounds of ammunition between March 1909 and April 1910. Border gangs and raiding parties increased accordingly, and the government of India had good reason to believe they were incited and armed by Kabul. Habibullah was, of course, careful never to give his British Resident-keeper proof of treachery, having learned swiftly the tricks of Western diplomacy. His humiliating impotence and that of his nation led him after 1907 to turn elsewhere than to British tutors for aid in bolstering Afghanistan's defenses.

The Ottoman Turkish Caliphate to his west was the first land to which Habibullah looked for help. Seven Turkish "immigrants" arrived in Kabul in 1907, "one of whom, Mahmud Sami, a gymnastics instructor, was put in charge of training the military forces of Kabul; another, an engineer, took care of the power plant that provided the palace with electricity, and a third, a physician, took charge of Kabul's hospital."[20] Frustrated in his friendly overtures and appeals for modernization, feeling betrayed by British duplicity, Habibullah looked to the Universal Brotherhood of Islam for help in leading his land toward a richer, happier future.

Pan-Islamic revival the world over had been initiated by Sayyid Jamal ud-din Afghani (1828–97),[21] whose name alone appealed to Afghan loyalties and pride, though he had actually been born in Persia and had traveled through India, Saudi Arabia, Turkey, and Egypt before settling in Kabul, where he was employed in Dost Muhammad's service. Afghani developed an intense hatred for Western imperialism,

especially its Anglo-French varieties, and called upon Muslims everywhere to rise against the "unbearable tyranny" of Western "infidel
rule." He even went to St. Petersburg and tried in vain to enlist the
tsar's aid for his mission. Millions of South Asian Muslims, mostly
from the Punjab and along the Frontier, were to become ardent supporters of Pan-Islam during the pre- and post-World War I era under
the charismatic leadership of the brothers Mohammad Ali (1878–
1931) and Shaukat Ali (1873–1938), founders of the *Khilafat* movement. But Habibullah's support for Pan-Islam was mitigated by his
stronger nationalist sentiment, which remained the primary passion of
his life. The Turco-Italian and Balkan Wars immediately preceding
World War I intensified Pan-Islamic fears of the West throughout
Asia.

The last European power to enter the Great Game was Germany.
On the eve of World War I, Field Marshal Helmuth von Moltke noted
the obvious advantage to be gained for his kaiser from a Pan-Islamic
Jihad to be called by the Ottoman Caliph. German intelligence in Constantinople learned that the amir would require little encouragement
for a strike against India. This proved to be wishful diplomacy, however, as Habibullah never felt quite strong enough to launch an attack
over his eastern passes during the war, when British garrisons throughout India were most dangerously depleted. Several Turco-German expeditions to Afghanistan were, nonetheless, sent through Turkey and
Persia in 1915, arriving in Kabul before the end of that year. Werner
Otto von Hentig, leader of the German expedition, informed Hallibul-
lah that "the Central Powers recognized him as an independent and
sovereign ruler and invited him to join in defeating his traditional enemies; his reward would be—in addition to independence—territorial
concessions along the Indian Frontier and a free port at Karachi."[22]
Habibullah "stressed that while the Afghan people were a formidable
force when it meant defending their own soil, they were less effective
in fighting a European force in a conventional war. A war against
India would be a grave risk as it would mean the loss of the British
subsidy; besides it would involve Afghanistan in war with Russia.
Without massive aid from the Central Powers, no guarantee for suc-

cess existed."[23] In his own way, Habibullah thus rejected the German offer of martial peanuts.

Much as Habibullah hated the British by now, he still vividly remembered the power of their Imperial army, which he had seen with his own eyes in 1906–7. Hentig wore a spiked helmet in Kabul, but was only thirty-two years old and had no more than a handful of small-armed German soldiers in his meager and exhausted escort. He did, however, draft a German-Afghan treaty, promising Afghanistan all the arms and money it needed in addition to complete independence. Habibullah supposedly signed it in January 1916, and Hentig transmitted it to Germany. British anxiety over the amir's meetings with the Germans, as well as over reports reaching Simla of Turks addressing large crowds in Kabul mosques, calling for *Jihad* against Britain and Russia, led to a most unusual personal appeal to Habibullah from King George V. The British decided at this juncture to raise Habibullah's annual subsidy by no less than 200,000 rupees. Germany's unexpected entry into the Great Game thus served, at least initially, to fatten the Afghan goat. The amir would not live very long to enjoy that added bounty, however. Hentig's treaty had promised £10 million and 10,000 troops, but neither ever reached Kabul.

The Bolshevik Revolution of 1917 put an end to the Anglo-Russian Convention, as it did to other tsarist treaties. The Cossack Brigade barracked north of the Oxus dispersed, and Austro-German prisoners held in Central Asia wandered south to Afghanistan with Muslim refugees, looking to the amir as their Pan-Islamic leader. The German and Ottoman defeat the following year gave Habibullah reason to pause, though many of his countrymen and close advisers urged him to lead a *Jihad* against British India. Had he acted earlier he might have done considerable damage to the Raj, but fear and indecision frustrated his plans. Perhaps he even imagined Britain would give him the total independence he sought for his nation if he remained neutral just a bit longer. Woodrow Wilson had stirred such hopes in India as well with the last of his inspiring Fourteen Points, self-determination. The Paris Peace Conference was ready to free the world, after all, was it not, now that the "War To End All Wars" had been won by such idealistic Allies!

On February 2, 1919, Habibullah wrote India's new viceroy, Lord Chelmsford, and demanded "absolute liberty, freedom of action, and perpetual independence" for Afghanistan. He never received a written reply. Eighteen days later, before dawn, Habibullah was murdered, apparently by one of his own trusted guards. The amir and his camp were on a "hunting trip" at Qala-i-gush in Laghman District near the British Indian border. Had Habibullah gone there to rouse the tribes, resolved after hearing no word from the viceroy for two weeks that he could wait no longer for the "perpetual independence" he yearned to bring his troubled land? His assassin fired a single bullet point-blank into Habibullah's sleeping brain.

The actual killer and motive never came to historic light, though a number of political conspiracy theories alternately blaming Pan-Islamic, Soviet, or British sources were soon current in the bazaars of Kabul and Jalalabad. Habibullah's religiously conservative brother Nasrullah, who had been along on the hunt, immediately proclaimed himself amir and cabled India's viceroy, informing Lord Chelmsford of his investiture. The viceroy, in turn, promptly cabled London that "It would be dangerous to hold up our acknowledgment. What we want are a peaceful succession and a friendly Amir. If the former were hanging in the balance, delay might turn the scale."[24] Was this sudden change of amirs simply a new chapter in the old Nabob Game? Chelmsford's lightning response to Nasrullah, whom he immediately addressed as "Your Majesty," must have made poor Habibullah's other relatives wonder why the British viceroy had been so slow in answering earlier messages from Kabul.

Amanullah Khan, youngest son of the murdered amir, was in Kabul that bitterly cold February morning. It did not take him long to decide that whoever had actually pulled the tirgger, his Uncle Nasrullah was the traitor responsible for his father's death. Proclaiming himself amir, Amanullah swore on his naked sword to avenge that murder and ordered his uncle arrested. He raised the pay of his army then stationed in Kabul, and in a week his hated uncle was in custody. A week later, Amanullah wrote the viceroy to inform him that Afghanistan considered itself a totally "independent and free Government."

A department of Foreign Affairs was established for the first time in Kabul, headed by Mahmud Tarzi (1866–1935), who had been Habibullah's leading adviser and was now Amanullah's foreign minister. Tarzi wrote to the president of the Russian Republic, calling for direct relations between the two neighboring states. Amanullah then seized "the opportunity of my accession to announce to the Russian Republic my strong adherence to the principle of equality of all men and peaceful union of all people. Afghanistan has hitherto stood apart from all other nations, but now that Russia has raised the standard of Bolshevism, I hasten to add that she has earned the gratitude of all the world."[25] On April 15, the Soviet press reported Afghanistan's "independence." Amanullah also wrote to Persia and Turkey, France, the United States, and Japan. At this time, he issued a revolutionary proclamation, informing his people and the rest of the world that the "Government of Afghanistan shall be internally and externally independent and free, that is to say, that all rights of Government that are possessed by other independent powers of the world should be possessed in their entirety by Afghanistan."[26] A month later Amanullah proclaimed *Jihad* against British tyranny, and with spring's thaw he ordered his troops to move east in three columns.

The third Afghan War began on May 6, 1919, as Amanullah's troops crossed the Durand Line at several points north and south of the Khyber. A mass uprising had been planned in Peshawar's bazaar for May 8, when the Afghan troops were supposed to reach that capital of the North-West Frontier Province. British intelligence got early warning of the Peshawar plot, however, and cut off the city's water supply, closing its gates on May 7. At Landi Kotal, Pathan Khyber Rifles started deserting their posts, singly at first, then in large numbers, as word of *Jihad* spread with the wind across the Hindu Kush. The commandant was soon obliged to disband his once much-touted Rifles, in effect burying Curzon's militia system. Heatstroke and cholera claimed as many British lives in that last of the Anglo-Afghan wars as Pathan marksmen. The British Royal Flying Corps (RFC), just a year earlier, had flown its first squadrons of Vickers' bombers to India from the Mesopotamian sector. A Frontier "aerodome"[27] on the Tochi road, about five miles out of Bannu, based these modern weapons within range of both Kabul and Jalalabad. Though high altitudes and extremes of heat and cold made flying most precarious in this part of the world, British pilots successfully bombed Jalalabad and Kabul, returning safely from both raids after thoroughly terrifying and demoralizing their tribal Afghan enemies. Amanullah appealed for an armistice on May 28, 1919. The British, tired of fighting and fearing a more extensive uprising along the entire Frontier as news of mounting tribal restlessness reached Peshawar, agreed. Both sides met in Rawalpindi that August to draw up a treaty that ended Kabul's subsidy from Simla with the war and declared Afghanistan a "fully sovereign State."

The Great Game was over. A number of smaller, nationalist games had, however, only just begun.

SIX

The Impact of Nationalisms

Amanullah's effective assertion of Afghanistan's national independence from British suzerainty sent a thrill of hope and excitement throughout British India's Hindu as well as Muslim population. "The Afghans have a bad Government," wrote Mohandas K. Gandhi (1869–1948) in his *Young India* in 1919, "but it is self-Government. I envy them." India's Muslims were far more enthusiastic and within a year of Afghanistan's independence started a *hijrat* over the northwest passes to the new *Dar-ul-Islam,* a Pan-Islamic Khilafat pilgrimage aimed at bolstering the crumbling Ottoman Caliphate with a growing army of Muslims, marching across Islamic soil to the Sublime Porte.

The seeds of nationalism had been sown in South Asia soon after the British Raj started to consolidate its Imperial power over the subcontinent early in the nineteenth century. Westernized Hindu Brahmans of Calcutta gathered in elite societies to study their great and tolerant Sanskrit tradition with fresh pride as Christian missionaries labored to save their "benighted souls" through conversion. A veritable renaissance of Hinduism had taken root in Bengal by 1830. Local Muslim mullahs and alims from the Frontier to Assam were by then angrily proclaiming British India a "Land at War" (*Dar-ul-harb*), calling upon their peasant followers to rise in *Jihad* against *feringhi kafirs* who exploited them. Deposed princes, disgruntled aristocrats, and impoverished peasants all longed with nostalgia for the glorious golden past that may have existed only in their dreams, but was made poignantly beautiful by the freedom from foreign rule it invariably embodied.

Ardent nationalists like Veer Savarkar (1883–1966) called the Anglo-Indian War of 1857–58 the "Indian War of Independence," insisting "that vast tidal wave from Peshawar to Calcutta" could only have "risen in blood" for the two great principles of Hindustan, *Sva-dharma* ("Our Own Religion") and *Sva-raj* ("Our Own Rule").[1] Whatever may be said for the historic accuracy of Savarkar's thesis, there is no denying that in the aftermath of that war, fought to restore the Mughal padishah and Maratha peshwa to their thrones of power, new forces of national consciousness roused "Young India" from its political lethargy, giving birth to the Indian National Congress (in 1885), and later to the Muslim League (in 1906). Congress and the League would subsequently serve as institutional rallying standards for the leaders of the independent nations of India and Pakistan, born from the fission of the British Empire in 1947.

Initially, both Congress and the League owed as much to the positive inspiration of British Western institutions and ideas as they did to the rejection of British power and its arrogant, racist Raj. For the first two decades of its existence, in fact, Congress remained a predominantly loyal political club for upper-middle-class, Western-educated, secular-minded Hindu, Parsi, Jain, some Muslim, and a few Christian Indians. Well read in Shakespeare, Milton, both Mills, Burke, Macaulay, and Morley, India's mostly moderate young Liberals of the National Congress wanted, as their first president, Barrister W. C. Bonnerjee (1844–1906) of Calcutta, put it, "the basis of the Government . . . widened" to give others of the same good sense, manners, and erudition "their proper and legitimate share in it." They wanted the British Crown to live up to the letter of its Company's noblest promises, especially the lofty Liberal Charter of 1833 and Queen Victoria's own lovely words in her Proclamation of 1858:

> We hold ourselves bound to the natives of our Indian territories by the same obligations of duty which bind us to all our other subjects. . . . We declare it to be our royal will and pleasure

that none be in anywise favoured, none molested or disquieted, by reason of their religious faith or observances, but that all shall alike enjoy the equal and impartial protection of the law. . . . And it is our further will that, so far as may be, our subjects, of whatever race or creed, be freely and impartially admitted to offices in our service, the duties of which they may be qualified, by their education, ability, and integrity, duly to discharge.[2]

What more could any bright, ambitious young Indian ask for—except actual implementation of such a policy?

'Twixt the word and its augmentation, however, fell the shadows of mediocre men on the spot, too insecure, fretful, or nervous to trust any native with a position of power, authority, or great responsibility. The "Turtons and the Burtons" always remembered the "Sepoy Mutiny," when those trusted by Christian colonels to be "true to their salt" faithlessly stabbed those very sahibs and their memsahibs in the back. Those who knew India best, including many English born there, cautioned recently arrived would-be reformers against any excess of intimacy. Indians made decent bearers, cooks, and clerks, but they had no place in one's club, officer corps, or the highest echelons of the Civil Service, as the old boys who presided over such exclusively male British preserves were careful to ensure.

When brilliant young Indians like Surendranath Banerjea (1848–1926) proved themselves exceptions to such rules of British prejudice and supremacy, gaining entry to the coveted Indian Civil Service, they were soon ousted for trivial infractions of regulations. "I had suffered because I was an Indian," Banerjea concluded, after he was "disgraced" by dismissal from the Service and then denied permission to enter the Bar. "The personal wrong done to me was an illustration of the helpless impotency of our people."[3] Driven out by the British, he became a leading Indian nationalist, using his gifts of golden oratory to rouse millions of Bengalis to a fever pitch of patriotism during the anti-partition movement in his home province after 1905. A decade earlier, presiding over the eleventh annual session of the Indian National Congress, Banerjea urged, "It is never too early to raise the cry for reform. We must cry betimes, cry late, cry incessantly, fill the air with our importunate clamour, and then only can we hope to move the Government to take any action. . . . They never move except under the irresistible pressure of a public opinion which will admit no delay.''[4]

Some incessant and "importunate clamour" for reforms of every sort, from more jobs for Indians to less money for the military and "Home charges" that drained India's wealth for the benefit of Great Britain, made Congress less popular with each succeeding viceroy, his commander-in-chief, and their lieutenants. In 1905, much sharper lines of conflict were drawn after the first partition of Bengal, the parting gift of Lord Curzon's administration to India's nationalist movement. With a population over 85 million and hundreds of thousands of square miles of what are now four states, pre-1905 Bengal was, as the government insisted, administratively cumbersome and inefficient. However, the partition line severing West Bengal from the newly created province of Eastern Bengal and Assam came to be viewed by a majority of Calcutta's intellectuals as nothing less than the Caesarian severance of their Mother, British *divide et impera* tactics of the most blatant sort. For that British partition line cut right through the center of the Bengali-speaking heartland of the province, whose extremities included three other major language regions, Bihari, Oriya, and Assamese, all subsequently to become separate provinces. Many of Congress's most articulate critics of government were, moreover, Bengali Hindus from Calcutta, who felt doubly discriminated against, for in their rump province of West Bengal they were a minority and in the new province of Eastern Bengal, whose capital was Dacca, there was a Muslim Bengali majority. "A cruel wrong," Congress President Gopal Gokhale (1866–1915) called the partition, one that would "always stand as a complete illustration of the worst features of the present system of bureaucratic rule—its utter contempt for public opinion, its arrogant pretentions to superior wisdom, its reckless disregard of the most cherished feelings of the people, the mockery of an appeal to its sense of justice, its cool preference of Service interests to those of the governed."[5] For all its severity of language, however, Gokhale's critique remained that of a true liberal believer in the ultimate justice of British rule, its wisdom, and fair play.

A tougher, harsher, more revolutionary "New Party" emerged within Congress, however, in the wake of this major crisis of confidence. Bal Gangadhar Tilak (1856–1920), Gokhale's Poona colleague-competitor, was founding father of that revolutionary movement. He viewed foreign rule as the single simple cause of all of India's suffering. "Your industries are ruined utterly, ruined by foreign rule," Tilak argued. "The remedy is not petitioning but boycott. We say prepare your forces, organise your power, and then go to work so that they cannot refuse you."[6] He was joined by a growing army of young Bengalis, Punjabis, and Maharashtrians, who came to think of themselves for the first time as *Indians,* children of mother India, to whose sacred freedom they dedicated their lives, determined to drive out the foreign intruders by whatever means.

Boycott of everything foreign was the first revolutionary method employed. National education, at schools and colleges founded by those who had thrown off the chains of studying in British schools and universities, became popular across the land. India's youth learned to glory in their own historic and religious traditions rather than trying to imitate and assimilate those of others. The boycott movement had its nationalist economic counterpart as well, called *Sva-deshi* ("Of Our Own Country"), which encouraged the production of India-made goods, especially cotton cloth and other textiles. Manchester imports soon became a glut on the market, and British-made saris and clothes already owned by Indians were thrown onto mass sacrificial altars, burned as patriotic offerings to India's gods, as the ancient Aryans had sacrificed wealth in propitiating Vedic deities.

"I want to have the key to my house and not merely one stranger turned out of it," insisted Tilak, as the tide of cultural nationalist opposition to British rule mounted to flood level in 1907. *Sva-raj* became the revolutionary mantra of the New Party, which challenged Congress's old guard of moderate leadership as well as the British Raj. "We shall not give them assistance to collect revenue and keep peace," shouted Tilak. "We shall not assist them in fighting beyond the frontiers or outside India with Indian blood and money. We shall not assist them in carrying on the administration of justice. We shall have our own courts, and when the time comes we shall not pay taxes. Can you do that by your united efforts? If you can, you are free from tomorrow."[7] As nationalist fervor mounted to new levels, cults of the bomb and pistol were added to those of moderate and revolutionary rhetoric. British-official lives were claimed in Poona in 1897, the first since Lord Mayo's assassination, and in 1907 several non-official women were added to the list of Western victims of Indian political-terrorist activity.

Official British response to intensified nationalist protest was basically harsh and repressive in India, moderate and reformist in London. "Preventive detention" arrests of thousands of political activists, mostly in Calcutta, Dacca, Poona, Lahore, and Amritsar, filled British Indian prisons without imposing any strain upon the courts, since such "criminals" never had to be charged as long as officialdom considered them a threat to "His Majesty's Government." Leaders of the New Party were either deported, as were Tilak and Lala Lajpat Rai (1865–1928) to Burmese prisons, or fled the country in disguise. Among the latter, Bipin Chandra Pal (1858–1932) went to London, while a young Bengali terrorist colleague changed his name to Sri Arabinda and founded what was to become a world-famous *ashram* in the French enclave of Pondicherry.

Whitehall's Liberal secretary of state for India, John Morley (1838–1923), tried to rally moderate Congress support for British rule in this era of mounting disaffection, with a number of important reforms.[8] The Indian Councils Act of 1909 expanded central and provincial legislative councils throughout British India, introducing directly elected representatives of the people to such councils. Morley also appointed the first Indian members to his own council in Whitehall and got Minto to appoint an Indian to his Calcutta Council as well, changing the government of India's lily-white complexion. Such enlightened measures advanced British India's Constitution toward responsible parliamentary government, but they were only palliative "pills for the earthquake" of India's nationalist movement, which could not be stopped by legislation.

There were, in fact, at least two nationalist movements well underway within the womb of British India by the time Britain's mountainous bureaucratic machine ground out its mouse-size reforms. Muslim modernist leadership had been slow to emerge, but before the end of the nineteenth century an Indian Muslim of towering stature and foresight appeared to urge his Islamic brethren to take full advantage of Western education as a providential benefit of British rule. Sir Sayyid Ahmad Khan (1817–98) was one of the first Mughal aristocrats to join the British Service, where he rose to positions of trust and power. Sayyid devoted the last half of his life to reversing post-1857 British prejudice against their loyal Muslim subjects and in 1860 published his important *Essay on the Causes of the Indian Revolt,* in which he argued that "faithless Brahmans," not Mughal Muslims, were the real instigators of revolt. In 1869 Sir Sayyid was knighted in London, and while in England visited Oxford and Cambridge. Most favorably impressed with the vitality of those educational environments, Sir Sayyid returned home to found the Anglo-Muhammadan Oriental College at Aligarh, some seventy-five miles south of Delhi, in 1875. Sayyid hired a British principal for his new college, which was soon to become the cradle of Muslim modernism and the Pakistan movement.

In 1886 Sir Sayyid started a Muslim Educational Conference, whose annual sessions were held at the same time as those of the Indian National Congress and were designed to serve as an institutional alternative for modernist leaders of the Muslim community. Sayyid launched a number of uncompromising attacks on Congress, whose aims and objectives he denounced as "based upon an ignorance of history and present-day realities." He insisted that "India is inhabited by different nationalities," one of which was Muslim. Congress critics attacked him as a tool of British imperialism. Orthodox Muslims considered him dangerously anti-traditionalist for his modern *Commentary* on the *Qur'an.*[9] Sir Sayyid's faith in science was, however, equal to his belief in the healing and illuminating powers of education, and undaunted by criticism, from whatever source, he worked until his death to encourage his friends and followers of the Muslim minority to trust in both modernizing forces.

Not every modern Muslim in British India agreed with Sir Sayyid's position. Congress's third president, Budruddin Tyabji (1844–1906), for example, was a Bombay Muslim barrister who argued, "I, for one, am utterly at a loss to understand why Mussulmans should not work shoulder to shoulder with their fellow-countrymen, of other races and creeds, for the common benefit of all."[10] Tyabji's unitary-nationalist speech was heard and applauded by no less than 80 Muslim delegates, out of a total of 607 Congress members, who met in Madras in 1887. Seven years later, however, there were only 20 Muslims among the 1163 delegates to the tenth Congress, undeniably reflecting diminished Muslim interest in or attachment to India's major national organization. Hindus and Parsis continued to dominate Congress sessions. Two of Congress's greatest early leaders were Bombay Parsis Dadabhai Naoroji (1825–1917) and Sir Pherozeshah Mehta (1845–1915), both of whom inspired their brilliant Muslim disciple, Muhammad Ali Jinnah (1876–1948), future *Quaid-i-Azam* ("Great Leader") of Pakistan, to start his political career as a member of Congress. Mr. Jinnah's early London experience and legal training at Lincoln's Inn, and his Shi'ite rather than Sunni family background, predisposed him to feel most at home among Congress's Anglophile, secular, liberal leadership. He was President Dadabhai's secretary at the Calcutta Congress of 1906, the year in which the Muslim League was born in neighboring Dacca, now capital of Bangladesh.

The League, like Congress at its inception twenty years earlier, was founded by a small group of moderate, upper-class Muslims, whose primary interest was in securing more jobs in expanding government services and councils for the relatively backward, hence neglected members of their minority community. As soon as word of Morley's planned Reforms bill reached Muslim ears, in fact, Nawab Mohsin-ul-Mulk (1837–1907), Sir Sayyid's successor at Aligarh, organized a prestigious Muslim Deputation to Simla, led by His Highness the Aga Khan (1877–1965). Thirty-five Muslims, who two months later would form the nucleus of the League, arrived at the viceroy's palace in the high Himalayas in October 1906 to plead for affirmative action for their community. Numbering some 62 million, Muslims comprised between 20 and 25 percent of the entire population of the British Indian Empire. The Deputation to Simla thus argued: "We, therefore, desire to submit that under any system of representation, extended or limited, a community in itself more numerous than the entire population of any first class European power except Russia may justly lay claim to adequate recognition as an important factor in the State." They went a step further, requesting "representation . . . commensurate, not merely with their numerical strength, but also with their political importance and the value of the contribution which they make to the defence of the empire." Finally, they appealed to the viceroy's paternalism and British official distrust of and disgust with Congress troublemakers and the unrest they were causing. "The Mohammedans of India have always placed implicit reliance on the sense of justice and love of fair dealing that have characterised their ruler, and have in consequence abstained from pressing their claims by methods that might prove at all embarrassing."[11]

The warmth and generosity of Lord Minto's official response to the Deputation exceeded their fondest expectations. "You point out that in many cases electoral bodies, as now constituted, cannot be expected to return a Mahommedan candidate, and that, if by chance they did so, it could only be at the sacrifice of such a candidate's views to those of a majority opposed to his own community, whom he would in no way represent," noted Lord Minto, adding, "I am entirely in accord with you." Then he promised the "Mahommedan community" to "rest assured that their political rights and interests as a community will be safeguarded by any administrative re-organisation with which I am concerned, and that you, and the people of India, may rely on the British *Raj* to respect . . . the religious beliefs and the national traditions of the myriads composing the population of His Majesty's Indian Empire."[12]

The viceroy's statement was hailed by his own staff as an "act of statesmanship . . . nothing less than the pulling back of sixty-two million of people from joining the ranks of the seditious opposition." Effusive historic credit for a single statement, no doubt. But the Muslim Deputation was sufficiently encouraged to plan its follow-up founding meeting of the Muslim League for that December. Minto's *ex cathedra* promises also ensured introduction of a separate Muslim electorate formula within the Indian Councils Act of 1909, and its expansion in the Government of India Acts of 1919 and 1935. Separate electorates irrevocably tied political office and power to Muslim religious identity in the minds of all Muslims enfranchised for the next four decades under the British Raj. Leaders of Congress saw this formula as further blatant proof of "perfidious" Albion's "divide and rule" technique of retaining power, denouncing the Muslim Deputation and its political offspring as nothing but "an official cat's paw."

To the 58 Muslim League founding delegates assembled at Dacca, however, their raison d'être was communal self-defense rather than special interest. As the League's first president, Nawab Viqar-ul-Mulk (1841–1917), put it, should British rule "at any remote period" cease to exist, India would "pass into the hands of that community which is nearly four times as large as ourselves. Now, gentlemen, let each of you consider what will be your condition if such a situation is created— . . . our life, our property, our honour, and our faith will all be in great danger."[13] The choice of Dacca as site of that historic first meeting was significant. Since the 1905 partition of Bengal, Dacca had emerged from its provincial backwater to the exalted new status of capital of the Muslim-majority province of Eastern Bengal and Assam. For Dacca real estate and the fortunes of local political leaders, like "Nawab" Salimullah Khan, landed baron and British adviser extraordinaire, partition brought an unprecedented boom. Historians of Bangladesh will one day, no doubt, trace the political roots of their nation, first born in 1971, to this seminal half-decade of precocious Bangladeshi political consciousness, even as the roots of Pakistan have their origin in this era.

But just as Muslim political hopes and dreams soared with that first partition, they crashed with its revocation by the British government in 1910. "No bombs, no boons!" cried the nawab of Dacca in bitter despair, attributing the change of heart his British friends suddenly displayed to Hindu Bengali terror tactics. Reunification brought a bitter pill to Calcutta as well, for British India's capital was moved to a new city, begun the following year on Delhi's vast plain: New Delhi. Politically and economically, the shift of government housing and business proved most deflating to Calcutta's condition and egotistical self-image. Strategically and psychologically, moving the center of British official power and gravity some 800 miles northwest of its Bengali metropolis to a grandiose new urban microcosm of the world's mightiest empire meant shifting the head and focus of the Raj toward the Frontier, Afghanistan, and their Muslim majorities and viewpoints. Almost on the eve of World War I the British Empire started raising its own Imperial mausoleum, phoenix-like, on the rubble-strewn plain that had served as a burial ground for no less than ten previous empires over the past three thousand years. A scant two decades after that magnificent shell of pink sandstone and white marble was to be completed, the British Raj would join its preceding Mughal incarnation on that historic pyre.

With the declaration of World War I in 1914 few would have dreamed that the twin-headed dragon of the subcontinent's nationalist movement would topple valiant Saint George from the mount on which he seemed so firmly set. The initial response of all parties, all shades, all classes of Indian opinion to that war against Prussian "barbarism" was, indeed, so positively supportive that India helped, in fact, save the entire Allied cause, on the Western Front, the Home Front, in Egypt, Mesopotamia, and Greece.[14] Forty-five thousand of India's best troops embarked within the first month for the Western Front. Without India's Punjabi, Pathan, Baluchi, and Sikh muscle and blood, Falkenhayn's awesome army might actually have reached Calais. Without Indian princes' money and hospital ships, more of the troops who were sent would have died. Without India's wheat, Great Britain might have starved. Without Indian leather goods, there would never have been enough shoes and martial belts for the Allied forces. Before the war was over, more than a million men, soldiers, coolies, non-combatant support of every variety had been shipped from India to every front on which World War I was fought. South Asia was mined of its wealth and natural resources. Congress and League leaders felt they had good reason, therefore, to expect their just reward of freedom once the war was won. The British gave them, however, not self-government but the sword.

By 1916, thanks primarily to Mr. Jinnah's initiative and energy, Congress and the League agreed upon a single scheme of nationalist constitutional demands to present to the government of India. Jinnah had joined the League in 1913, after it adopted self-government as its ultimate goal, Muslims having become more revolutionary in their protests following their 1910 disillusionment with British promises. With the Caliph on the side of the Central Powers, moreover, Indian Muslim distrust of British rule often exceeded that of the most radical Hindus. Muslim troops remained loyal, however, and Muslim politicians closed ranks behind the Raj, trusting, even as Tilak did, that British gratitude in victory would amply reward their patient friendship. In August 1917 they even had the secretary of state's word on it. "The policy of His Majesty's Government," Edwin Montagu stated in Parliament, "with which the Government of India are in complete accord, is that of the increasing association of Indians in every branch of the administration and the gradual development of self-governing institutions with a view to the progressive realisation of responsible government in India as an integral part of the British Empire."[15] What could be clearer? Indians, of course, only read "responsible government," British officialdom focused on "gradual development."

Armistice brought increased repression of the most brutal sort to India. Perversely, soon after the Central Powers surrendered, early in 1919 the British government of India extended wartime martial law for another six months. The hated Rowlatt Acts, denounced as "Black Acts" by Indian leaders, triggered a universal response of outrage, violent and non-violent, among Indian patriots. "The fundamental principles of justice have been uprooted and the constitutional rights of the people have been violated," cried Jinnah, resigning his Muslim-member Central Legislative Council seat, "by an overfretful and incompetent bureaucracy, which is neither responsible to the people nor in touch with real public opinion."

A more revolutionary response to passage of those Black Acts came from *Mahatma* ("Great-Souled") Gandhi, who had recently returned to India after a long interlude in South Africa and now emerged as a new leader of Congress. Gandhi called for a halt to all business throughout India, a religious strike (*hartal*) to demonstrate the depth of popular feeling against the government's "Satanic Acts." He appealed to his followers to prepare for their strike with special prayers and fasting. It was a new mode of political action, evoking India's most ancient yogic powers of concentration, suffering, self-purification, and restraint to bring the giant machine to a grinding halt, pitting unarmed India's "Soul Force" against the world's major power.

Mahatma Gandhi's method of *Satyagraha* ("Hold fast to the Truth") evolved out of his own "Experiments with Truth," as he called his autobiography. It was a uniquely Hindu method of struggle, based on the twin foundations of *Satya*-Vedic reality, hence Truth, and *ahimsa*—non-violence or, in Gandhian terms, Love. In some respects it was singularly suited to India's population and condition, for it evoked a rich spectrum of religious symbols, stirred popular emotions and passions, yet stressed the non-violence that most realistically elicited the strength of Indian society under the iron heel of British repression.

The Mahatma, who looked and dressed like a Hindu sadhu, used a sadhu's "weapons": celibacy, poverty, fasting, silence, *ahimsa,* suffering. Earlier leaders of Congress had trained themselves in meticulous English, aping the dress and manners of viceroys, governors, collectors and seeking to replace them by becoming as "good" as them. Gandhi turned his back on all the trappings of Western civilization, marching to his own drumbeat, stripping himself of all clothes but a few bits of cotton he had spun and woven with his own hands. He taught his disciples to live as he did, aspiring to less and smaller, rather than more and bigger. He abandoned all machines but those he could operate by hand. He traveled over the subcontinent by foot, the way Hindu pilgrims did, or in third-class rail carriages when he had to move a bit faster. He appealed to Hindu India's peasant mass by becoming one of them. They adored him as a *mahatma* and followed him through fire or flood, for he taught them to "forget fear," his ultimate goal—as their own—being the final extinction or "blissful cessation" of *Moksha*, not the Muslim or Christian Paradise. His leadership techniques and the method of struggle he popularized were totally foreign, virtually incomprehensible, to men like Mr. Jinnah and Secretary of State Montagu.

To British officers in the field, Gandhian non-cooperation was intolerable. When Satyagraha Week started in April 1919 they resolved to crush it with every weapon at their command. In the Punjab, whose lieutenant-governor, Sir Michael O'Dwyer, was one of Curzon's sunbaked old Frontier agents, the crackdown was harshest. Demonstrations were banned, nationalist leaders jailed or deported. The sacred Sikh temple city of Amritsar ("Nectar of Immortality") became the immortal shrine of Indian nationalism. The two most popular local leaders were deported, inciting a protest march by their followers toward the collector's bungalow in the camp. The collector's guards were ordered to stop the mob at the bridges separating the old (native) from the new (British) cities. Trigger-nervous soldiers opened fire, killing several demonstrators and sending the rest back in panic and rage through their own city bazaars and wards, burning banks, attacking the handful of English people they could find. The army was called in, a full brigade of Gurkhas and Baluchis to whom the people of Amritsar were almost as foreign as Russians.

The British brigadier in charge, General R. E. Dyer, had missed his chance to fight on the Western Front, being obliged to stick out the war in Indian hospitals after his horse fell back on him and crushed his groin. But he was deemed fit for action against unarmed natives. They had gathered in the Jallianwala *Bagh* ("Garden") that afternoon of April 13, 1919, mostly peasants from neighboring villages. It was a Hindu festival day. None of them had guns or weapons of any kind. But General Dyer had ordered "no meetings," and viewed this one as a "seditious conspiracy of troublemakers." He believed they were "testing my resolve." He would later be called before a Royal Committee of Enquiry to explain his actions of that bloody afternoon—what Viceroy Chelmsford was to call his "error of judgment."[16]

Dyer drove with 50 armed troops to the single narrow entrance of the Bagh. His troops lined up across the full width of the entrance, also the only exit from that otherwise totally enclosed area, walled in by several-story brick houses. Without ordering the crowd to disperse, without warning of any kind, the brigadier told his men to open fire. They fired, and kept firing, live ammunition, point-blank at their human targets until they had used almost all the bullets they had brought. The murderous orgy lasted only ten minutes, but when it ended some 400 Indians lay dead and over 1200 wounded on the blood-soaked ground that has since become a national shrine. The general drove back to camp with his troops as the sun set over Amritsar, sending no doctors to minister to the mortally wounded, whose cries of anguish could be heard all night.

"I ordered the least amount of firing . . . to produce the necessary moral and widespread effect," the deranged general later testified. When news of the massacre was made public, the moral effect was, indeed, widespread. Indians who had taken no interest in non-cooperation before, men as wealthy, conservative, and loyal to the Raj as Barrister Motilal Nehru (1861–1931), father and grandfather of Indian prime ministers-to-be, turned overnight into followers of Gandhi. British barbarism had proved itself no better than the Prussian variety. Non-cooperation was the only alternative left to human beings of pride who wished to retain their sanity.

Dyer was urged by his commander-in-chief to retire a bit early from India, but returned home to a hero's welcome and was presented with a lavish purse raised by his Tory friends and a gold sword, inscribed to the "Savior of the Punjab." His "prompt action," argued Viceroy Chelmsford, had "saved the situation from being infinitely worse." "This Government must go and give place to a completely responsible Government," Mr. Jinnah declared when he had learned all the lurid details of those "celebrated crimes," as he called the

Amritsar Massacre and its martial-law aftermath, "which neither the words of men nor the tears of women can wash away."[17]

Mahatma Gandhi launched his first great nationwide *Satyagraha* on August 1, 1920, the day Tilak died. "We were full of excitement and optimism and a buoyant enthusiasm," recalled Jawaharlal Nehru (1889–1964), just then returned from Harrow and Cambridge. "We sensed the happiness of a person crusading for a cause. We were not troubled with doubts or hesitation; our path seemed to lie clear in front of us."[18] Gandhi promised them freedom in "just one year." The multiple boycott he called for brought students out of schools and colleges, lawyers out of courts, legislators out of councils. British jails filled with protestors who lay motionless on railroad tracks until trains steamed to a stop, symbolizing to those exhilarated youths exactly what was going to happen to the British Raj in 1921. They reckoned without awareness of the tenacity of power or the complexity of governing any large number of people, especially the more than 280 million of India's pluralistically divided, impoverished, still mostly illiterate society.

Ahimsa was the first rule of *Satyagraha* broken in the course of that passionate upsurge of national feeling and emotional struggle. How could it not be, asked young enthusiasts like Bengal's Subhas Chandra Bose (1889–1945), who had joined Gandhi's movement rather than the Indian Civil Service for which he had qualified. Tough-minded, passionate, violent, Bose agreed with Stalin that it was no more possible to make a revolution without breaking heads than it would be to make an omelette without breaking eggs. The Mahatma disagreed. "Violence is the law of the beast," he said, "Non-violence the Law of Man." Without *ahimsa*, argued Gandhi, there could be no *Satyagraha*, for Truth and Love were one and the same force—Soul Force—and together they could "move the World." False or evil means, Mahatma Gandhi argued, would never lead to true or good ends. When he learned, therefore, of a number of cases of murderous violence committed by supposed *"Satyagrahis"* in several provinces of India, he called off his campaign, crying "I have committed a Himalayan blunder!'' Gandhi now agreed, as Jinnah and other moderates had often earlier warned him, that India's masses were hardly ready for non-violent rule. Early in 1922 he withdrew from the field of political conflict to his idyllic village *ashram* to train disciplined followers in the "spiritual purification" and "constructive hand-labor" he now considered prerequisite to any future *Satyagraha* campaigns.

The Khilafat movement, which Gandhi had embraced as the "first plank" of his own *Satyagraha* campaign, also quickly led to violence and bitter disillusionment. The Ali brothers were jailed for inciting violence, and British officials cracked down most harshly on Muslims throughout the Punjab and all along the Frontier. The third Afghan War was viewed by the government of India as "proof positive" of the "treasonous character" of the Pan-Islamic movement, which was, moreover, believed to be inspired by Bolsheviks, since Muslim League President Hakim Ajmal Khan explained in 1919 that "Islam is . . . a system which knows no colour nor race," and within the Muslim brotherhood everyone was assured "equality of treatment." [19] British Intelligence feared that the red shirts worn by many Pathan Khilafatists along the Frontier were also political symbols. Soviet publication of the secret clauses in the Allied wartime Treaty of Sevres, which divided Islam's holy places between Britain and France, brought the mass of South Asia's Muslim population solidly behind the sacred Khilafat cause. By allying himself with the Khilafat cause, Gandhi swelled the ranks of its advocates with his own mass following, and for the first time since 1857 Hindus and Muslims joined in a struggle against British rule. Superficially it seemed a united national front, but the Mahatma's most devout Hindu followers could never stop asking him why he embraced Pan-Islam, just as the Ali brothers' orthodox Muslim adherents never approved their alliance with a sadhu. The Hindu-Muslim marriage of convenience was soon to sour.

In the summer of 1920, over 20,000 penurious Muslim Khilafatists climbed the Afghan passes to enter their neighboring brotherland, and Amir Amanullah initially welcomed them warmly. Many Muslims urged Amanullah to stand forth as Caliph at this time, viewing Afghanistan as the heart and the light of world Islam. The Indian refugees soon imposed considerable strain on Kabul's marginal economy, however, for they had come without possessions, requiring everything from land to food, clothing, and building supplies. Many brought disease as well, and by mid-August Amanullah ordered his border roads closed, barred with barbed wire by soldiers who faced their British Indian brothers with rifles. Close to 50,000 Khilafatist pilgrims flooded Afghanistan that summer, but by early fall most of them headed home, bitter, frustrated, exhausted, hating their Khilafat leaders at home as much as they had hated their Afghan hosts. The *hijrat* failed miserably, bringing in its wake the worst wave of Hindu-Muslim communal conflict British India ever experienced. Many pilgrims had sold their lands and other worldly possessions to Hindu neighbors or moneylenders before setting off on their fruitless journey, and they could get nothing back except by force. Long before "Khalif" Mustafa Kemal Ataturk himself proclaimed an end to the Caliphate in 1924, the mass movement in India had lost its heart and political steam.

Almost equally disillusioned with Gandhian *Satyagraha* and Pan-Islamic Khilafatism, the Muslim League, under Jinnah's vital leadership, was soon to chart a separate nationalist path for Indian Muslims, the painfully hard road that led to Pakistan. For though the British had tried to recapture the allegiance and confidence of their once loyal subjects, World War I and its aftermath had proved too devastating a series of historic blasts to the empire's bastion of power. All that remained to the once seemingly imperishable Raj was now little more than two decades of life.

SEVEN

Freedom and Fragmentation

The last quarter-century of British rule in India was a political holding action fought by a dwindling line of stiff-upper-lip Imperial managers, who pretended they would never leave but knew that nationalism's charge would soon crush them if they didn't step aside. Not that all shades of British political opinion agreed on how, when, or to whom the government of India should transfer its power. Had Curzon and Churchill dominated more post-World War I British Home governments, British troops might still be in India. More would certainly have died there. Liberal and Labour Cabinets were, as a rule, more sympathetic to Indian nationalist aspirations and demands, though the India Office, like the Foreign Office, tried to remain above the turbulence of shifting party winds.

The Government of India Acts, two massive British Indian constitutions, were passed by Parliament in 1919 and 1935, the latter remaining the highest law for the Dominions of both India and Pakistan after they attained independence in 1947. Both Acts introduced more potent measures of elected representation to expanded council chambers in New Delhi and the provinces, and both tried, but failed, to bring the princely states into an all-embracing Indian Federal Union. The princes could never agree on their appropriate titles, or the number of gun salutes each merited, or how and where they should sit when meeting in the same room, so they remained outside the new constitutional system, puppet potentates pretending to enjoy great power.

The major new idea in the postwar Acts was a British brainstorm called "Dyarchy"—dual rule—turning certain provincial departments of government over to elected Indian administrators to run in 1919, then doing the same at the center in 1935. Such phasing in of Indian administrators was supposed to smooth the transition process, giving the new boys time to learn under the seasoned supervisory eyes of the wiser old boys. It sounded most impressive in theory but did little to avert disaster throughout the closing cataclysmic years and final holocaust days of the Raj, when the British left India almost as frantically as they had evacuated Dunkirk.

As the tide of Indian opposition to the Raj mounted, British officials intensified frenzied efforts at securing the dikes. Waziristan remained the most troublesome sector of the Frontier. Britain relied' more and more upon air bombardment to pacify that hotbed of unrest, but as the number of bombing missions escalated so did "mistakes" based on understandable errors, since British bombs were usually just tossed out of still-primitive planes by "observers." By 1923 a standard "scale of reparations" was drawn up by the government of India for use throughout the North-West Frontier Province. Any Pathan life erroneously taken during an air raid was worth 3500 rupees, a human limb lost equated to slightly less than half that amount, a horse at 200 rupees, a donkey 100 rupees. British pilots also often "strayed" over the Durand Line into Afghan air space in pursuit of their tribal prey, but there was nothing Amanullah could do to stop such "accidents," and no reparations scale was devised for Kabul. Despite the amir's profession of innocence, British officials suspected he was secretly stirring up trouble, continuing to arm Pathan raiders sent into their tribal zone. The government of India sent another mission to Kabul in 1921, desperately trying to win Amanullah's confidence and support, to wean him from closer ties and dependence on Russia. The British now offered their once-hated enemy an annual subsidy of 4 million rupees, purchasing his quiescence if not active support.

Amanullah signed a treaty with the British in 1922 that soon brought him the advantages of modern civilization, including two war planes, flown from Peshawar to Kabul, where they became the first wing of Afghanistan's air force, piloted by German émigrées. By allying himself with the British, however, the man who could have been Caliph lost the faith of his own mullahs and border tribals. The Mangal Revolt that flared up in Khost in 1924 was fired by proclamations of *Jihad* against the "infidel" amir, who was seen as having sold out to his *kafir* Imperial neighbor, punishing his own tribal brethren for killing sahibs in their territory. Amanullah managed to crush that rebellion with the aid of those "hell-sent" weapons, raining fire from the sky. But bombing his own people only made more of them lose confidence in his Islamic claim to their allegiance. He and his wife Sorayya had by now become Western in dress and manner. She abandoned her veil and appeared bare-faced in public, violating the tenet of orthodox Muslim tradition governing female attire. Much like the British in India, Amanullah could still subdue his people, but he could never recapture their affection or loyal trust and support. In 1927 he took his Western-clad wife on the Grand Tour of Europe, journeying over the British border at Quetta, from there by special train to Karachi, by boat to Bombay and Suez, and on to London, Paris, Rome, Berlin, even Moscow. He wanted to visit the United States as well, but Washington refused to host his trip. Driving home through Persia in his Rolls-Royce, Amanullah's first message to his people was, "Rouse yourselves from your deep sleep." It only intensified their distrust of him, inspiring fresh revolt.

A water carrier's son, the bandit Bacha Sacao, led the revolt that toppled Amanullah from his throne in 1928–29. Bacha kept in close contact with Sir Francis Humphreys, Foreign Minister Curzon's representative in Kabul, whose key position in Kabul's diplomatic colony at the time allowed him to evacuate Westerners and their families by air before the city came under full rebel siege. T. E. Lawrence (Lawrence of Arabia) was at the RAF's most advanced air base of Miranshah, ten miles from the Afghan border, during this year of civil war, and there was suspicion within Afghanistan and India that the fine hand of secret British diplomacy had pulled the violent rebel strings that forced Amanullah to flee his capital and country early in 1929. Amanullah stopped running in Rome, having found Mussolini the most congenial among the European rulers he had met on his Grand Tour. Amanullah would never set foot in Afghanistan again, dying in penurious exile in Italy three decades later.

Within India itself, nationalist pressure against British rule was reduced. Gandhi called a halt to *Satyagraha* in 1922; the Caliphate died in 1924. Mass emotions and political energies suddenly diverted from British targets, however, could not be easily harnessed or tamed. Hindus and Muslims turned upon one another in the latter half of the 1920s, venting their frustrations in orgies of religious hatred and violence that British officials could do little to suppress. By remaining cool above the communal fray, of course, the British could always present themselves as impartial arbiters of Hindu-Muslim conflicts, as the one force left in South Asia capable of running its pluralistically muddled affairs.

From his prewar "experiments" in South Africa, Gandhi early recognized the primary importance of Hindu-Muslim cooperation in a truly Indian nationalist struggle. He spoke of each community as a vital limb of Mother India's body, and made Hindu-Muslim unity the keystone of his political struggle. Jinnah, it is often forgotten, felt much the same way. Even after he was elected president of the Muslim League in 1924, the still ardently Indian nationalist Jinnah warned that

> one essential requisite condition to achieve *Swaraj* ["Freedom"] is political unity between Hindus and Mohammedans; for the advent of foreign rule, and its continuance in India, is primarily due to the fact that the people of India, particularly the Hindus and Mohammedans, are not united and do not sufficiently trust each other. . . . *Swaraj* is an almost interchangeable term with Hindu-Muslim unity. If we wish to be free people, let us unite; but if we wish to continue slaves of bureaucracy, let us fight amongst ourselves and gratify petty vanity over petty matters, Englishmen being our arbiters.[1]

Such prophetic warnings went unheeded. Militant Hindus organized into paramilitary parties, the most famous of which—the Hindu Mahasabha and Nagpur's Nation-Saving Society (RSS)—would include among its later members Mahatma Gandhi's assassin. These young men often "trained" by parading noisily in front of mosques at time of prayer, inciting Muslim worshipers to rush out at them and join in mortal combat. Or they waited in ambush to "liberate" cows being led to Muslim slaughterhouses or holiday sacrificial altars. Muslims retaliated violently, and in districts with Muslim majorities initiated attacks against Hindu temples or Hindu girls. Sacrilegious looting or rape usually provoked widespread communal violence, for reports of each incident were invariably magnified, made to sound more dreadful, with each recounting. Often it was financial trouble that stimulated the religious hatred. Muslim peasants found themselves obliged to borrow from Hindu moneylenders, whose subsequent demands for usurious interest payments triggered violence. In many parts of South Asia, peasants or landless Muslim laborers worked soil owned by Hindu landlords. During years of drought, flood, and famine, communal violence was thus compounded by economic deprivation and exploitation. Similarly, raucous Hindu wedding music, played within earshot of mosques filled with Muslims at prayer, and voluptuous Hindu images of gods and goddesses incited the wrath of iconoclastic Muslims.

British officials were not all insensitive to the tragic human suffering caused by this self-perpetuating epidemic of communal conflicts, but as Indian seas became stormier it was harder for them to save themselves and the Raj from going under. They were never more than a tiny beleaguered garrison, after all, scattered across a continent. They clung with bulldog tenacity, trying as did E. M. Forster's "fictional" young Ronny Heaslop, to do their best to "civilize" the natives. " 'We're not pleasant in India, and we don't intend to be pleasant,' Ronny explained to his irksome mother. 'We've something more important to do.'."[2] Ronny was never quite clear about what that was, but India's foreign secretary in this era, Sir Denys Bray, certainly seemed to understand. Simply writing about new roads in Waziristan made Sir Denys wax poetic over "the grand work of civilisation. . . . Come what may, civilisation *must* be made to penetrate these inaccessible mountains," insisted Bray in 1923. "It may be thought visionary to talk of the civilisation of the Mahsud. But . . . the Mahsud . . . the Mahsud, for all his barbarity and ignorance, is a man of magnificent virility and courage."[3]

Bray typified the Forward mentality of the Raj in the postwar era. "In the domain of India's foreign politics," he insisted, "I know of one fixed and immutable rule only: What India has, let India hold." Afghanistan was still considered an essential buffer to Frontier security, but Bacha proved too unreliable, too mercurial, for British statesmen to depend upon. Before the end of 1929, that "bandit usurper" would be ousted from Kabul's throne by Amanullah's powerful cousin, Nadir Khan (1883–1933), who restored the Durrani dynasty with the support of Waziris and Mahsuds, paid handsomely with British money and armed with British .303 rifles. As soon as Kabul was liberated, British residents returned to their quarters and the new amir confirmed all prior Anglo-Afghan agreements, assuring the viceroy of his strict neutrality, which satisfied Simla and London enough to restore the full flow of money and arms.

Amir Nadir was the sort of solid strong man the British liked for a neighbor, born to the right aristocratic family, a general by profession, conservative religiously, a cautious modernizer, anti-Bolshevik. Though Moscow concluded a non-aggression pact with him in 1931, Russia's press branded him "feudal and reactionary," and called him "a tool" of British imperialism. In November 1933 he was assassinated by a young Kabul student named Muhammad Khalq, whose last name, meaning "masses," was later to be adopted by the ruling faction of Afghanistan's pro-Moscow People's Democratic party. Nadir's son Zahir, only nineteen at his father's death, succeeded to Kabul's throne with immediate and continuing British support. Amir Zahir's powerful uncle, Hashim Khan, was prime minister and became the effective ruler of Afghanistan's new administration through World War II.

While British officials worked so assiduously to save Afghanistan and the Frontier, with each passing year most of them lost touch with South Asia's most popular internal leaders. The heads of Congress and the League similarly lost touch with one another, moving farther away from the unity they had briefly enjoyed from 1916 to 1919. Motilal Nehru and his remarkable son Jawaharlal led the Congress after Gandhi withdrew from active politics. Both were secular-minded, the elder of Liberal, the younger of Fabian Socialist-Labour political predilection. "Many a Congressman," however, as Jawaharlal admitted in his autobiography, "was a communalist under his national cloak."[4] While Congress professed to be totally a-religious, therefore, its Hindu-majority membership often led, in practice, to adoption of pro-Hindu, anti-Muslim positions. The League, whether in reaction or anticipation, moved simultaneously toward the opposite end of India's religio-political spectrum, until in 1930 President Dr. Muhammad Iqbal (1877–1938), the Punjab's poet-philosopher, inquired from its rostrum: "Is it possible to retain Islam as an ethical ideal and to reject it as a polity?" His erudite and elaborate analysis in response led to a negative conclusion under any circumstances, but most emphatically within a Hindu-majority India. "The principle of European democracy cannot be applied to India without recognizing the fact of communal groups," argued Iqbal. "The Muslim demand for the creation of a Muslim India within India is, therefore, perfectly justified."[5] Then he added that he would like to see the Punjab, North-West Frontier Province, Sind, and Baluchistan "amalgamated into a single State," thus delineating for the first time the provincial perimeters of modern Pakistan.

In 1930 Mahatma Gandhi returned to the helm of Congress, demanding "complete freedom" from British rule. He launched his second nationwide *Satyagraha* by leading a march from his *ashram* in Gujarat to the sea at Dandi. This non-cooperation campaign was aimed at the recently augmented British monopoly tax on salt. The salt tax was the Raj's third largest source of revenue. Its burden fell most heavily on India's poorest peasantry, whose unrelenting labor under South Asian suns made substantial daily doses of salt requisite to survival. British law made Indian "stealing" of salt of any sort, including the surf-dried variety found on beaches, a crime punishable by heavy fine or jail. Gandhi set out in openly proclaimed defiance of that "Satanic" law on his historic Salt March, reported regularly in the American as well as Indian and British press. Once again he had selected an issue that would appeal to Muslims as well as Hindus, one that vitally affected most of India's over 300 million peasants. By the time he reached Dandi, his message was clear, and within weeks of his "illegal" taking of salt from the whitened sands, a million of his followers had done the same. British jails filled to capacity again. Still they continued marching to seashores with their containers and sacks, defying the mighty Raj with their silent, non-violent persistence, proving the strength of the weakest among them to provoke, frustrate, cripple the vast machine.

In Peshawar, so many Pathan *Satyagrahis* in their red shirts gathered after the arrest of the "Frontier Gandhi," Abdul Ghaffar Khan, leading Pathan advocate of non-violent resistance in the name of Islam, that terrified officials called in airborne machine-gun fire to disperse the "mob." On the Frontier at this time, a company of sepoys from the United Provinces refused to fire at unarmed civilians, and the British braced themselves for another mutiny. The Frontier rang with cries of *"Inquilab Zindabad!"* ("Victory to the Revolution!")

London decided it was time to try diplomatic negotiation rather than risk further bulldog confrontation and escalating violence. Viceroy Lord Irwin released Gandhi from jail and embarked upon a series of direct personal talks with the Mahatma, despite Churchill's expressed "revulsion" at the sight of a "half-naked *fakkir*" rushing up the steps of Government House. A pact was reached between Gandhi and Irwin in 1931 calling off *Satyagraha* and releasing political prisoners, and Gandhi sailed for London to attend a Round Table Conference on constitutional reforms. Jinnah was already there, as was the Aga Khan, other Indian princes, and representatives of all other parties and minorities, as well as British officials. Gandhi went as sole representative of Congress. He failed, of course, to convert officialdom to his demand for "complete freedom" and exhausted himself in the process, losing the support of his more radical followers, who accused him of becoming a British tool. As soon as he set foot once more on Indian soil, he was arrested. This time far fewer *Satyagrahis* rushed to follow their Mahatma. The British Raj survived, alternating carrot and stick to coax the vast bullock cart of India to move forward at its command. The wisest of the Imperial managers certainly knew their years were numbered. But who would inherit the glittering giant machine, railway-linked, that had been put together over more than a century? Surely no natives could manage so magnificent a show as the British Raj had become!

In England's Cambridge a young group of militant Muslim students, led by Chaudhri Rehmat Ali, demanded the creation of a Muslim fatherland in northwestern India in 1933. They wanted to call it PAKISTAN, an acronym, each of whose letters stood for one part of the nation they envisioned: *P*unjab, *A*fghania (the North-West Frontier Province), *K*ashmir, *S*ind, and Baluchis*TAN*. In Persian, the name means "Land of the Pure." The Pakistan Manifesto charged that

> Our brave but voiceless nation is being sacrificed on the altar of Hindu Nationalism not only by the non-Muslims, but also, to their lasting shame, by our own so-called leaders . . . at the Round Table Conference. . . . They have agreed . . . to the perpetual subjection of the ill-starred Muslim *Millat* ["Nation"] in India. They have accepted, without any protest . . . a constitution based on the principle of an All-India Federation. This acceptance amounts to nothing less than signing the death-warrant of Islam and of Muslims in India.[6]

Such harsh criticism hardly endeared Rehmat Ali to Jinnah or the Aga Khan or other prominent leaders of the League. Within seven years of that first articulation of the Pakistan idea, however, it would be adopted as the single, ultimate goal of the Muslim League.

The concept of the "All-India Federation," accepted by Mr. Jinnah and other delegates to the Round Table conferences, was never fully realized because of princely squabbles, but the British India portion of it was inaugurated in 1935 as the Government of India Act. Sind emerged at this time as a separate province and Burma as a separate colony. The eleven provinces of British India were granted full, responsible cabinet government, though governors retained veto powers over all legislation, even as the viceroy did at the center. Those official veto powers made Nehru initially condemn the Act as a "charter of slavery," threatening a Congress boycott. By 1937, however, when elections were finally held, Nehru and Gandhi agreed to give the new Constitution a try. Congress emerged victorious in seven provinces, each of which then came under the control of its own mini-cabinet of elected ministers. The separate electorate formula was retained and extended to several other minorities.

The Muslim League did not win control of a single province at this time, since many other local Muslim parties competed with it for the Muslim minority vote. Jinnah still hoped it might be possible for a single Indian nation to emerge from the British Empire's ashes and appealed to Nehru to form coalition governments in Congress provinces that had substantial Muslim minorities, such as the United Provinces. Nehru dismissed that suggestion out of hand, however, arrogantly insisting there were only two parties left in India: Congress and the British. Jinnah soon proved to him that the Muslim League was, in fact, a formidable third party.

"The present leadership of the Congress, especially during the last ten years, has been responsible for alienating the Musalmans of India more and more by pursuing a policy which is exclusively Hindu," proclaimed President Jinnah at the Muslim League's annual meeting in 1937. "Musalmans cannot expect any justice or fair-play at their hands."[7] He thus set the tone for what was to remain the League's basic theme of anti-Congress criticism for the next decade, that a *Hindu* Congress would mean a *Hindu* Raj, which would bring *no* justice to Muslims. With Liaquat Ali Khan (1896–1951), Pakistan's first prime minister-to-be, to assist him in organizing the League nationwide, Quaid-i-Azam Jinnah toured Muslim districts of British India for the next two years, reiterating that fearful theme and calling upon Muslims to wake up by joining the League, before it was too late.

Congress provincial governments inadvertently proved to be the League's best helpers. Ministers newly appointed to posts of power, enjoying political patronage for the first time, gave most of their plums, peaches, and mangoes to members of their own communities and castes, if not families, generally ignoring the qualifications of minority applicants and the pleas of minority suppliants. The League kept files and records of all such common abuses of power, compiling extensive reports that were published for distribution to the Muslim press and read from League platforms or at open meetings. The Muslim cry of "Religion in Danger" echoed across the Punjab and all along the Frontier, and radiated from Dacca to the most remote of East Bengal's village hamlets. British officials watched, if not with actual gloating and smug satisfaction at the bickering mess Indians made of things once they took the reins of power, then at least without interference. It was Congress's turn at bat, after all, and the long-abused Ox-bridge collectors, commissioners, and judges, who saw all the blunders being made by their most vocal critics of yesteryear, would have to have been more than human not to have enjoyed that two-year interlude.

The outbreak of World War II further accelerated Congress's fall from power as well as from national trust. The viceroy, Lord Linlithgow, proclaimed India at war with the Axis powers in September 1939, without first consulting Gandhi, Nehru, or any political leader of India. Congress's central working committee was so outraged by that autocratic act that they called on all provincial ministries under their control to resign within the month. It was a major political blunder. Jinnah turned the resignations of Congress ministries to the League's political advantage, urging Muslim's to observe a prayerful "Day of Deliverance" on Friday, December 22, 1939, thanking God for delivering them from the shackles of the "Hindu Raj." A few months later, at a special meeting in Lahore in March 1940, the League passed its Pakistan Resolution. British officials were more favorably disposed to helping the League achieve its goal, especially given the importance of Muslim military cooperation throughout the war, than they were to worrying about "treacherous" Congress criticism or anti-Pakistan positions at subsequent Imperial conferences.

Congress leaders, however, could not forget the British betrayal of their loyal support during World War I and resolved, therefore, to lift no finger to help the Allied cause in World War II, after Linlithgow's initial snub to them. Many Congress leaders spent most of the war behind British bars. Hitler's lightning charge across France and devastating air assault upon London combined with Japan's equally stunning military conquest of most of Southeast Asia only confirmed, at least initially, what Gandhi, Nehru, and others considered to be the wisdom of their wartime non-cooperation posture. Early in 1942, therefore, when the British Cabinet sent Sir Stafford Cripps, then Lord Privy Seal, to India to confer with leading nationalists of all parties on a new constitutional offer the British government was ready to make, Gandhi treated Cripps's mission with contempt. "A post-dated cheque on a bank that is failing," the Mahatma called Cripps's offer of full dominion status for India as soon as the war ended. The tacit acceptance of the idea of Pakistan particularly offended Congress, since provinces that wished to do so could vote to "opt out" of that Dominion. "Why did you come here, if this is all you have to offer us?" Gandhi asked, after meeting with Sir Stafford, who quickly flew home.

For Afghanistan, World War II brought ardent new international courtship. Germany vied with Great Britain for Kabul's hand, offering the government of Zahir Shah (he was now king, not just amir) military as well as economic support. Joachin von Ribbentrop even tried to convince Stalin, during the brief Russo-German honeymoon in late 1939 through early 1940, to invade Afghanistan from the north. Russia soon found itself invaded by Germany, however, and then had all it could handle in defending Moscow, Stalingrad, and Leningrad from Hitler's armies.

Afghanistan reaffirmed strict neutrality during the war, but, ever-sensitive to British power in South Asia, recognized early in 1946 that the Raj's demise was imminent. Kabul hoped to capitalize on Great Britain's withdrawal from India at least to the extent of reabsorbing the tribal areas that had been under Britain's control since the second Afghan War. Thus Kabul strongly sponsored, if not actually initiated, a separatist *Pashtunistan* ("Land of the Pashtus" or Pathans) movement, calling for the creation of a Pathan nation that would integrate the Pashtu-speaking tribes of the North-West Frontier. Abdul Ghaffar Khan became the Frontier's most popular leader of this new nationalist movement, which was viewed as so serious a territorial threat by the

Muslim League that after Pakistan's birth in 1947, trade with Afghanistan was cut off. The North-West passes were closed as virtual frontier war erupted. So bitter was that conflict, that Afghanistan was to be the only nation in the United Nations Organization (UNO) to vote against admitting newborn Pakistan to the world organization.

Great Britain, of course, proved more tenacious and powerful than Indian Congress leaders had anticipated, and after the United States joined the war the balance soon tipped against Axis powers on both sides of the world. Most of the Indian Army remained loyal, though some 60,000 Indian troops captured by the Japanese in Singapore were turned over to former Congress President Subhas Bose, who escaped house arrest in Calcutta and raised the banner of "Free India" (*"Azad Hind"*) over the Andaman Islands, with General Hideki Tojo's support. *Netaji* (Leader) Bose's Indian National Army marched up the Malay peninsula and across Burma in 1944, getting as far as the outskirts of northeast India's Imphal, where the British garrison held out long enough for the torrential monsoon rains to give them three months more respite. After the rains, fresh Allied air support forced Bose and his dispirited army to flee back the way they had come. Netaji himself died in Formosa soon after the overloaded "last plane" out of Saigon he had boarded crash-landed. Underground Indian terrorists did whatever damage they could to British communications and personnel throughout the war, blowing up railroads and bridges, tossing bombs into British barracks and theaters attended by troops, taking a not inconsiderable toll in lives and property. But they couldn't seriously diminish the machine's capacity to provide ample replacements and essential matériel. Gandhi launched the last of his *Satyagrahas*, but those too were contained by a British Raj that was secured under Viceroy General Wavell's martial command and functioned as a military base of operations. It was, however, the Raj's final phase, its last holding action. The muscle remained taut, but the heart had gone out of Imperial housekeeping, and though Gandhi had coined the slogan "Quit India" for his own campaign, it became the goal of most British officials long before the war ended.

In the wake of the Allied victory, Churchill's coalition government was voted out in 1945, and Clement Attlee's Labour Cabinet came to power in London. Attlee favored cutting the Indian albatross from Britain's ship of state as quickly as possible and soon after coming to office sent a Cabinet mission of "Three Wise Men" to New Delhi. Secretary of State Lord Pethick-Lawrence led the mission, but Stafford Cripps was author of its consitutional proposal, Great Britain's parting gift of statesmanship to South Asia. The Cabinet Mission Plan might well have saved South Asia's subcontinent decades of tragic conflict, still unresolved. Unfortunately, it was never implemented.

The three-tiered Federal Union government proposed was to have embraced the modern nation-states of Pakistan, India, and Bangladesh, each of which would have been a "Group" under the central "Union" umbrella. Within each Group were to be provincial divisions, much the same as those of British India. The Groups would have been virtually autonomous, a weak Union administration managing only foreign affairs and defense for the subcontinent as a whole. Hindus and Muslims were to have, in effect, joint control of the Union government, enjoying separate autonomy over their own majority Group and provincial administrations. The Plan would have maximized South Asia's defense capability while reducing communal conflict to a bare minimum. "If there is to be internal peace in India," the Mission concluded, "it must be secured by measures which will assure to the Muslims a control in all matters vital to their culture, religion, and economic or other interests."[8] Pakistan, however, was rejected, for its creation "would not solve the communal minority problem." Over 40 million Muslims would remain "dispersed" throughout India, while more than 15 million Hindus and Sikhs would remain under Pakistan's wings. "The Indian Armed Forces," moreover, wrote the Three Wise Men, "have been built up as a whole for the defence of India as a whole, and to break them in two would inflict a deadly blow on the long traditions and high degree of efficiency of the Indian Army and would entail the gravest dangers." Pakistan's two wings would, of course, also "contain the two most vulnerable frontiers of India and for a successful defence in depth the area of Pakistan would be insufficient."[9]

Mahatma Gandhi was overjoyed with the Plan, wisely perceiving that "It contains the seeds to convert this land of sorrow into one without sorrow and suffering."[10] Nehru and Congress reluctantly bowed to Gandhi's judgment, though many conservative Hindu leaders in Congress feared it gave too much of India to Muslim Group dominance. The Muslim League had by now emerged as the major party of South Asia's Muslims, having swept the separate electorate polls in the winter elections of 1945–46. Quaid-i-Azam Jinnah could have stubbornly insisted on Pakistan, but rose to the peak of his diplomatic stature, accepting the Plan on behalf of the League, even though he had earlier said, "We stand for Pakistan, and we shall not falter or hesitate to fight for it, to die for it if necessary."[11]

Before the new Constitution could be confirmed by its newly selected delgates, however, Jawaharlal Nehru held a press conference on July 10, 1946, insisting in response to questions that Congress had made "no commitment" to any "prearranged Plan" that would "bind" members of the Constituent Assembly. What drove Nehru to so rash and tragically foolish a statement remains a mystery, though he himself later acknowledged it to be one of the worst mistakes of his public life. As Congress's new president he was, of course, believed to be spokesman for his party, and when he said its members would be free to decide whatever they wished concerning the actual form of free India's new government, he in effect threw all the delicate diplomatic papers and labors of the Cabinet Mission onto the rubbish pile of history. Jinnah read Nehru's remarks, understandably enough, as "a complete repudiation of the basic form upon which the long-term scheme rests."

Quaid-i-Azam bid goodbye to constitutinal methods, proclaiming August 16, 1946 as "Direct Action Day" on behalf of the Muslim League. The only tribunal, Jinnah insisted, to which his party and people could now turn for justice was the "Muslim Nation." This marked the end of diplomatic negotiations on the transfer of power and the dawn of a bloody year of civil war of succession for the subcontinent. Calcutta's "Great Killing" on that August 16 alone claimed over 5000 lives, leaving another 100,000 homeless as rampaging mobs of looters, killers, and rapists roamed that "City of Dreadful Night." Orgies of communal violence were triggered across the subcontinent, from Bengal to the Frontier, from Kashmir to Hyderabad. Wherever Hindus lived in close proximity to Muslims, passions flared beyond the boiling point. Centuries of neighborly coexistence ended overnight. Hatred and distrust ran wild. The birth pangs of Pakistan had begun long before British India's last viceroy, Lord Mountbatten (1900–79), flew into New Delhi in March 1947.

Mountbatten's royal birth and "fatal charm" gave him unique powers in effecting Britain's final transfer of power in South Asia. He had his Cabinet's carte blanche, and parliamentary permission to take until June 1948 to complete his mission. But soon after he arrived in India and surveyed the swiftly deteriorating situation, he decided to advance his timetable to August 1947, fearing a South Asian Dunkirk if he waited any longer. As a military commander, his first concern, of course, was for the safety of British forces. Were that his only concern his decision would have been sound. Millions of Indians, especially in the soon-to-be-partitioned Punjab and Bengal, however, were left to the never-tender mercies of their communal antagonists, without even a pretence of British border-guard protection. Before 1947 was over, South Asia erupted with volcanic violence, tearing itself apart. Had the Britisih waited another six months they could not have stopped the violence, but they might have reduced post-partition civilian slaughter.

After meeting several times with Gandhi, Nehru, and Jinnah, Mountbatten concluded that South Asia's partition into separate Dominions of India and of Pakistan was inevitable. Jinnah fought hard against accepting a "moth-eaten Pakistan," stripped of Eastern Punjab and Western Bengal districts that had Hindu and Sikh majorities, but finally had to capitulate to tough Congress bargaining. "Frankly, Your Excellency," a tired Quaid-i-Azam told Mountbatten, "the Hindus are impossible. They always want seventeen annas for the rupee." (There were only sixteen annas to a British rupee). By late April, Nehru was also ready to agree to partition. "The Muslim League can have Pakistan," Panditji said, "but on the condition that they do not take away other parts of India which do not wish to join Pakistan.'' Gandhi alone remained unreconciled to what he called the "vivisection" of his "sacred Mother.'' He was actually prepared to let Jinnah preside over a united India, if that was the only way of preventing partition, and seriously urged Mountbatten to invite Jinnah to serve as free India's first prime minister. Nehru would certainly not have appreciated turning over his job to his arch-rival, however, and Lord Louis refused to consider the Mahatma's idea as anything more than a playful suggestion, never even communicating it to the Quaid-i-Azam. Jinnah would most probably not have accepted such an offer, yet the stakes were so high that any possibility of averting the holocaust that followed partition should have been considered. Denied the prospect of becoming India's prime minister, Jinnah assumed the office of Pakistan's first governor-general and remained its Quaid-i-Azam.

By mid-July 1947, frenzied Hindus, Muslims, and Sikhs started to leave their ancestral village homes, moving like a dark cloud of locusts across what were to become the new international borders, cut like earthquake scars through the Punjab and Bengal. Rumors and reports of communal slaughter, rape, looting moved with the terrified peasant armies of refugees that hot and dust-dry summer. In the Punjab, an inadequate Boundary Force retreated to their barracks' shelter, leaving unarmed refugees to fend for themselves. Most of those troops and officers, like Colonel Mohammad Ayub Khan (1907–72), Pakistan's future field-marshal "president," were "infected with communal virus" and did nothing to calm the rising fever of hate and fear that raged across the land. In Lahore and Amritsar arson and stabbings were endemic throughout July, but few criminals were apprehended as fireballs were hurled through urban skylights and North India's cities turned into blazing funeral pyres. Cyril Radcliffe, the British judge who chaired the Boundary Commission that drew the dissecting east and west lines, had never visited India before 1947 and had time to see nothing of the terrain he divided, except from the air on days obscured by dust. His boundaries were, therefore, hardly perfect, leaving entire villages, even subdistricts, full of Hindus and Sikhs to Pakistan, assigning others that were preponderantly Muslim to India.

Gandhi and Jinnah both signed an appeal to their people to abjure

lawlessness and violence, denouncing "for all time" the "use of force
to achieve political ends." It was too late. The volcano, once it had
erupted, could not be capped. An estimated 10 million refugees started
out to cross the new borders. A million of them died before reaching
their new homeland. "I have given up the hope of living 125 years,"
the Mahatma confessed as he witnessed the mad orgy of murders and
looting in Delhi. "I have no wish to live if India is to be submerged
in a deluge of violence, as it is threatening to do." His *Moksha* would
come soon enough, also violently, at the hands of a hate-crazed Poona
Brahman, on January 30, 1948. After the assassination, Prime Minister Nehru told his nation,

> The light has gone out of our lives and there is darkness every-
> where. A madman has put an end to his life, for I can only
> call him mad who did it, and yet there has been enough of
> poison spread in this country during the past years and months,
> and this poison has had an effect on people's minds. . . . The
> first thing to remember now is that none of us dare misbehave
> because he is angry. We have to behave like strong and deter-
> mined people, determined to face all the perils that surround
> us. . . . We must hold together and all our petty troubles and
> difficulties and conflicts must be ended in the face of this great
> disaster.[12]

The British Raj ended at midnight on August 14–15, 1947. The
Union Jack was taken down from Delhi's Red Fort, and India's Dominion tricolor was raised in its place. Nehru told his Constituent Assembly that day,

> When the world sleeps, India will awake to life and freedom.
> . . . We end today a period of ill fortune and India discovers
> herself again. . . . We have to labour and to work, and work
> hard, to give reality to our dreams. Those dreams are for India,
> but they are also for the world, for all the nations and peoples
> are too closely knit together today for any one of them to imag-
> ine that it can live apart. Peace has been said to be indivisible;
> so is freedom, so is prosperity now, and so also is disaster in
> this One World that can no longer be split into isolated frag-
> ments.[13]

Yet even as he spoke, the new Dominion of Pakistan, two isolated fragments of what had until that day been British India, came to life on either side of the new India set perilously, threateningly, between its west and east wings. "It will be our constant endeavour to work for the welfare and well-being of all the communities in Pakistan," said Quaid-i-Azam, inaugurating Pakistan's Constituent Assembly in Karachi that day. "The tolerance and goodwill that great Emperor Akbar showed to all the non-Muslims is not of recent origin. It dates back thirteen centuries ago when our Prophet not only by words but by deeds treated the Jews and Christians, after he had conquered them, with the utmost tolerance and regard and respect for their faith and beliefs. The whole history of Muslims, wherever they ruled, is replete with those humane and great principles which should be followed and practised."[14] Words and sentiments as noble as Nehru's, yet before the next year ended, Governor-General Quaid-i-Azam Jinnah, like Mahatma Gandhi, would also be dead. Thus, India and Pakistan, so early orphaned, were left to rear themselves under less wise, less tolerant leaders.

EIGHT

South Asia at War with Itself

Britain's postwar withdrawal from the subcontinent left South Asia weakened and vulnerable to divisive pressures. Pakistan and India fought over residual princely-state fragments of the Imperial puzzle that refused to fall neatly into place in the Dominions. Foremost among these states was Kashmir, the jewel of contention that triggered the first two India-Pakistan Wars. At least as important a potential threat to world peace was removal of all British support from Afghanistan and the unleashing of Pathan Frontier tribal unrest in the shifting borderland domain of "Pashtunistan." Pakistan itself was a nation born divided into distant, linguistically different segments. The Bangladesh timebomb, bearing further national divisiveness, was to go off almost a quarter-century after the British retreat. From 1947 through the end of 1971, then, South Asia was a torn and weary subcontinent at war with itself.

The first and second India-Pakistan Wars of 1947–48 and 1965 were fought over Kashmir. Geographically contiguous to both new Dominions, Kashmir could have joined either Pakistan or India. But its Hindu maharaja, ruling a population overwhelmingly Muslim (77 percent of the 4 million Kashmiris in 1947), was unable to decide which way to jump by August 15, 1947. He chose instead to sign a "standstill" agreement with both New Delhi and Karachi, hoping that international inertia would allow his state to remain independent, the Switzerland of Asia. He reckoned without the passion of Pakistani feelings, however, for the Muslim League considered Kashmir as integral to Pakistan's body politic as its initial "K" was central to Pakistan's name. All the waters of the Indus River and its mighty tributaries flowed through Kashmir's mountain gorges. Pakistan's very soil was for the most part Kashmiri sediment.

Less than a month after Pakistan was born, Muslim peasants of southern Kashmir rose in rebellion against their tyrannical Hindu landlords. From the North-West Frontier, Waziri and Mahsud tribals, those same fierce *Mujaheedin* the British had earlier armed to liberate Kabul, jumped into British lorries to volunteer their services in "freeing" Kashmir from its Hindu maharaja's rule. Trucks filled with armed tribals crossed the Indus at Attock and headed east to Muzaffarabad, down the Baramula road toward Srinagar, Kashmir's capital, in late October 1947. There were still enough British officers serving Pakistan's Frontier Province at this time to ensure that the lorries were well fueled and the tribal rifles well fed with ammunition. Pakistan's government formally denied supporting these invaders until the United Nations sent its first commission to South Asia to try to resolve the Kashmir conflict.

Maharaja Hari Singh, spurred to action, now formally acceded his state to India, appealing to Mountbatten, who had remained in Delhi as India's first governor-general, for military aid. Lord Louis's stunning martial response was to airlift the First Sikh Battalion to Srinagar, just as its tribal invaders were approaching the outskirts of that city. Had Mountbatten waited a day, it would have been too late for India to "save" Kashmir.

When Mountbatten returned to London the next year, he found that many members of his Tory party considered him a traitor. The royal family threw a party to welcome him home, but as he approached, Winston Churchill pointed a foreboding finger toward him and "raised his voice so that all other chatter stopped," shouting, "Dickie, stand there! What you did in India was like running your riding crop across my face!" The ex-prime minister then turned and strode off across the hall in the opposite direction, "and it was the last

word he spoke to me for six years."[1] Churchill had been most encouraging to Jinnah.

When Governor-General Jinnah learned of the Indian airlift, he
tried to hurl the full weight of Pakistan's army into the field to support
his *Mujaheedin* volunteers. Field Marshal Sir Claude Auchinleck, supreme commander of all British forces in South Asia, flew to Lahore
to inform Pakistan's Quaid-i-Azam, however, that since Kashmir's
accession was "legal," any Pakistani order to "invade a sister Commonwealth Dominion" would automatically and immediately require
"withdrawal of every British Officer serving with the newly formed
Pakistan Army."[2] The most Jinnah could do was privately encourage
units of Pakistan's armed forces to volunteer their services, as many,
of course, immediately did. The war raged for months before a de
facto new border was stabilized along the Uri-Poonch line, with Pakistan's *Azad* ("Free") Kashmir to its west, with Muzaffarabad as capital, and the remaining three-quarters of the old state of Kashmir, including Srinagar, to the east, permanently integrated into India.

India brought Pakistan's "aggression" in Kashmir to the United
Nations Security Council on the last day of 1947, but soon regretted
having done so. Pakistan's foreign minister, Sir Muhammad Zafrullah
Khan, presented his side of the argument so brilliantly that most delegates at Lake Success soon viewed the problem of Kashmir as an
international extension of the communal conflict that had given birth
to Pakistan, which should be resolved through a plebiscite of its own
people. Nehru insisted that India had no objection to holding a plebiscite, but first wanted Pakistan to "vacate its aggression." Pakistan,
however, argued that to withdraw its troops without first impartially
polling Kashmir's population would simply be turning over the rest of
the state to India's "Army of Occupation." The Security Council appointed a United Nations Commission on India and Pakistan (UNCIP)
to visit South Asia and arrange for a free and fair plebiscite throughout
Kashmir. A cease-fire line was agreed upon in January 1949, but no
agreement has ever been reached on a Kashmir plebiscite. West Pakistanis have never stopped feeling bitter toward India about Kashmir,

and most of them continue to believe that India "treacherously stole Kashmir" from the Muslim nation within which it properly belongs.

Kashmir remained a dormant volcano, the major point of diplomatic contention between India and Pakistan, erupting once again into actual war in 1965. Two years before that war started, Field-Marshal "President" Ayub Khan assured his nation that "we have not abandoned the cause of our Kashmiri brothers and sisters in bondage." India had kept at least 100,000 of its best troops stationed around Srinagar since 1948, but Ayub felt confident that "even this show of force no longer intimidates the brave people of Jammu and Kashmir." Since allying himself with the United States in 1954, General Ayub had received several billion dollars' worth of the Pentagon's most modern weapons, including fighter bombers, heavy tanks, and 100-pound guns. By 1965 he was convinced that, despite India's more than double numerical advantage in troops, Pakistan's army could "lick them in the field" and "win back" Kashmir. UN Kashmir observers reported an alarming increase of over 2000 "violations" of the cease-fire line in the first half of 1965. New Delhi noted over 300 "incidents" against its forces in Kashmir in May. Pakistan charged India with launching a "major assault" in Kargil on May 17, 1965, when Indian army units captured three strategic Pakistani outposts overlooking the Srinagar-Leh road.

In the summer of 1965 persistent reports reached India and the UNO that Pakistan had a "substantial guerrilla force" under training in "battalion strength" at its hill station of Murree, close to Rawalpindi Army Headquarters, for "infiltration" of Kashmir's Vale to "soften up" Srinagar.[3] UN observers reported armed men in civilian clothes crossing the line from west to east in the first week of August. Pakistan Radio announced a spontaneous uprising in Kashmir a few days later, calling it "an all-out War of liberation against Indian Imperialism." Within Kashmir itself, a "Revolutionary Council" suddenly surfaced, broadcasting daily to urge Kashmiris to "rise to a man to fight" for freedom and honor. Zulfikar Ali Bhutto (1928–79), Ayub's minister at the UN at the time, spoke of Kashmir's uprising against "tyranny and subjugation," but denied any direct Pakistani role. On August 15, 1965, however, India's prime minister, Lal Bahadur Shastri (1904–66), announced that Pakistan had invaded Kashmir, promising his people that "force will be met with force," and "aggression against us will never be allowed to succeed." Shastri claimed that India had captured 83 officers and men of Pakistan's army inside Kashmir and killed another 126 such "infiltrators."

On August 30, 1965, India reported sending forces over the cease-fire line near Uri "to clear up the Pakistani raiders established in the Uri-Poonch bulge." The following day, India held about 200 square miles of Azad Kashmir. On September 1, regular units of Pakistan's army crossed the line into Kashmir's southernmost Chhamb sector, hoping to cut off the rest of Kashmir state from India in a strategic move that Pakistan called "Operation Grand Slam." Ayub insisted that Pakistan launched none of its regular martial units prior to India's aggression.

Indian strategists refused to allow their forces to become bogged down in the Kashmiri conflict alone, however, and before dawn on September 6 a three-pronged, tank-led Indian army moved west across the Punjab, headed for the teeming city of Lahore. Ayub solemnly informed his nation, "We are at war," and urgently called Washington for help. The U.S. put all arms shipments to both sides under embargo, however, as soon as this fiercest South Asian war began. With 900,000 men in arms, India enjoyed more than a two-to-one advantage over Pakistan during the war, which raged unabated for three weeks in September. Though neither side won a decisive victory, the 1965 war helped to dispel the British myth of "martial races, castes, and tribes," which Pakistan had tried to perpetuate.

India claimed to have knocked out 472 Pakistani tanks, Pakistan claimed 516 of India's, while more objective assessments indicated both sides lost about 350 tanks each, Pakistan Pattons, India Centurions. For India, such loss was roughly one-quarter, for Pakistan one-third, of its total tank force. At cease-fire in late September, India claimed to hold 700 square miles of Pakistan, Pakistan claiming 1600 square miles of India (mostly Rajasthani desert) and 340 square miles of Kashmir. India, however, held the strategic Uri-Poonch bulge.

Each side admitted just over a thousand troop fatalities, India some 70 airplanes lost, Pakistan only 20. Operation Grand Slam had ended in stalemate. Ayub and Shastri met in Russia's Tashkent at the invitation of Premier Kosygin to sign an agreement the day before Shastri died there, pledging to withdraw all armed personnel to pre-August 5, 1965, positions on the subcontinent by February 25, 1966. Kashmir thus reverted to its prewar cease-fire-line division, much like South Asia as a whole, a state divided against itself.

Afghanistan decided to recognize Pakistan in June 1948, formally giving up any claims Kabul hitherto had asserted to Pakistan's Frontier territory in return for Pakistan's reopening of trade and offers of aid to Zahir Shah. A year later, however, Kabul proclaimed the Durand line "imaginary" and refused again to recognize it or any similar line, thus stirring up dormant Pashtunistan agitation among the tribes. In 1950 Afghanistan was actually flying red Pashtunistan flags from some of its public buildings in Kabul, openly funding Pathan raids into Pakistani territory. War was almost declared between these two neighboring Sunni Muslim nations, and hundreds of Afghan tribal "bandits" were killed crossing Pakistan's western border.

Though Afghanistan always based its support for Pashtunistan on what it called the "just claims" of the Pashtu nation, Kabul was clearly willing to incorporate that entire region into its own nation, if Pashtu independence proved utterly impractical. Afghanistan was, moreover, anxious to secure direct access to the Arabian Sea and hoped eventually to incorporate all of the Baluchistan Frontier region as well as the Pathan North-West Frontier within its suzerain, if not sovereign, control. Pakistan refused to concede to Pashtun (or Pakhtoon) separatist demands, although they almost seemed to have been inspired by the demand for Pakistan itself.[4] Pakistanis argued that Pathan claims of racial or ethnological homogeneity of the some 190,000-square-mile region were spurious, since many non-Pathans, including Brahuis, Baluchis, and Jats, inhabited the Frontier zone. Pakistan also noted that *its* North-West Frontier peoples *had* been polled on their political preferences prior to British India's partition, opting to join Pakistan, and asked when Kabul would allow the Pathans living along *its* side of the Durand Line similar self-determination. Legally and historically, moreover, Pakistan was sole legatee to the northwest British Indian domain up to the Kabul-approved Durand Line. Pashtunistan advocates countered by reminding Pakistan that more than half of the Frontier Pathans had abstained from voting in 1946, since their only options at the time were to join either India or Pakistan and most wanted a nation of their own. They also asked if Pakistan was satisfied with India's claims that Indian-controlled Kashmiris had, in fact, often expressed their political satisfaction with their current status in a number of plebiscites, i.e., regular Indian elections.

The Pashtunistan issue remained a constant source of irritation between Afghanistan and Pakistan, periodically inflamed and often causing fever and pain, at times stimulated, Pakistanis charged, either by New Delhi or Moscow or both in order to threaten or embarrass Pakistan's administration. On October 16, 1951, when Prime Minister Liaquat Ali Khan was assassinated in Rawalpindi by an émigré Afghan Pathan, Saed Akbar, some Pakistanis feared that "Pashtunistan" was the cause of that crime. Subsequent investigation, however, revealed that the assassin, instantly shot dead by a police guard, had been living on a Pakistani pension in Peshawar, had quite a bit of money in large bills in his pocket, and belonged to one of Pakistan's extremist Islamic fundamentalist parties, whose leaders considered Liaquat Ali a heretical traitor to Islam. Amir Maulana Abul A'la Maududi (1903–80), founding head of that *Jamaat-i-Islami* ("Islamic Party"), had also challenged Quaid-i-Azam Jinnah's Islamic credentials and had spent the first two years of Pakistan's independence behind bars, released a year and a half prior to Liaquat Ali's assassination with a halo of noble (*amir*) martyrdom.

Liaquat Ali's assassination seemed almost to signal the start of a fundamentalist Islamic revolt that soon spread across most of West Pakistan. The Shi'ite cosmopolitan sect of *Qadian Ahmadis,* a small but powerful group of Muslim followers of Mirza Ghulam Ahmad (1835–1908), who was born in Qadian, became the principle targets of orthodox Sunni attacks throughout the Punjab and Sind. Foreign Minister Zafrullah Khan was the most prominant Ahmadi at this time.

Maududi's party and the Punjab's orthodox *Ahrars* ("Nobles") joined forces in the worst anti-Ahmadi riots in 1953, turning Lahore into a nightmarish inferno, demanding exile or death to all "heretics," and calling for the conversion of Pakistan into a proper Islamic state, where the legal Code of Islam alone would be followed by all. Pakistan's administration, however, especially the top echelons of its military as well as civil leadership, remained in the mold of British Service dress and traditions, whose model, Mr. Jinnah, had much more in common with Eden and Churchill than with Maududi.

Governor-General Khwaja Nazimuddin (1894–1964), who succeeded Jinnah in 1948, had been Home and prime minister in Bengal before the British left India and was appointed prime minister after Liaquat Ali's death. Pakistan's third governor-general, Ghulam Muhammad (1895–1956), was Punjabi-born and trained in the British Civil Service in finance. In 1953 he became Pakistan's strong man by dismissing Bengali-born Prime Minister Nazimuddin and appointing his own protegé, Mohammed Ali Bogra (1900–63), then serving as ambassador to Washington. The ideological gulf between such sophisticated Westernized leaders and the mass of Pakistan's then 75 million Muslims remained almost as great as that which had kept the British so remotely out of touch with South Asia's population. This continuing distance and tension between Pakistan's modernized leadership and still-traditional populace imposed growing strains on governmental machinery, leaving most of the dissatisfactions and frustrations that led to Pakistan's birth undiminished and unresolved. The long and arduous freedom struggle brought no better or higher standard of living to most Pakistanis or, indeed, Indians—at least for these initial decades of upheaval, internal conflict, and inexorable population growth.

Thanks to Nehru's seventeen years at the helm of India's government, New Delhi enjoyed much more administrative stability than did Karachi-Islamabad. But India's leadership also remained mostly Westernized, made up of secular modernists seeking to drag a peasant, religious, and impoverished society out of its rural ruts onto concrete highways and airstrips. There were new faces, mostly in hand-spun, tight Gandhi caps and loose Nehru shirts, occupying the old British bungalows and new national flags flying from the fast-moving official cars that also went with Cabinet office, but the old problems remained: poverty, provincialism, caste and class inequities, illiteracy, lack of technology, insufficient application of scientific knowledge and skills, nepotism, sexism, insufficient water, never enough drains, epidemic diseases, heat, filth, bureaucratic incompetence. The British had gone home. The mess they had found and brought remained, in some ways diminished, in others augmented.

Pakistan's civil bureaucratic leadership was given only one decade to try to pull the country together and keep the lid on mounting opposition, East and West. The basic character of Frontier and fundamentalist religious opposition forces that racked the West has been noted above. Mounting disaffection in East Pakistan was, however, far more serious, reflecting the seismic historic power of a separate national movement. Though East Pakistan (formerly East Bengal) embraced merely 55,000 square miles, it sustained a larger population than that living within West Pakistan's 310,000 square miles. Virtually all of Pakistan's "Easterners," moreover, spoke Bengali, yet Urdu was made the national language of Pakistan, despite the fact that less than 10 percent of West Pakistan's population spoke it in 1947. Ethnically, most Easterners looked just like their West Bengali Indian neighbors, whose original gene pool they shared. They were generally smaller, finer-featured, darker-skinned than either Frontier Pathans or Punjabis, many of whose ethnic ancestors came from farther west. The one unifying characteristic shared by East and West was, of course, Islam, but even there it must be remembered that most Easterners were descendants of relatively late Sufi converts.

The twin sources of East-West tension and conflict were economic and political ones. Usually heavy annual monsoon rains combined with the flooding force of the Brahmaputra River and its tributaries flowing through East Bengal's low-lying deltaic soil allow this region to enjoy a virtual world monopoly of raw jute production. East Pakistan's jute became Pakistan's major source of hard-currency foreign exchange. Yet, though East Bengal annually often supplied about two-thirds of Pakistan's total exports,[5] it rarely received more than one-third of the nation's overall imports. West Pakistani government officials, who dominated Dacca's bureaucracy as well as Karachi's, in part because of greater Western patronage and their natural advantage in taking central government service examinations in Urdu, were viewed by Bengali nationalists in much the same way Indian nationalists saw the British—as foreigners who drained the wealth of the "colony" they ruled.

Whether West Pakistani officials pumped more development money into dams, roads, bridges, and factories in the West than they allocated to the East because they truly believed the West a better investment or strategically more important really made no difference to irate Bengali feelings of "Imperial exploitation" suffered at the hands of those who were supposed to represent their government. Eastern political leaders hoped, however, to set the balance straight by using their region's demographic advantage to win control of Pakistan's central government. But for precisely this reason Pakistan's Constituent Assembly had great trouble reaching any agreement on a national constitution. The Republic of India emerged as a stable polity under its own Constitution in 1950, but East and West Pakistan never really agreed upon a single constitution that worked for more than a few months. Eastern representatives wanted a constitution that would create a government responsible to the majority will of its people, while Westerners, who knew that would mean losing their power, tried to find a formula to avert such a "disaster." In 1955, they finally came up with the "One Unit" administrative amalgamation of all four Western provinces, tied to the idea of East-West parity in a central parliament that would have exactly the same number of representatives from each Unit, thus, in fact, downgrading the value of each Bengali franchise. Frontier Pathans and Baluchis of Baluchistan were even more unhappy about the One Unit experiment than Bengalis, but everyone was so sick of wrangling about elaborate constitutional formulas while the country was tearing itself apart for lack of popular government, that they all finally agreed to give it a try. They even raised Bengali to co-equal status with Urdu as Pakistan's second national language.

Dr. Khan Sahib (1882–1958), brother of the Pashtunistan movement's then-exiled leader, Abdul Ghaffar Khan, was appointed chief minister of West Pakistan's One Unit by the governor-general in an obvious political bid for Pathan support. The Pashtun Fraternity (*Vror Pakhtun*), however, remained vigorously and vocally opposed to the One Unit idea after Khan Sahib's appointment, which succeeded only in drastically shortening his life, ended a few years later by a knife in the hand of his most trusted Pathan servant. Kabul immediately broke off diplomatic relations with Pakistan in the wake of the One Unit proclamation, viewing it as an act primarily aimed at crushing the Pashtunistan movement entirely and even drying up the remaining provincial wellsprings of Frontier political power and support. Actual open war between Afghanistan and Pakistan at this time was averted only by a strong British and American reaffirmation of the Durand Line's "inviolable" international status. Turkish mediation was employed by Anglo-American diplomacy to bring Afghanistan's prime minister to Karachi in December 1956 for the first high-level talks between those neighboring states since 1948. The talks, and considerable pressure from Washington, convinced Pakistan of the need to assist its neighbor economically by reopening trade across the border, which, in effect, was greatly subsidized. The old British system of bribing the amirs and their "wilder" tribes was thus resurrected. In 1958 King Zahir himself visited Pakistan, fully reestablishing diplomatic relations, and Pashtunistan agitation calmed down all along the Frontier.

Bangladeshi nationalism was not as easily silenced. Pakistan's only popular prime minister since the death of Liaquat Ali was Husain Shaheed Suhrawardy (1894–1963), Bengal's "Big Daddy," who was invited to take the helm of Karachi's government in September 1956. "I realise that Democracy has its weaknesses for Democracy is human," Suhrawardy admitted in his first address to the nation, "but it is the only sure road to progress and evolution. . . . We are one

Nation. We are all Pakistanis.'' But Suhrawardy survived as prime minister for only one year before Maududi's orthodox opposition and Right-wing Punjabi landlord pressures in the West combined with Left-wing Bangladeshi separatist impatience in the East to topple his precarious coalition government. Though Shaikh Mujibur Rahman (1920–75), Suhrawardy's leading lieutenant and general secretary of the *Awami* (''People's'') League party of the East, staunchly supported his chief, floods and famine in Bengal severely eroded their base of popularity. Suhrawardy lost a vote of ''confidence'' in October 1957 that brought both extremes of Pakistan's political spectrum into alliance against the political middle just long enough to tear down Karachi's elaborately designed, arduously constructed representative government. It would never really be given another chance. I. I. Chundrigar (1899–1960) and Malik Firoz Khan Noon (1893–1970) both tried to patch it up, pulling together ministries that clung to the sagging rafters for a few months, but the roof had collapsed, the foundation was sinking, and the military was tired of waiting.

United Pakistan's last civil prime minister was Sir Firoz Khan Noon, a knight of the old school tie and a seasoned diplomat. He planned to call Pakistan's first nationwide general elections, apparently hoping they would return Suhrawardy to the premiership, allowing Noon to step aside to the less-pressured post of president. But Commander-in-Chief General Ayub Khan got wind of that plot and decided it wouldn't do. ''There would be large-scale disturbances all over the country,'' wrote Ayub, seeking to justify his coup to Western readers of his autobiography, ''and civil authority, already groaning under the heels of the politicians, would be incapable of dealing with the situation. Whether the army liked it or not it would get embroiled, because in the final analysis it would become a question of maintaining some semblance of law and order in the country.''[6] Ayub had just completed a most successful tour of the United States, which was then closely allied to Pakistan. He had golfed with General Nathan Twining and General Omar Bradley at Burning Tree, dined with Allen Dulles, director of the Central Intelligence Agency, and watched El Paso's super-guided-missile show at Fort Bliss. When he got back to Karachi to find ineffectual tea-drinking politicians fiddling with talk of elections, he advised his martial colleague, President General Iskandar Mirza, to activate the plan they had drawn up years before.

Mirza proclaimed martial law throughout Pakistan on October 7, 1958, dismissing central and provincial governments, abolishing all assemblies, and appointing General Ayub "Chief Martial Law Administrator," i.e., military dictator of Pakistan. "The ruthless struggle for power, corruption, and shameful exploitation of our simple, honest, patriotic and industrious masses," General Mirza announced over Radio Pakistan, "the lack of decorum, and the prostitution of Islam for political ends . . . These despicable activities have led to a dictatorship of the lowest order." Obviously unconscious of the double meaning of his last remark, Mirza then stated his decision to cancel elections, since they would only create "greater unhappiness and disappointment leading ultimately to a really bloody revolution."

The coup was carried out with martial efficiency. Ayub had moved a crack brigade the night before from Quetta to Jungshahi, outside Karachi, to handle the "unforeseen." But Sir Firoz Khan offered no resistance. Even Dacca silently bowed to the awesome sight of American tanks in strategic squares and at highway junctures. Pakistan's Constitution was replaced with twenty-nine Martial Law Regulations, violations of which were punishable by death, rigorous imprisonment, deportation, or whipping. Special military courts were created to expedite punishment, especially the death sentence for recalcitrants, who were defined as "Any external enemy of PAKISTAN and mutineers or rebels or rioters and any enemy agent." Ten years' imprisonment was meted out to any one guilty of making a speech deemed prejudicial to "good order or the public safety." The same punishment went to any striker or agitator. Fourteen years was the punishment for troublemakers, who "By word of mouth, or in writing or by signals, or otherwise . . . spread reports, calculated to create alarm or despondency amongst the public, or calculated to create dissatisfaction towards the Armed Forces and Police, or any member thereof."

Hoarders, price gougers, and black marketeers found themselves in similar jeopardy, and consumer prices dropped about 25 percent within the first 100 hours. The army seized millions of rupees worth of smuggled gold, jewels, cloth, and other goods, putting them on the market at fair prices. Consumer-buying sprinted, and within two weeks stocks of virtually everything were exhausted in the bazaars of Karachi, Lahore, Pindi, and Dacca. Pakistan's business world came to a standstill. Merchants were either too frightened or their stocks too depleted to sell anything. The army, of course, could create no consumer goods, only devour them. Were it not for massive and continuing U.S. aid, Pakistan's economy would have collapsed.

Twenty days after announcing his coup, President Mirza appointed Ayub the new prime minister. That night three of Ayub's colleagues drove to Mirza's house to "advise" him to leave the country. "It seems that he realized the gravity of the situation," Ayub delicately noted, recording how Mirza resigned the next morning and flew to London three days later, where he remained in exile until his death. Ayub decided to appoint himself president, preferring that title, explaining to his nation that "What we are practicing is also democracy." With the aid of Madison Avenue he devised a scheme called "Basic Democracies," which he promulgated on the first anniversary of the second phase of his coup, when he also promoted himself to field marshal.

Ayub moved his capital north to Rawalpindi Army Headquarters, where he felt much more at home than in low-lying, humid Karachi. Son of a Spin Tarin Pathan, who had served in Hodson's Horse as a *risaldar* ("sergeant") major, Ayub loved the North-West, and decided to build his own new capital just a few miles from Pindi, devoutly named Islamabad ("City of Islam"). His Basic Democracies scheme was an elaborate, five-tiered chain-of-command system of indirect elections, designed to reduce Pakistan's some 80 million populace to a more manageable 80,000 Basic Democrats, who would then be the only ones enfranchised to vote for new representatives and the president. It worked beautifully. In their first secret-ballot vote, 75,084 out of the 80,000 Basic Democrats voted for Ayub for president.

Ayub launched Pakistan's Second Five-Year Plan in 1960, projecting an overall expenditure of $5 billion, designed to increase food production by 21 percent, industrial output by 50 percent, and per capita income by 13 percent. Over 70 percent of all funding was to come from foreign aid and loans, channeled through the World Bank and other U.S. agencies.[7] In 1954, the World Bank, which had also been invited to mediate a major economic dispute within South Asia several years earlier over how to share the Indus River's waters, proposed a solution to that problem. It was not until 1960, however, that India and Pakistan signed the Canal Waters Agreement, and then only after Ayub had squeezed several hundred million dollars more from the Bank's president than had been offered. "People have told me very plainly that if they have to die through thirst and hunger they would prefer to die in battle," Ayub warned the World Bank. "So this country is on the point of blowing up if you don't lend a helping hand."[8] The blackmail worked. Another $200 million went to funding the Punjab's Tarbela Dam, which soon helped spark West Pakistan's development. Ayub and his concrete-construction-business family took keen personal interest in the new Indus Waters projects that would include several multi-million-acre-feet storage dams, five barrages, and eight link canals, each 400 miles long. Virtually none of the new construction money went to the East, however, where only the population continued to make rapid advances, periodically cut back by hurricanes, floods, and tidal waves.

Ayub flew to East Pakistan in October 1961 and urged the need for greater unity and solidarity, warning that if Pakistan's two wings were separated "the lives of the people" would be "endangered." Pakistan, he noted, was "surrounded by enemies."[9] Three months later, ex-Prime Minister Suhrawardy, obviously considered one of those enemies, was arrested. Suhrawardy's incarceration triggered protests throughout East Bengal, and in February student opposition was so widespread that Dacca University's campus was closed for "indefinite vacation." The "wild horse," Ayub's metaphor for the nation he chose to ride, "had been captured but not yet tamed."[10] To help speed up national integration, Pakistan International Airlines (PIA) inaugurated its first jet service between Karachi and Dacca in 1962, cutting flying time between both wings to 165 minutes. Western troops could be flown in to "secure" Dacca's campuses more swiftly. But East Bengal's national protest over Suhrawardy's arrest spread to other cities and their campuses as well, Chittagong, Barisal, Khulna, Noakhali, Sylhet, Kushtia. Mujib was also arrested, as were lesser leaders of the Awami League. East Pakistan's jails filled to overflowing. The new jets flew in tear gas with their troops. *Dawn* was amazed at the persistence of the opposition, calling it *"Incomprehensible"* by April 1962, noting "the student situation in East Pakistan, instead of getting better, seems to be getting worse."[11]

Suhrawardy was finally released from detention in August 1962, and immediately organized a "National Democratic Front" of the most prominent Pakistani political leaders from the West as well as the East, all of whom called upon Ayub to scrap his "Constitution," dismiss his government, which had no popular base of support, and hold fresh elections. The martial farce had continued long enough. Fortunes were wasted, fields and factories left empty and idle, prisons filled, streets jammed with shouting mobs of protesters. Even the army was demoralized. The field-marshal president had reaped a fortune for himself, his friends, his family, as all could see, but Pakistan was no stronger, no richer, no happier. It was a shambles. One of Suhrawardy's lieutenants was knifed in the back, most of the others were arrested, and Suhrawardy himself died of heart attack on December 5, 1963. Charged with subversive activities, the National Democratic Front was banned. Still, Ayub promised to restore democratic rule to Pakistan, perhaps to make Washington feel better about having invested so heavily in a martial dictatorship that was breaking down.

Bhutto became Ayub's foreign minister in 1963 and flew to China, where he negotiated a Sino-Pakistan boundary agreement (March 2, 1963) that turned over several thousand square miles of Indian-held northern Kashmir and Ladakh to the People's Republic of China. Bhutto masterminded the Sino-Pakistani connection in the wake of the Sino-Indian border war of 1962. The humiliating Chinese invasion of India's North-East Frontier Agency in October-November of that year had brought Nehru's prestige, at home and abroad, to its lowest point, burying, with India's slaughtered troops on the Northern Tier, the much-touted *Panch Shila* ("Five Principles") of Sino-Indian coexistence and Third World friendship and cooperation. In the wake of Beijing's unilateral decision to withdraw its victorious army, the U.S. invested heavily in India, arming and training ten new mountain divisions of Indian troops for the Northern Tier. Bhutto urged Ayub to turn to China in response, and by August 1963 Sino-Pakistani friendship and trade had accelerated to the point of opening direct civil flights between Dacca and Canton and Shanghai, and Rawalpindi and Beijing. Zulfi Bhutto had learned his Berkeley lessons in political theory and *realpolitik* well. He soon reported the "complete breakdown" of a series of Kashmir talks he had embarked upon with India's Sikh foreign minister-to-be, Swaran Singh.

In February 1964 the UN Security Council met to discuss Kashmir. Bhutto presented Pakistan's position there, eloquently appealing "in the name of humanity" for "an honourable and just solution . . . in the interest of peace in Asia." Ironically, in the light of what was happening within Pakistan at this time, especially in East Bengal, Bhutto's conclusion to his impassioned appeal for Kashmiri self-determination was: "Freedom can be delayed by oppression, but it cannot ultimately be denied. The course of history is relentlessly so set."[12] Premier Chou En-lai flew to Pindi a few weeks later for direct talks with Ayub. In April 1964 Shaikh Muhammad Abdullah, the "Lion of Kashmir," ex-premier of the state and its most popular leader, who had been incarcerated for more than a decade by India, was released. A South Asian summit meeting of Ayub, Nehru, and Abdullah was suggested at this critical juncture to try to resolve the Kashmir dispute before it boiled over into war again. Nehru's death the following month put an end to that last hope for a peaceful Kashmiri settlement. The second India-Pakistan War over Kashmir, as already noted, exploded the following summer.

Victory in Kashmir would have brought Ayub's martial administration such overwhelming popularity in the West that Bengali opposition could have been ignored much longer with impunity. Stalemate brought only compounded bitterness and a search for scapegoats that would soon end with Ayub himself. The Tashkent agreement reached with India in January 1966 was viewed in West Pakistan as nothing more than a sellout of Pakistan's "sacred claims" to Kashmir. Orthodox Islamic opposition in the West joined forces with radical student leadership on campuses from Karachi to Lahore. Police opened fire on demonstrators at Lahore University's campus on January 13, 1966, drawing the first blood that would flow into a river from every major city of Pakistan before year's end.

Bhutto now abandoned Ayub's side, shrewdly recognizing that his leader's ship was sinking fast, and resigned from the Cabinet in June, "for medical treatment."[13] Zulfi wrote his *Myth of Independence* at this time, his political brief against Ayub, sensing the popular disillusion with a Pathan general as big as Ayub who couldn't defeat a Hindu Brahman as small as Shastri, either on the field of battle or at the table of diplomacy. Ayub had lost his mandate. India, Bhutto warned, "will now seek to convert Pakistan into her satellite by holding out inducements of peaceful cooperation. How can any sensible person object to it? It would appear unreasonable to ignore the extended hand of friendship. India, however, plans to enter by the back door, like a burglar. In this she would be aided and abetted by foreign powers."[14] Bhutto meant Russia and the United States, which he saw joined in "unholy alliance" with India against Pakistan and China. His analysis played uniquely upon popular West Pakistani fears, both radical and orthodox, and rallied student intellectuals and unlettered mullahs to his new Pakistan People's party.

In East Bengal, Mujibur Rahman's Awami League passed its Six-Point Program, calling for virtual Bengali autonomy, in March 1966. Separate currency, full powers over taxation and revenue collection, total control over its own foreign exchange, a separate militia, universal and direct adult suffrage—all administered in the Bengali language—remained the platform of Mujib's party from this date until the birth of Bangladesh. Mujib and his followers were arrested, a general strike ensued throughout "Bangladesh" in June, and eleven Bengalis were killed when the military opened fire. Ayub reaffirmed "the indivisible unity of East and West Pakistan."[15] The East was ravaged once again by floods, which destroyed the homes of an estimated 13 million Bengalis. Washington had provided over $14 million to West Pakistan that year for "salinity control and reclamation," bringing the decade's total U.S. Agency for International Development support to West Pakistan for minor irrigation schemes alone to $56.7 million. But no U.S. funding for flood-control works was expended in the East. "We must evolve a synthesis between economic growth and moral and spiritual values," Ayub wrote in his forward to the revised Third Five-Year Plan, calling for the attainment of "Islamic social-ism" in Pakistan.

Shastri's heart attack and death in Tashkent in January 1966 brought Indira Gandhi (b. 1917), Jawaharlal Nehru's only child, to the head of India's Congress government. Mrs. Gandhi, though a widow (her deceased husband, Firoze, was no relation of the Mahatma), won the unanimous support of her party's elected members of Parliament as heir to her father's socialist ideals, charisma, and international rep-utation. She was also considered unassuming, shy, and easily man-aged by Congress party President K. N. Kamaraj, who lived to revise that judgment. Mrs. Gandhi was, however, far more radical than her only competitor for the prime ministership, conservative Brahman Morarji Desai (b. 1897). Her first trip abroad, nonetheless, was to Washington, where she secured some 12 million tons of U.S. wheat to help her famine-gripped nation survive, as well as over $400 mil-lion in other non-military support.

"India, like the United States," Indira assured U.S. audiences during her 1966 visit, "is wedded to the democratic ideal." She would look more to Moscow for military, technological, and diplo-matic sustenance, however, throughout the ensuing decade of her in-creasingly centralized power. A supreme pragmatist, Prime Minister Gandhi never hesitated to seek assistance from any source, internal or international, that could help to further her own political and India's national goals. She saw no dichotomy, in fact, between the two, and soon behaved as if she truly believed her chosen Congress President D. K. Barooah's pithy Emergency aphorism: "India is Indira, and Indira is India." She managed, by the end of 1969, to move her gov-ernment's program of economic reforms so far to the Left—national-

izing Indian banks, stripping former maharajas of the pensions her
father had paid them, lowering landholding ceilings dramatically—that
the old guard of her own party expelled her for "indiscipline." But
instead of humbly bowing her head to such chastisement, Mrs. Gandhi
fought back. She took her platform over the heads of New Delhi's
political pundits directly to the people, appealing for their support for
change that would bring, she promised, "food to the famished" and
"jobs to the jobless." "Madam" proved herself as good a politician
as her father, and just a bit tougher. She ran with her own New Congress on a radical platform that brought a few communist and several
regional party allies to her coalition and soon smashed Morarji's conservative Old Congress at the polls.

India's move to the Left coincided with Pakistan's shift even farther to the political Right of total martial dictatorship. Bhutto formally
launched his People's party in 1967 and was soon jailed for "inciting
the masses." In Karachi alone, where Bhutto's power base of Sindhi
support was strongest, the death toll rose above 20 in twenty-four
hours. In Dacca, more than 100 Bengalis were killed as Mujib went
on trial for "treason." Strikes now alternated with street protest
marches, East and West and East again. Ayub blamed all the trouble
on "enemies of the country," but as his decade of "strong rule"
ground to its tormented close it became obvious, even to his own
military colleagues, that President Ayub was not the rider to tame
Pakistan's "wild horse." Too much Basic Democracy, some feared,
had softened him. On March 24, 1969, Ayub stepped down, turning
his reins of faltering power over to Pakistan's Commander-in-Chief
General Aga Mohammad Yahya Khan (b. 1917). Yahya immediately
proclaimed full martial law.

"We in the Armed Forces had hoped that sanity would prevail and
this extreme step would not be necessary," Yahya told Pakistan in his
first broadcast on March 26, 1969, "but the situaton has
deteriorated."[16] It would soon deteriorate further. U.S. military support had started flowing to Pakistan again early in 1968, and within a
month of Yahya's takeover, Secretary of State William Rogers flew to
Islamabad. Yahya assured him he would only retain power long

enough to "restore . . . normal democratic life" to Pakistan. President Nixon visited Pakistan that August to recruit Yahya as his middleman in launching top-secret talks with Mao. General Yahya soon announced that Pakistan's first nationwide elections would be held in October 1970. Then he issued what he called his "Legal Framework order," to set legal guidelines for Pakistan's new Constitution. The first guideline was preservation of Pakistan's Islamic ideology, and the second was to ensure "national integrity and solidarity." Addressing his armed forces in Pindi on March 23, 1970, Yahya declared that "no power on earth" could separate East from West Pakistan, insisting they were "two limbs of the same body."[17]

Severe cyclones hit Chittagong and Dacca in October 1970, and a hurricane, followed by a tidal wave, struck East Pakistan the following month. Elections were postponed until December. Mujib's Awami League won 160 of the East's 162 seats in the National Assembly, which was to have met the following March. In the West, Bhutto's party won 81 of the total of 138 seats. On the Frontier, Abdul Ghaffar Khan's son, Abdul Wali Khan, won 6 seats for his National Awami party, the "Pashtunistan" party. Mujib's victory was unprecedented. He was "overwhelmed by a deep sense of gratitude to Almighty Allah and to my beloved countrymen." Yahya flew to Dacca to confer with him in January, and then referred to him as Pakistan's future prime minister. Bhutto, however, refused to concede defeat. After he and Yahya had met for many hours, they decided to fly to Dacca together to speak again with Mujib, who soon detected a conspiracy between the Sindhi landlord and the general to disenfranchise Pakistan's majority by postponing the Assembly. Mujib called upon his followers in Bangladesh to stop cooperating with the "unlawful tyranny" of Yahya's forces. Pakistan's army filled every PIA flight with "special-services" soldiers. Dacca became a bristling garrison. Some 60,000 of West Pakistan's best U.S.-armed troops held the East in a grip of steel as the deadline approached for convening the National Assembly. It was never to meet.

Shortly before midnight on March 25, 1971, Pakistani forces rolled their U.S. M-24 tanks onto the grounds of Dacca University and opened fire on Iqbal Hall, one of the student dorms. Some 200 students inside that dorm were dead when the tanks moved on to other "hotbeds" of "treason." Simultaneously, other armored units opened fire with machine guns and cannon in predominantly Hindu sections of the sleeping city bazaar. At 1 A.M. an armored column rolled to Mujib's suburban home to arrest him. The election game was over. A new kind of "Legal Framework order" had begun. Estimates of the number of Bangladeshis killed that dreadful night vary from thousands to more than a hundred thousand. No actual count could be made at the time, for the military continued to fire for several days, "cleaning up" many "pockets of treason." Yahya broadcast from Pindi the next morning, blaming Mujib for having "created turmoil, terror and insecurity."[18] Bhutto, interviewed in Karachi that day, said of the preemptive military strike, "By the Grace of Almighty God, Pakistan has at last been saved."

Shortly before his arrest, Mujib had issued a proclamation to his people, which informed them:

> You are citizens of a free country. . . . Today the West Pakistan's military force is engaged in a genocide in Bangla Desh. . . . They have unleashed unparalleled barbarity on the golden Bengal. . . . You should not be misled by the false propaganda of the military rulers. Our struggle is most rewarding. Certain is our victory. Allah is with us. The world public opinion is with us. JAI BANGLA ["Victory to Bengal"].[19]

The flood of panic-stricken refugees from East Pakistan poured across the Indian border, a million in the first month, 60,000 a day by April 1. There were an estimated ten million Hindus in East Pakistan at this time, and all of them seemed determined to leave that country before being slaughtered either by West Pakistan's terrifying army or by Bangladesh's inexperienced Liberation Force (*Mukti Bahini*) that was being trained and armed close to India's border. Chaudanga became Bangladesh's first provisional capital, Tajuddin Ahmed, that nation's first provisional prime minister. The latter appealed to the world for recognition. New Delhi was first to respond. The Nixon administration remained dumb.

As the refugee flood tide from Bangladesh reached its peak, Yahya reported that Dacca was returning to conditions of normalcy. He still promised to transfer his power to elected representatives, insisting that "We shall not allow the result of these elections to be destroyed." Hindus moved like an army of locusts into refugee camps set up around Calcutta, already the world's most overpopulated metropolis, bringing their hunger, cholera, and other epidemic diseases with them. About 3.5 million Bangladeshis had arrived by May 1971. Congressman Cornelius Gallagher, chairman of the Asian subcommittee of the House Foreign Affairs Committee, visited the refugee camps in June and returned to Washington to report: "I am now convinced that terrorism, barbarities and genocide of no small magnitude have been committed in East Bengal." Still, U.S. arms flowed to Pakistan unabated. Nixon needed Yahya to help conclude his China visit plans and sent Kissinger to Pindi that July to take a secret Beijing shuttle while he was reportedly "unexpectedly delayed" in Pakistan because of "an intestinal affliction."

Mrs. Gandhi signed a twenty-year Treaty of Peace, Friendship, and Cooperation with the Soviet Union on August 9, 1971. If either party was "subjected to an attack or a threat thereof," under that treaty, Moscow and Delhi would "immediately enter mutual consultations in order to remove such threat and to take appropriate effective measures to ensure peace and the security of their countries." It was the end of India's "non-aligned" era.

By September 1971 it was costing India approximately $200 million a month to feed the almost 9 million refugees from Bangladesh settled on its soil. The entire 1965 war with Pakistan had cost only $70 million. Indira's advisers warned her that the economic burden of Bangladeshi refugees could destroy India more rapidly than any Pakistani army. In October, after the monsoon ended, the Indian Army rolled its heavy new Russian guns and tanks closer to the Bangladesh border. Thirty to forty thousand Mukti Bahini guerrillas were now inside Bangladesh, equipped and trained to blow up bridges, mine roads, and snipe at Pakistani soldiers in order to paralyze the country-side. Indira flew to Washington for talks with Nixon on November 4. "We are told that the confrontation of troops is a threat to peace," she informed the National Press Club as she prepared to fly home the next day. "Will the world [i.e., the White House] be concerned only if people die because of war between two countries and not if hundreds of thousands are butchered and expelled by a military regime waging war against the people? . . . Who is more important to them, one man and his machine or a whole nation?"

On November 23, 1971, Pakistan's ambassador to Washington called a press conference, reporting that Indian troops of three divisions, supported by heavy armor and MIG air cover, had crossed the border and attacked in the East. "How imminent is war between India and Pakistan?," asked one reporter. "I am surprised to hear this question," His Excellency, General Raza, replied. "The war is on. It is not only imminent, but it is on!" Soviet-built trucks towed 105-mm. artillery down the Jessore road. Turbaned Sikhs drove the endless line of jeeps mounted with recoilless cannon. Cumbersome trailers dragged pontoon bridges to ford rivers whose glistening ribbons sliced the skirt of Bangladesh's soil in a thousand places. In Dacca, Pakistan's commanding General Niazi had bragged, "I am so happy if they attack," and promised his troops would hold them off, fighting, if necessary, "to the last man." In the basement of the White House, Henry Kissinger told the Joint Chiefs in the Situation room: "I am getting hell every half-hour from the President that we are not being tough enough on India. . . . He wants to tilt in favor of Pakistan." The nuclear-armed carrier USS *Enterprise* of the Seventh Fleet was ordered to leave the Pacific and head for Chittagong. By the time it reached the Bay of Bengal, the Bangladesh War would be over.

The Indian Army rolled through Jessore on the road to Dacca, greeted less by bullets than smiling faces and shouts of *"Jai Bangla!"* From every village hut and city house the red, green, and gold flag of Bangladesh flew triumphant. On December 7, Yahya appointed Bhutto his foreign minister and sent him to the United Nations to plead Pakistan's case. The Security Council debate was long and bitter, and Bhutto finally tore up his notes, crying, shouting: "Mr. President, I am not a rat. I've never ratted in my life . . . but I am leaving. . . . I find it disgraceful to my person and to my country to remain here a moment longer."[20] In Dacca, on December 15, 1971, Niazi surrendered, turning over his pearl-handled pistol and some 78,000 troops to General Sam Manekshaw of the Indian Army. Mrs. Gandhi declared a unilateral cease-fire and victory to her wildly cheering Parliament. Yahya resigned and turned what was left of Pakistan over to Bhutto, who promised "to pick up the pieces, very small pieces," and with them build "a new Pakistan—a prosperous and progressive Pakistan, a Pakistan free of exploitation." It was an emotional, moving speech, the best Bhutto ever made. "We have to rebuild democracy," he told his people. "We have to rebuild confidence, we have to rebuild hope in the future. We have to rebuild a situation in which the common man, the poor man in the street, can tell me to go to hell."[21]

The People's Republic of Bangladesh was born with a population of 75 million, initially a "secular, democratic" republic (four years later changed to an "Islamic Republic"), out of Pakistan's East wing. Mujib was released and flew home to a hero's welcome in Dacca early in January 1972. He became prime minister and was hailed as "Nation-Unifier" by his people. Before March 25, 1972, the first anniversary of Bangladesh, all 9,774,140 refugees had returned to their homeland, most of them by special Indian trains. Fifty other nations had followed India's lead in recognizing the new state by then, but Washington waited a bit longer, until April 4, 1972. In New Delhi, Indira was acclaimed a military genius and political savior, all but worshipped as the Mother Goddess-incarnate by her adoring populace.

Thus by the end of 1971, India had emerged the supreme single power of South Asia, its grateful neighbor-ally Bangladesh to the East, its disgracefully defeated, much-diminished enemy Pakistan to the West. Independent and friendly Afghanistan, moreover, posed no threat or concern to New Delhi, for King Zahir, much like Mrs. Gandhi herself, was most warmly supported, cordially welcomed, and "assisted" by Moscow.

NINE

Washington's South Asian Policy

The United States had no South Asian policy prior to 1947. After the demise of the British Empire, Washington found itself faced with two competing, angry, jealous Dominions. The puzzle of how to please one without offending the other would have challenged the reputed wisdom of King Solomon. It proved more than Harry Truman, Dwight Eisenhower, and all their successors and diligent Cabinet advisers combined were capable of solving. Unless partition was undone, or the divided status of Kashmir at least accepted as widely in Pakistan as in India, it was chimerical to expect New Delhi and Karachi-Islamabad to respond with equal ardor to the courting of Washington. Critical interludes of weakness and singular incompetence, nonetheless, have alternately turned an admittedly difficult foreign assignment for Washington into a shambles of neglect or a disaster area of inept intervention.

The focus of U.S. foreign policy at the historic birth of India and Pakistan as independent nations was Europe and its postwar division into a free West and an enslaved East. Russian wartime hatred of Germany and lust for reparations combined with Soviet paranoic fears of encirclement led to the swift absorption of Eastern Europe into Moscow's iron orbit and a Cold War aftermath to dampen the joys of Allied victory. India and Pakistan seemed quite remote from the next possible center of global conflict and were a bit too puzzling and certainly too poor and weak to worry Washington. The UN seemed a more appropriate forum for handling such emerging nations and their squabbles. The Kashmir conflict, however, proved tougher to subdue than the Japanese navy had been for Chester Nimitz, who was appointed UNCIP's plebiscite administrator, but never got to fire his first salvo.

By mid-1950, U.S. success with its European recovery program (the Marshall Plan) of economic aid to Western Europe encouraged Congress to pass the Act for International Development, Point Four of which authorized the President to initiate programs in underdeveloped nations. This act was to become the major arm of peaceful U.S. policy in Asia, and its introduction to South Asia was assigned to the vigorous, ambitious first U.S. ambassador to India, whose fame spread beyond the hallowed halls of Foggy Bottom. Chester Bowles flew into India in 1951, with his winning smile, Yankee common sense, and mandate to spend lots of money. He soon became one of Jawaharlal Nehru's most trusted and appreciated foreign advisers. He even thought of Nehru's daughter as a close friend, but learned better after she became prime minister.[1]

Point Four was not meant to be simply a charitable dole to the have-not nations of the Third World. It was designed to stimulate economic development and improve the climate for the private investment of capital wherever its seed money was planted. Private American foundations, especially the Ford Foundation, thus often proved at least as influential and effective in encouraging economic growth as did government programs. Douglas Ensminger, the Foundation's first director in New Delhi, for example, funded India's important Community Development and Rural Extension programs, launched in 1952 on Mahatma Gandhi's birth anniversary. Ensminger remained in India much longer than Bowles and got even closer to Nehru before Nehru's death.

U.S.-Indian relations remained most cordial during the first three years of the 1950s, in fact, until Eisenhower's secretary of state, John Foster Dulles, tried to persuade Nehru to join at least one of his new Asian pacts, which were to serve as a martial link fence for the containment of Russian imperialism. Fabian Socialist that Nehru was, he refused to buy any of Dulles's dire warnings of "Hell and brimstone" that would fall over India once the "Red Russian Menace" started moving south instead of west. Nehru was, moreover, eager to lead the Third World of non-aligned nations of Asia and Africa away from the threats to peace that he firmly believed superpower confrontation posed. He was at any rate hardly ready to join the Southeast Asia Treaty Organization (SEATO) or the Central Treaty Organization (CENTO) or their South Asian equivalent, all of which Dulles pushed on his first tour of Asia.

Pakistan, however, was delighted to accept membership in both SEATO and CENTO, signing a Mutual Defense Agreement with the United States in 1954, reaping the Pentagon's most modern and sophisticated arms and other economic support in return. Pakistan even agreed to lease part of its terrain, near Pindi, to the U.S. for launching and landing pads for U-2 spy planes that surveyed the Soviet Union from what were believed to be "untouchable" altitudes—until a plane was shot down in 1960, after which Russian protests and Pakistani fears dismantled that monitoring base.

As most South Asian scholars had anticipated in 1954, the U.S. military alliance with Pakistan first antagonized India, rapidly escalating the South Asian arms race, soon turned New Delhi toward Moscow in search of military supplies and support, and ultimately alienated Pakistan as well. It was surely the worst single blunder in U.S. South Asian policy and easily the most costly. Unfortunately, it was not to be the last. The price tag for arming Pakistan with weapons that would be used against India—in the Rann of Kutch mini-war in 1965 as well as in Kashmir—and against Bengalis in East Pakistan in 1971 totaled nearly $2 billion.

Russia wasted no time in offering more aid to India as well as Afghanistan in the immediate wake of Pakistan's alliance with the U.S. In the summer of 1955 Nehru flew to Moscow, saying, none too cryptically: "Countries make pacts and alliances often through fear of some other country or countries. Let our coming together be because we like each other and wish to co-operate and not because we dislike others and wish to do them injury."[2] Nehru's meetings with Nikita

Khrushchev and Nikolai Bulganin at this time opened the door to Indo-Soviet friendship and cooperation which was to bring Soviet MIGs as well as steel plants to Indian soil in the following decade. The Russian plant at central India's Bhilai was the first major offspring of this new era of Indo-Soviet cooperation. Were it not for the stimulus provided by Dulles's "containment" chain of alliances stretching from Turkey to Pakistan—with links missing across Afghanistan and India—it would have been hard to imagine Russia investing so heavily in Indian development.

Such Russian aid, moreover, only stimulated escalation of U.S. Point Four and World Bank investments in New Delhi's Five-Year Plans, thus doubly taxing American citizens for every dollar spent arming Pakistan. By 1957 Nehru told his nation that since U.S. arms to Pakistan were "a menace to India", his government felt obligated "to spend more and more on armaments." [3] Washington's costly policy, launched to contain Soviet expansion, thus served to stimulate Moscow's massive and effective diplomatic and economic intervention there. "By the use of many types of maneuvers and threats, military and political, the Soviet rulers seek gradually to divide and weaken the free nations and to make their policies appear as bankrupt by overextending them," John Foster Dulles wrote in March 1954. "It is not easy to devise policies which will counter a danger so centralized and so vast, so varied and so sustained. It is no answer to substitute the glitter of steel for the torch of freedom," he wisely concluded. [4] Too bad he couldn't practice what he preached.

Mohammad Ali Bogra, Pakistan's prime minister from 1953 to 1955, when the U.S. alliance was concluded, made no secret of the fact that he allied his nation with Washington primarily because "we apprehended a threat of our security from India." [5] Ever since the first India-Pakistan War, the bulk of India's army and armor had been deployed along West Pakistan's eastern border, from Kashmir to Sind. The same held true for Pakistan's forces, most of which faced east rather than west, and have remained so to this day. By joining forces with the Free World, Pakistan also received much-needed non-military economic assistance. Famine had stalked that land in 1953, and U.S.

gifts of wheat alone saved countless Pakistani lives. U.S. non-military aid in loans and gifts during the first decade and a half of Washington's alliance with Pakistan came to more than $4 billion. Aid of every sort accelerated after 1958, when the martial coup of Generals Mirza and Ayub replaced Karachi's civil government with its more "efficient" Pindi machine. Ayub's personal approach to foreign influence was, "I believe we should adopt good things wherever they can be found."[6]

John Kennedy's presidential victory in 1960 brought Chester Bowles to Washington as Dean Rusk's undersecretary of State, shifting the focus of U.S. interest and concern in South Asia back to India. Russia's downing of an American U-2 flown by Gary Powers and based in West Pakistan earlier that year proved alarming to all nations concerned. Islamabad alone ran the risk of incurring Russian wrath and retaliation, however, and Ayub later apologized to Premier Kosygin, claiming that "the U-2 incident . . . had been as much of a shock to us as it was to the Soviet Union."[7]

John Kenneth Galbraith was Kennedy's choice as Indian ambassador, and in his pre-assignment briefing from John Sherman Cooper, who had served Eisenhower in Delhi, learned that Cooper had already informed Nehru "that his [Cooper's] position on the Pakistan arms buildup was not the same as that of Dulles and that he was urging a change."[8] Galbraith was totally to reverse the balance, with an unexpected assist from China the following year. Galbraith and the Peace Corps soon conspired to break some of the diplomatic ice Dulles had brought to Indo-American relations, though misadventures like the Bay of Pigs proved embarrassing setbacks. U.S. military commitments to the jungles of Southeast Asia were starting to spread, moreover, like a cancerous growth through the bloodstream of Indo-U.S. relations, sapping all potential for strong and healthy development. Nehru had met Ho Chi Minh, who had visited India, and knew he was first a Vietnam nationalist, that his struggle against French Imperial rule and for reunification of his country was much the same as India's struggle against the British. India and Vietnam soon would have even more in common: their most feared and hated northern neighbor, China.

Ironically, Nehru and India had been China's foremost champions in the UN and elsewhere during the first decade of statehood for the People's Republic, while Washington had led the Western world in refusing to recognize its existence. In 1954 Sino-Indian relations seemed firmly set upon a friendly course of peaceful coexistence, based on the famous Five Principles (*Panch Shila*) that promised "mutual respect for each other's territorial integrity and sovereignty," and "non-aggression," promises that were rearticulated at the Afro-Asian Bandung Conference in 1955. New Delhi hailed this era of "Indo-Chinese Brotherhood" (*Hind-Chin Bhai Bhai*) as the dawn of a new age of peace for Asia. Such optimism proved unfounded. China's cartographic claims to 55,000 square miles of British India Imperial real estate along the Northern Tier, from Ladakh to Assam, were made with deadly bullets in October 1959. Subsequent attempts by Indian border patrols to drive Chinese units from several advanced posts led to the massive invasion of India's North-East Frontier Agency three years later.

From New Delhi, the Chinese invasion, coming so soon after Pakistan's alliance with Beijing, looked almost like the start of a three-front assault against India. Nehru's old Cambridge buddy Krishna Menon, the most virulent anti-American in the Indian government, was forced from the helm of Defense, and Nehru himself was finally jolted from non-alignment and faith in *Panch Shila*. Washington had to reassess its South Asian alliance with Pakistan, since the latter seemed poised to use American arms in support of Asia's leading communist power. Not the least disconcerting to Indo-U.S. strategists was the fact that India dared not remove any units from three full divisions based along the West Pakistan border, despite heavy losses and continuing Chinese advances in the northeast.

Before the end of 1962, U.S. arms and planes started flowing to India, a steady stream of C-130s loaded with enough equipment to outfit and support ten new mountain divisions, which were to be raised

and trained over the next half-decade. Pentagon technicians and train-
ers started arriving with the new equipment, and by 1963 New Delhi
had more U.S. brass than Islamabad-Pindi. Ayub's reactions were pre-
dictably irate. He had never believed that China's strategic objective
was anything other than to secure its claims to disputed border territory, especially in the Aksai Chin region of Ladakh. He saw no valid
basis for the U.S. rush of military aid to India on a scale that reflected
Washington's anxiety about a major war with China.[9] New Delhi,
many Pakistanis now felt, had made the most of its weakness in 1962
in order to build up its armed forces with both U.S. and Soviet aid,
not so much to guard against any improbable future threats from China
as to "dismantle" Pakistan.

Galbraith's hope was to press Nehru into some sort of settlement
in Kashmir once the Chinese tide flowed out, and ultimately to establish a subcontinental "defensive relationship" with Pakistan. He urged
both but achieved neither. He soon found it impossible, in fact, to
control "our own military invasion" of India.[10] After having called in
the Pentagon, it was not so easy to keep colonels and generals from
sending more and more experts to do the job properly. Billions of
dollars worth of U.S. hardware thus kept flowing into India long after
the Chinese had withdrawn their last soldier. Galbraith and Kennedy
overreacted as wastefully in India's "defense" as Dulles and Eisenhower had done earlier in "protecting" Pakistan—each, of course,
from communism. Galbraith was replaced by Bowles in mid-1963, but
neither brilliant Yankee was sharp enough to get Nehru to move beyond discussion of Kashmir and related matters before "Panditji" died
in 1964.

South Asia's stage was set by then with two armies, each heavily
supplied and partially trained by the U.S. and eager to go at one another. In 1965 they did, first in the Rann of Kutch, the lowest point
along the India-Pakistan border, then in Kashmir, the highest point.
Fighting in the sub-sea-level Rann ("Salt Marsh") erupted in April
over a disputed area of the border that had never been clearly demar-
cated, since it was flooded for much of each year. Pakistanis in U.S.
Patton tanks blasted Indians in U.S. Shermans. The Pattons won, pen-

etrating some ten miles into Indian territory by April 25, when Ayub proposed a cease-fire. India agreed to submit the disputed territory to an impartial commission for arbitrated delineation.

Pakistan, apparently encouraged by its easy victory in the Rann, pushed ahead with plans for the liberation of Kashmir. India's strategy, however, appears to have been to attempt not more than a token stand in the Rann, suspecting perhaps that the Pakistani assault there was, in fact, diversionary. When Pakistan's forces moved in the north, therefore, they found themselves facing a much tougher and better-prepared army. The ensuing three-week war that ended in stalemate might have lasted much longer had the U.S. not enforced a strict embargo on all military shipments to both India and Pakistan soon after the actual fighting started. Without a steady flow of parts to keep them in effective operation, many Indo-Pakistani weapons soon ceased functioning because of systemic breakdown. Pentagon supplies of ammunition were, moreover, calculated to limit to three weeks of heavy firing any brush wars between Washington's weapons' clients.

Pakistan felt betrayed by Washington's even-handed policy in 1965, and Ayub wondered of what use his government's long-standing martial alliances with the U.S. had been, and whether Nehru had not been wiser to remain sufficiently non-aligned to procure every sort of aid from both sides. Russia had begun building its MIG factory in India by this time, and shortly before the actual war started, Moscow concluded an agreement to sell Russian submarines and destroyers to India's navy. Shortly after the 1965 war ended, therefore, when Russia's Premier Kosygin invited Ayub and Shastri to the Soviet Central Asian capital of Tashkent for a peace conference, both leaders accepted. It was Soviet Russia's first major diplomatic initiative toward South Asia as a whole and proved remarkably successful.

Washington was left out in the cold. After having earned the antipathy of both India and Pakistan through the misguided generosity of excessive military support, the U.S. played no visible role in helping South Asia find peaceful formulas for resolving its outstanding problems. Secretary of State Rusk was too busy worrying about South Vietnam and the Congo, which he viewed as the world's "two most dangerous centers of infection''[11] at this time, to give any constructive thought to India or Pakistan. The pendulum of U.S. policy suddenly swung from its peak of overcommitment and inept intervention to the opposite extreme of total abdication of constructive responsibility.

Pakistani fury at feeling betrayed and abandoned by its U.S. ally in 1965 exploded violently in Karachi and Lahore, where rampaging mobs of young men burned the United States Information Service (USIS) Library and American Consulate buildings. American employees were stoned and chased whenever sighted in Pakistan during that anguished aftermath of bitter non-victory viewed throughout West Pakistan as defeat and dishonor. Indians in Calcutta and Delhi became almost as outraged against "Imperialist U.S. intervention" when several Indian newspapers reported that Rusk had called a Kashmiri plebiscite "an essential ingredient" to South Asian peace. Instead of attempting to argue and defend that obviously valid position, the State Department's press officer issued a disclaimer of the "rumor." The U.S. had by now given India some $2.5 billion in non-military capital goods and technical assistance alone, over 58 percent of the total foreign assistance received by the nation, the "world's largest democracy," as Washington called it. Yet now that the time for peacemaking was at hand, Russia was left to wear the laurel wreath of international glory, and a U.S. secretary of state was afraid of admitting he favored holding a plebiscite. Hardly surprising to find America reviled on both sides of the river Sutlej.

The conference at Tashkent opened on January 4, 1966. Premier Kosygin welcomed "our southern neighbours" and made a point of reminding them that "The peoples of our country . . . have long maintained the closest trade and cultural contacts with the peoples of Pakistan and India. . . . Normalization of relations between these two countries, which the coming talks should promote, will lead to even greater development of the Soviet Union's friendly relations with Pakistan and India."[12] Prime Minister Shastri hailed Russia's "bold initiative," assured Ayub that "we unreservedly accept Pakistan's sovereignty and territorial integrity," and called for "peaceful coexistence" and an end to "the atmosphere of cold war." "Instead

of fighting each other, let us start fighting poverty, disease and ignorance," India's frail second prime minister added, in his last and
greatest speech, "The problems, the hopes and the aspirations of the
common people of both the countries are the same. They want not
conflict and war, but peace and progress. They need, not arms and
ammunition, but food, clothing and shelter."

Ayub agreed. "Our aim is to compose our differences with India
not to perpetuate them," insisted Pakistan's president.

> The prosperity of six hundred million people of India and Pak-
> istan depends on peace. Both of us have suffered under long
> and dark periods of foreign domination. It is after centuries
> that we have regained our freedom. We must live in peace to
> be able to devote all our energy and resources to the liquidation
> of the grim heritage of colonialism and to open avenues of
> happiness and progress for our peoples. . . . There is no prob-
> lem between us which cannot be solved peacefully and hon-
> ourably. . . . The terms of peace are equality and justice.

The next four days, however, were wasted in wrangling over whether
to include Kashmir on the agenda for discussion. Kosygin personally
was obliged to shuttle between Ayub and Shastri to bring the two
leaders face to face for a closing day's signing of the agreement that
declared their "firm resolve to restore normal and peaceful relations."
In addition to the withdrawal of all armed personnel to prewar positions, Shastri and Ayub agreed that future relations between India and
Pakistan be "normalized," negative propaganda discouraged, and
conditions created by both neighbors to "prevent the exodus of people."

After signing the Tashkent Agreement, Lal Bahadur Shastri went
to sleep, awakened only briefly by a fatal heart attack. Much was
hoped for, much said and written of the "Spirit of Tashkent" that was
to usher in an era of peace for South Asia. Unfortunately, that spirit
barely survived the death of Shastri. His successor, Indira Gandhi,
mentioned it often in her early years of precarious power, but seemed
less concerned about it as she grew stronger. Mrs. Gandhi visited
Washington soon after taking high office, securing some twelve mil-

lion tons of wheat for India's famine-gripped land and over $400 million in civil aid for her nation's Fourth Five-Year Plan. "India, like the United States, is wedded to the democratic ideal," she assured American audiences. As if to offset the impact of that visit, Russia sent heavy road-building equipment to Pakistan over the new highway it had been building across Afghanistan. The following September, Ayub flew to Moscow for a second visit, thanking Kosygin for "your initiative which led to the Tashkent meeting" and appreciating the "development of friendly relations between the Soviet Union and Pakistan." [13]

Washington's futile escalation of the war in Vietnam by late 1967 only further alienated Pakistan as well as India. Pakistan recalled its representative to SEATO and refused to attend any meeting of CENTO in 1967. Had U.S. intervention in Southeast Asia proved more effective, Ayub might have been more supportive, but still blistering as he was from Washington's embargo in 1965, he was certainly in no mood to help the Pentagon fight a losing war. Prime Minister Gandhi considered American intervention in Vietnam completely unjustified by any criterion, urging some form of negotiated settlement and calling for the "immediate withdrawal of all foreign forces" to allow the people of Vietnam to "fashion their own destiny without any outside interference." [14]

The nadir of U.S. South Asian policy was reached during Nixon's tenure in the White House. Nixon and Kissinger had the unique capacity to pursue policies toward the subcontinent that alienated all three of its competing powers, India, Pakistan, and Bangladesh. How was it possible? The key to their Asian policy was to court China as a counter to Russia. Yahya Khan was Nixon's chosen instrument in arranging the top-secret China visit that culminated in U.S. recognition of the People's Republic in 1972. Nixon had liked Yahya from their first meeting. The short Pathan general was a man's man, a boon companion, who enjoyed a ribald joke, like Nixon, and a good time. The two hit it off famously. Washington more than doubled its annual allocation of aid to Pakistan during Nixon's first year in power, and the World Bank promised another $485 million. Yahya, in return, flew to Beijing, where he served as Nixon–Mao matchmaker and

promised elections to Pakistan's long-repressed populace. He spent
more time in China than in East Pakistan during 1970 and seemed
truly startled at the landslide victory of Mujib's Awami League that
December.

Soon after Yahya's army opened fire on Dacca University's campus in March 1971, U.S. consul in that nightmare city, Archer Blood,
cabled Washington, reporting the "mass killing of unarmed civilians,
the systematic elimination of the intelligentsia, and the annihilation of
the Hindu population." His cables were to remain buried in State Department files, and Blood himself was recalled to Washington for reas-
signment. That May, Senator Walter Mondale introduced the first
congressional Resolution to suspend all U.S. military aid to Pakistan,
"before we watch the burial of another generation of babies." In moving his Resolution 21, Mondale explained that such suspension was
vital "If America's claim to moral and humane values means anything." Secretary of State Rogers spoke at Colgate's commencement
that month on "Relating Our National Idealism to International Realities."[15] Rogers remarked:

> A dedication to peace, democracy, and international well-being
> arises naturally from our idealism. However, in many ways our
> idealism was too grandiose. . . . In the fast-changing world of
> today our idealism must constantly be augmented by realism.
> . . . Well, you might ask—where are we?

On the Dacca Massacre and Bangladesh, Nixon's White House remained dumb.

"We view what is going on in Pakistan as an internal matter," a
State Department spokesman announced several weeks after the massacre had started, as the refugee flood was rising. "We know that the
Pakistan army, equipped mostly with American arms and led by U.S.
trained officers, let loose a massive burst of violence on fellow Muslims," Senator Frank Church of the Foreign Relations Committee reported, seconding Resolution 21.

> Military largesse, costing the United States nearly $2 billion in
> arms was perennially justified to Congress and the American

people as a shield to protect the Pakistanis—and the United
States—against Communist aggression. . . . Far from containing the Russian bear or the Chinese dragon, however, Pakistan
has used its American-furnished military equipment first
against India in 1965 and now against its own people. Indeed,
in 1968, Pakistan unabashedly closed down our electronic listening post at Peshawar in order to placate Russian and
Chinese feelings. By all standards, then, our military assistance
policy has proved a failure—but it has been kept alive by the
persistence of our arms bureaucracy, and the insistence of the
Pakistan junta. . . . When a policy goes sour but is not
changed, the results are sordid.[16]

Instead of cutting off aid, Nixon's administration raised proposed
AID to Pakistan tenfold, inserting an extra $5 million for arms and
$250,000 for police training. Yahya's proposed military budget for
1972–73 was $26 million higher than the $425 million he had had in
1971–72. Peter Cargill, director of the World Bank's South Asia department, visited East Pakistan at this time and found the population
there "in a state of extreme terror," the economy a "shambles," and
the potential for epidemic disease and famine "dangerous." When
Cargill informed Yahya of this picture, the general "simply refused to
believe it." The White House and State Department were equally un-
impressed.

"Our Government goes to great pains to warn us of a fearsome
bloodbath that will befall the people of South Vietnam if the regime
there is left to fight on alone," Church continued in mid-summer,
"yet one of the worst manmade bloodbaths of our time is taking place
in East Bengal, administered by the Pakistan Army. The martial-law
ruler, General Tikka Khan, has been quoted recently as saying: 'We
will reduce you [Bengalis] to a minority.' . . . However, the administration is so unconcerned about events in Pakistan, as well as voices
of outrage in Congress, the press, and among private citizen groups,
that the transfer of arms to the transgressors continues on a 'business
as usual' basis. I understand an estimated $35 million is still in the
arms pipeline, and the President refuses to stop the flow." Kissinger
flew to Pindi for discussion with Yahya that July, but instead of per-

suading the latter to release Mujib and make peace with Bangladesh he played "sick" and flew to China. Nixon's paranoid preoccupation with secrecy obliged Kissinger to lie to the press in order to keep the forthcoming China visit completely under wraps until Nixon announced it on nationwide television and world radio on July 15.

Nixon's personal dislike of Mrs. Gandhi was even stronger than his affection for Yahya. She was too much the snob for him, a "socialist egg-head" like her father. Privately, he referred to her with various female expletives, some of which would later be "deleted" from his tapes. She was not insensitive to or unaware of such cold and hostile White House feelings toward her and the nation she represented. Nixon did more to strengthen the bonds of Indo-Russian friendship than any other President of the United States. His thunderous silence on the Dacca Massacre and continued arms aid to Pakistan accelerated Indira's signing of the twenty-year Treaty of Peace, Friendship, and Cooperation with Russia on August 9, 1971. Kosygin warmly welcomed Mrs. Gandhi to Moscow that September, saying,

> It is impossible to justify the actions of the Pakistani authorities which have compelled millions of people to leave their country, land, property, and to seek refuge in the neighbouring India. . . . Never before has there been such solidarity between the peoples of India and the Soviet Union in the struggle for peace and progress.[17]

Indira and Kosygin issued a joint statement on September 29: "Urgent measures should be taken to reach a political solution . . . paying regard to the wishes, the inalienable rights and the lawful interests of the people of East Bengal as well as for the speediest and safe return of the refugees to their homeland in conditions safeguarding their honour and dignity."

Senator Edward Kennedy spent a week touring Bengali refugee camps outside Calcutta and returned August 26 to report:

> Unfortunately, the face of America today in South Asia is not much different from its image over the past years in Southeast Asia. It is the image of an America that supports military

repression and fuels military violence. It is the image of an
America comfortably consorting with an authoritarian regime.
It is the image of an America citing the revolutionary past and
crowing about its commitment to self-determination, while it
services military juntas that suppress change and ignore a people's aspirations. . . . It is argued that the continuation of military aid to West Pakistan somehow gives us "leverage" to
constructively influence the military's policy in East Bengal.
Well, where is that leverage? Where is the leverage to stop the
use of U.S. arms which produce the refugees and civilian victims that we then must help support in India? . . . Where is
the leverage to prevent our humanitarian aid from being turned
into military equipment, when American relief boats are transformed into American gun boats? Why, if we have the leverage
to influence the government of Pakistan, must our great nation
assist in this shabby and shameful enterprise? It is time for
Americans to ask their leaders: "Just what kind of government
is it that we seek to influence—and for what purpose?" [18]

Many Americans asked those same questions, but Nixon was much
too busy worrying about Watergate and his cover-up to give any constructive thought to South Asian policy. He ignored Mrs. Gandhi's
personal appeals for aid in "saving humanity" in early November and
urged Kissinger to tilt toward Pakistan during the ensuing month's
war. Preoccupied with his own problems, fears of impeachment, fears
of prosecution, fears of further inadequacy and human failure at every
level, the President of the United States floundered, while India, Pakistan, and Bangladesh burned. On December 15, 1971, Prime Minister
Gandhi wrote "Mr. Richard Nixon" an open letter, "setting aside all
pride, prejudice and passion and trying, as calmly as I can, to analyse
once again the origins of the tragedy which is being enacted."

All unprejudiced persons objectively surveying the grim
events in Bangla Desh since March 25 have recognised the
revolt of 75 million people, a people who were forced to the
conclusion that neither their life, nor their liberty, to say nothing of the possibility of the pursuit of happiness, was available
to them. The world press, radio and television have faithfully
recorded the story. The most perceptive of American scholars

who are knowledgeable about the affairs of this sub-continent revealed the anatomy of East Bengal's frustrations. The tragic war, which is continuing, could have been averted if, during the nine months prior to Pakistan's attack on us on December 3, the great leaders of the world had paid some attention to the fact of revolt, tried to see the reality of the situation and searched for a genuine basis for reconciliation. . . . I undertook a tour in quest of peace. . . . It was heart-breaking to find that while there was sympathy for the poor refugees, the disease itself was ignored. War could also have been avoided if the power, influence and authority of all the States, and above all of the United States had got Shaikh Mujibur Rahman released. . . . Lip service was paid to the need for a political solution, but not a single worthwhile step was taken to bring this about. . . . The fact of the matter is that the rulers of West Pakistan got away with the impression that they could do what they liked because no one, not even the United States, would choose to take a public position that while Pakistan's integrity was certainly sacrosanct, human rights, liberty were no less so, and that there was a necessary inter-connection between the inviolability of States and the contentment of their people. . . . When Dr. Kissinger came in July 1971, I had emphasised to him the importance of seeking an early political settlement. But we have not received, even to this day, the barest framework of a settlement which would take into account the facts as they are. . . .[19]

Not only did India thus blame the U.S. for impotently refusing to take any action to avert war in South Asia in 1971, but Pakistan also blamed Washington for not backing its martial alliance more forcefully. The USS *Enterprise* arrived too late, after all, and then did nothing but steam about within range of India's eastern coastline, never launching a single nuclear missile or war plane! What sort of military support was that? As for Bangladesh, Washington did not as yet deign to recognize that nation other than by such occasional odd references to it, such as Dr. Kissinger's tasteless aphorism, "that international basket-case."

TEN

Emergence of Modern Afghanistan and Its Relations with Russia

The first Russo-Afghan Treaty of Trade and Friendship was signed in Kabul in 1920. Amir Amanullah had corresponded with Lenin the year before, and Lenin had replied warmly, writing of "mutual aid against any encroachment of rapacious foreigners" and concluding: "May the aspirations of the Afghan people to follow the Russian example be the best guarantee of strength and independence of the Afghan State."[1] Amanullah's global plenipotentiary, Mohammad Wali, was welcomed in Moscow by Lenin himself, sparking considerable anxiety in Britain's Foreign Office. The amir had, however, effectively asserted his national sovereignty and was determined to make the most of it. But in 1920 Soviet Russia could hardly afford to send any arms or aid to Kabul. Words alone did little to comfort penurious Kabul, especially when faced with the need to feed the Khilafat army of Indo-Muslim refugees, who arrived over the passes in 1920. When Soviet Russian troops marched against the Central Asian Muslim Khanates of Bokhara and Khiva in 1921, moreover, forcing the amir of Bokhara to flee south to seek asylum in Kabul, Amanullah's faith in Russian promises dissolved in the acid of his Islamic brother's plight.

The British government of India was only too happy to replenish Amanullah's arsenal, sending him an even more generous annual rupee subsidy than his father had received to ward off the Russian advance. Soviet troops, however, remained north of the Oxus, content slowly to digest their Khanates, one—or at most two—at a time. In return for Britain's renewed payments, Amanullah promised to keep Russian envoys out of his eastern cities. He did not, however, lose his passion for modernized reforms, which roused many of the most orthodox of his eastern tribal chiefs against his regime. Amanullah also hoped to open direct relations with Washington. A U.S. State Department representative, Cornelius Engert, was accommodated for a few months in Kabul in 1922, and his report urged his superiors to establish permanent relations with Afghanistan at once. Due to the nature of American interest in and concern with this part of the world at the time, however, no action was taken by Washington until 1934.

Amanullah's relations with the Russians improved by 1924, when Soviet pilots started to arrive in Kabul to help the amir put down his own orthodox Muslim rebels. Russian planes arrived as well, but they were still crated, having never been opened by the Russians, and took Afghan-Russian engineers several years to actually get off the ground. By 1927, however, regularly scheduled air service existed between Termez, on the Soviet border, and the Afghan capital.[2] Amanullah and his unveiled wife embarked that year on the Grand Tour, which did much to lessen their support among their own people. The "Red Amir," as some Simla officials called him, was soon to be driven into exile. With his ouster, Russian influence over Kabul went into temporary eclipse.

The Russians, like many Afghans, suspected Nadir Shah of coming to power in Kabul as a British puppet, but that did not deter Moscow from recognizing his regime and trying to expand relations with his government. In 1931, in fact, a Russo-Afghan non-aggression pact was signed. The following year, Russia bought Afghanistan's total supply of Qandahar wool produced for export, after the Indian market collapsed. An Afghan-Russian postal agreement was concluded at this time also, and Russian scientists were most helpful late in 1932 in teaching Afghans to cope more effectively with locusts. Nadir Shah's assassination by a pro-Amanullah student, in 1933, brought young Zahir Shah to the throne, and his uncle, Hashim Khan, to actual control over Kabul's government as its prime minister. Russian proximity, patience, and commercial and technical assistance inevitably tied Afghanistan closer to the Soviet Union throughout the 1930s.

A commercial treaty was signed in 1936 that significantly expanded trade between these neighboring states. Faced as they were with growing nationalist resistance within India, the British dared not dictate to Kabul in this era and, once World War II started, were satisfied with King Zahir's proclaimed neutrality, asking little more. German commercial penetration into Kabul in the mid-1930s had aroused considerable British anxiety, especially in 1938 with the completion of several German exploratory flights from Kabul to China. Substantial German credits to Afghanistan and almost 100 German advisers moved into Kabul on the eve of World War II. In the autumn of 1941, when Britain and Russia simultaneously demanded removal of all "Axis nationals," the Afghans "took umbrage at this enforced infringement of their neutrality."[3] As the tide of war turned toward the Allies, however, Kabul showed less interest in the Germans and renewed warmer relations with Russia and Britain.

Amanullah's secular reforms included the promulgation of an Afghan Constitution in 1923, which, while leaving the state an absolute monarchy in theory, introduced representative democratic councils and "consultative bodies."[4] Nadir Shah's Constitution of 1931, however, rescinded these attempts at representative government, returning Afghanistan's polity to rule by Hanafi Sunni orthodox Law and hereditary tribal chiefs' advisory councils, convened only at the will of the king, whose power was absolute, arbitrary, and final. The king and his royal family ministers ruled as they wished, in fact, subject only to assassination and the persuasive powers of foreign advisers, whose influence was generally commensurate with the largess provided by their home governments. Pashtu was made the national language of Afghanistan after 1931 and a "parliamentary facade" was written into the Constitution, theoretically creating an upper House of Nobles and a lower house called the National Assembly, whose members were to be elected for three-year interludes. No elections were held, however, until after the next Constitution was adopted in 1964.

Allied victory in World War II imposed greater pressures for change upon Afghanistan's absolute monarchy. It was, after all, hailed the world over as the victory of democracy over Axis tyranny, of freedom over slavery. The British Empire itself had caved in under that avalanche of idealistic rhetoric, popular enthusiasm, nationalist hopes, humanitarian dreams. Old Hashim Khan, tough though he was, could no longer withstand the assault of demands for reforms that echoed even in the hallowed halls of Kabul's royal palace. Early in 1946 he stepped down, turning Afghanistan's administration over to his younger martial brother Shah Mahmud Khan, whose premiership led Afghanistan toward greater interaction with the outside world. Washington had extended formal diplomatic recognition to Kabul in 1934, but no permanent U.S. mission was established there until 1943.

Under Shah Mahmud's aegis, U.S. AID began to flow onto Afghanistan's remote plateaus and barren plains. The most ambitious of America's early Afghan enterprises was in the Helmund River valley. The Boise, Idaho, firm of Morrison and Knudsen invaded there with their heaviest earth-movers and concrete mixers, promising to turn almost 40 percent of Afghanistan's desert soil into a blooming garden, capable of supporting almost 50 percent of the nation's population at a much higher standard of living than they had ever enjoyed or imagined possible. Unfortunately, costs skyrocketed, concrete results dwindled, and hopes diminished as the saline-polluted plains grew nothing but frustrations for all involved with that grandiose scheme. In some portions of the newly dammed valley, production of crops actually decreased by 50 percent. Many Afghans learned new skills, of course, and some grew rich on American know-how, but few villagers prospered from America's first major intrusion into their Hermit Kingdom.

Russian engineers and scientists opened their first commercial office in Kabul in 1952, starting less obtrusively than the U.S. had, with smaller projects designed to produce early, tangible benefits: machine shops, fertilizer plants, medical laboratories. "Young Afghan" leaders in Kabul staged a palace revolt in 1953, ousting Mahmud and bringing King Zahir's cousin and Military College classmate, General Mohammad Daoud Khan, to power as the "strong man" best qualified to guide Afghanistan's ship toward the world's ocean of rapid modernization.

During Daoud's first decade in power, Russian influence in Kabul increased more rapidly than that of the U.S. Moscow's aid was not only less obtrusive than Washington's, but usually came at lower interest rates. Khrushchev and Bulganin arrived in Kabul in 1955 to a warm welcome and promised another $100 million in long-term loans, to be used for modernizing Afghanistan's air and road facilities. The Russians built a new airport at Begram and improved the field outside Kabul, which proved very useful to them in 1979. Dulles tried to get Daoud to join the Baghdad Pact (CENTO) in 1955, but Afghanistan refused all of Washington's martial overtures to ally itself with the Free World's struggle against communist expansion, interested only in American arms to ward off attacks from Pakistan. U.S. military aid was, however, entering Pakistan's port of Karachi faster than it could be processed at this time.

As Daoud's support for "Pashtunistan" separatists became more vocal, Pakistan closed its border passes to all Afghan trade, trying to pressure Kabul to abandon the cause of its Pathan brethren. All that Pakistani tactic achieved, however, was to make Daoud and his government more dependent than ever on Russian support and Soviet assistance. Russia's portion of Afghanistan's overseas trade more than doubled from 1950 to 1956, jumping to over 30 percent by the latter year. Eastern European states also joined in aiding Afghanistan to weather the Pakistani blockade. Czechoslovakia, Poland, and Bulgaria helped Afghanistan develop technologically as well, sending engineers and scientists to Kabul with their state-trading officials. By the summer of 1961, no less than fifteen Russian planes were filled daily with Afghan fresh fruits, which were flown north to a Russian market hungry for the lush melons and citrus that Pakistan had rejected, to its own detriment.

In 1956, after Washington had turned down several requests from Kabul for "non-allied" arms and ammunition, Afghanistan appealed to Moscow for its military hardware. The Russians responded most generously and with "no strings attached." Moscow was only too happy to help convert Afghanistan's martial machine from its traditional dependence on British equipment and spare parts to ever-growing reliance upon weapons made in the Soviet Union. Soon after Kabul was totally weaned from its Western sources of martial nourishment, Russian military advisers would be able to convince their Afghan general-students that the most advanced of their Soviet-made radar equipment and anti-aircraft batteries required "special servicing," and they were all taken "off the line" on the eve of the Russian invasion.

U.S. non-military AID to Afghanistan continued throughout Daoud's decade as prime minister, and American technicians often found themselves working side by side with Soviet engineers and scientists on Kabul projects of modernization. Roads, airports, irrigation schemes, mines, and factories swiftly transformed the traditional face of Afghanistan, lifting it out of the wrinkled mold of its ancient past to a smooth new patina of modernization, stripping the veils and dark robes of orthodox Islam from the eyes and bodies of Afghan women. Muslim mullahs soon decried such un-Islamic behavior as clear proof of Russia's atheistic influence over Kabul, and Pakistan's *Ulama* echoed those charges. The examples of Russia's transformation of the former Islamic Khanates of Uzbekistan and Turkmen into Soviet Socialist Republics were powerful portents of the grim future that awaited all Muslims under Russian domination. Without U.S. CIA, International Cooperation Agency (ICA), or AID prodding or encouragement, Afghan and Pakistani religious leaders began to warn their flocks of the dangers of "Satan's helpers" who flew to them from "distant places." Traditional tribal chiefs felt equally threatened by the strong winds of change that blew down from the north, but kept so busy fighting one another across the Durand Line that they had little time to unite against the Bear. Then in 1963 Daoud, considered too pro-Russian and anti-Pakistani by his cousin, King Zahir, resigned, and Dr. Mohammad Yousuf, a "commoner," was appointed premier.

The Shah of Iran invited Pakistani and Afghan delegates to Tehran immediately after Daoud's resignation to mediate normalization of Afghan-Pakistani relations. The Teheran Treaty of May 1963 re-opened the Durand border to the free flow of produce, including millions of dollars worth of U.S. aid that had been shipped to Afghanistan but had been left rotting in Karachi warehouses. Yousuf's government received further commitments from Washington for a number of major new development projects to be funded by the International Monetary Fund, AID, and the World Bank. With many hundreds of millions of dollars worth of American goods flowing to Kabul, a small army of U.S. experts arrived to help train Afghans to use them properly. In 1964, a new Constitution was drafted, revised, and approved by the Grand Tribal Assembly (*Loye Jirga*), proclaiming Afghanistan a constitutional monarchy, whose "sacred religion" was Islam, an "independent, unitary and indivisible" State. Persian (*Dari*) now shared national-language status with Pashtu. Hanafi Law remained sacred throughout Afghanistan, but with elections and a bicameral Parliament (*Shura*), "New Democracy" came to Kabul, where almost 15,000 of only 40,000 eligible voters exercised their franchise.

American-educated Dr. Abdul Zahir was "elected" (he was actually chosen by King Zahir and later confirmed by popular mandate) president of the lower House of the People (*Wolesi Jirga*). His most articulate and troublesome opposition came from Marxists of the far Left, led by young Babrak Karmal (b. 1928). An impassioned speaker, Karmal roused students from Kabul University to pack the House's galleries, cheering his articulate attacks upon Yousuf and his "corrupt" choices for Cabinet posts, disrupting Parliament and the "New Democracy" before it got started. Believing they were really free to assert their new-born "constitutional rights," some students marched to Yousuf's home, shouting slogans and denouncing the premier in not very polite language. On October 25, 1965, Afghan government troops opened fire, killing "at least" three students, wounding "scores" of others.[5] Four days later Yousuf resigned, and the king chose his former ambassador to the United Kingdom and U.S., Mohammad Hashim Maiwandwal, as the next prime minister.

An AID-funded U.S. team of academic administrators from Indiana University was sent to Kabul in 1966 to help reorganize the university, but there was little any government could do to eliminate student unrest once martyrs' (*shaheed*) blood had been shed, short of granting demands or keeping all campuses closed. Much like the students of British India half a century earlier, whose youthful energy and intelligence had been fired by idealistic tomes and speeches on democracy, freedom, and liberty for all, these young Afghans, their nation's elite, woke up in 1964 suddenly to find themselves in the twentieth century. They could not so easily be stuffed back into medieval closets of obedient quiescence. Freedom's passions were contagious, as potent and heady as love of life itself. While the older, more jaded men cautioned moderation, urging patience and calm, the youth persisted in advocating the righteous wisdom of their wild, willful ways. It was easy enough for the balding graybeards of Kabul to blame these "hotheads" for all their nation's troubles, but harder for those who remembered the Boston Tea Party, the storming of the Bastille, and the Bolshevik Revolution, Jallianwala Bagh, and Wilson's Fourteen Points. Once the pandora's box of a representative, at least partly responsible government had been opened, even on Kabul's remote plateau, there was no one strong enough to clamp its lid shut again.

Many newspapers and political journals sprang to life after the birth of the new Constitution. One of the most outspoken, *Khalq* (*"Masses"*), was published by Nur Mohammad Taraki and lasted only for six issues, until mid-May 1966. The self-proclaimed "democratic voice of the people," *Khalq* hailed "the Great October Socialist Revolution" and called for an end to "the feudal system which dominates Afghan society."[6] Religious conservatives demanded the ban and withdrawal of government press funds used to print *Khalq*. The new political party founded by Maiwandwal, the Progressive Democratic party, was also attacked by traditionalists and conservatives as much too radical, since it advocated collective leadership. Prime Minister Maiwandwal, seeking to bolster his government's sagging economy, flew to Washington in March 1967 and met with President Lyndon Johnson, who promised him more AID to help launch Afghanistan's Third Five-Year Plan.

Afghanistan's huge northern neighbor remained the major market for Kabul's exports, however, and by this period continued annually to sell Afghanistan over one-third of all its imports, more than four times the U.S. input into that land. Russian President Nikolai Podgorny visited Afghanistan in May 1967 to attend the opening of a Soviet-financed power plant at Naghlu. By 1967, the Russians had invested $568 million in Afghanistan's developing economy, over 50 percent more than the U.S. total of $388 million to that date. For the following two years, Russian aid continued to leap ahead, $30.5 million in 1968–69 and almost as much again for the next fiscal year. U.S. support dropped precipitously, because of Washington's cancerous commitment to Vietnam, to $4.8 million in 1968–69 and to a mere $1.4 million in 1969–70.[7] Nixon's policy toward Afghanistan, much like his position on India, was one of malignant neglect.

Maiwandwal resigned in October 1967 as a new tide of student unrest mounted against him. His foreign minister, Nur Ahmad Etemadi, former rector of Kabul University, took up the burden of premiership. Russian interest in Kabul affairs continued to grow. Kosygin visited there in January 1968, assuring his neighbors of more and greater support. Indian interest increased as well. In 1969, Prime Minister Gandhi visited Kabul, and Indian imports jumped to almost one-fifth of Afghanistan's total for fiscal year 1969–70, second only to those from the Soviet Union. Kosygin arrived in Kabul again in May 1969 to celebrate the fiftieth anniversary of Afghan "independence." Pakistanis linked growing Indian interest with renewed Pashtunistan agitation, but Kabul insisted that Pathan nationalists in the North-West states of Dir, Swat, and Chitral had, in fact, been aroused that year by Islamabad's forced integration of those hitherto autonomous states into West Pakistan's provincial grip of steel.

Afghanistan's modernization and economic development inevitably led to closer, more permanent ties with the Soviet Union, simply by virtue of geographic proximity. In April 1968, for example, a 125-mile Russian pipeline was completed, through which Afghan natural gas has flowed ever since from the Shibarghan gas fields to the Russian border, thus permitting Kabul painlessly to repay many Soviet loans of the previous decades with gas valued at close to $15 million a year by 1971. Afghan hydroelectric power, similarly developed with Russian assistance, can easily be wired back to the country that helped harness it. The modern roads are also beneficial to both countries, especially the spectacular Russian-built highway from Kabul to the Soviet border, that includes almost two miles of the world's highest tunnel 25 feet wide and cut through the Hindu Kush at over 11,000 feet above sea level. Since the Salang Tunnel opened in August 1964, an average of 600 trucks a day have rolled through it. These veins, arteries, and central nervous system of modernity thus helped integrate the Soviet and Afghan economies for more than a decade before Russian tanks and planes rolled into Kabul.

New elections were held in Afghanistan in 1969, but they accomplished little more than to raise student hopes once again to fever point, terrifying government officials into closing universities. To no one's surprise, Etemadi remained in power even after the democratic exercise of counting ballots returned some new faces to the 216-member lower House of Kabul's Parliament. All the king's men (and the one woman) in his Cabinet were not the same people, yet they remained very much King Zahir's loyal servants. The internal political and economic tensions and conflicting external pressures that seemed daily to threaten to blow apart Afghanistan's brittle monarchy were intensified by natural disasters from 1970 to 1972, when drought and famine stalked that bleak, barren land. Etemadi finally gave up in mid-1971, and the king brought old Abdul Zahir back from his ambassadorship in Rome to try to pull a new cabinet together. The political game of musical chairs at the top of the pyramid failed, however, to silence popular demands for more real power, or peasant needs for more food and water. A year after he took over, Abdul Zahir resigned again, and another, equally impotent prime minister, Mohammad Shafiq, was appointed to stand up in Kabul's *Shura* to inform members who shouted protests at him that his government was trying its best to improve conditions.

By 1973, even King Zahir understood that time had run out for him and the ancient dynasty he embodied. He had been unable to transform himself into an Afghan model of Britain's truly constitutional monarch. The parliamentary facade he had erected, while afraid to enact legislation that would legitimize political parties or a free press for his politically repressed land, collapsed without crushing him, however, for he and his family had left on a "holiday trip" abroad—just in the nick of time! In Kabul, the king's cousin and brother-in-law, Lieutenant General Mohammad Daoud Khan, after ten years in quiet retirement, proclaimed himself prime minister and president of the "Republic" of Afghanistan, miraculously created overnight on July 18, 1973. The "old corrupt system," President Daoud announced, was "dead and gone," and a new "popular government" had emerged in its place, "in the genuine spirit of Islam." The grandson of one king, cousin of another, *Sardar* General Daoud, was born again, as a republican president! Some skeptics expressed disbelief. They were quickly silenced. Maiwandwal was arrested, but soon after that "hanged himself." The new president chose a brace of generals for his first Cabinet, to help him keep his "Republic" working most efficiently.

Daoud quickly reestablished the close relationship he had earlier enjoyed with Moscow, visiting there in 1974 and again three years later after the adoption of his new Constitution by the *Loye Jirga* he had convened early in 1977. The Constitution gave Daoud enhanced powers as president and head of state, reaffirming Islamic institutions. Several coups were attempted against Daoud, two late in 1973, another in 1976, but all proved abortive. Afghanistan's "strong man" seemed impervious to assault. His support came not only from his staff of well-paid, well-trained generals but from the remnant of Kabul aristocracy, who knew that whatever his title his blood remained royal, and from such flaming radicals as Babrak Karmal and his *Parcham* ("Flag") party of student Marxists, who viewed Daoud as a helpful tool of revolution, if not its ideal initiator. The president's trip to Moscow in April 1977 paid off handsomely with a twelve-year agreement between the neighboring republics on economic cooperation, Russia pledging to increase its support of Kabul annually and to consider renewal of the agreement two years before it expired. What more could any Afghan politician, regal or plebian, ask for or require?

A year later, however, on April 27, 1978, Daoud and several hundred of his closest relatives and supporters were killed in Kabul's bloodiest coup to date. The mastermind behind that coup was none other than Taraki, who quickly emerged at the head of a 35-man Revolutionary Council, proclaiming Afghanistan a "Democratic Republic," and himself its president-prime minister. Kabul's palace got a new red flag, with an upper corner emblem of sheaves of wheat wrapped in green ribbon and curved like two horns toward a gold star between them, that bore a striking resemblance to the regional emblems of several Soviet Central Asian republics. The single Pashtu word under the star was *"Khalq,"* though the banner at the bottom of the oval carried a longer Arabic inscription celebrating the "April 1978 Revolution." The "Imposter-Monarch" or "cruel *Sardar,"* as Daoud soon came to be called in Kabul's press, was dead. Afghanistan's true revolution had begun, under Taraki and his People's Democratic party, which now included Karmal's Parcham wing merged with the *Khalq* body.

"Comrade Taraki," as the *Kabul Times* called him, was hailed a "True Son of the People" and "Great Leader."[8] The Revolutionary Council swiftly banished all "rotten customs" from Afghan law, including traditional Islamic dowry and money exchange on engagement or marriage. Peasant indebtedness was also abolished, and all workers, peasants, toilers, and homeless civil servants were promised "safe homes" as soon as possible. Landless peasants were promised land. Kabul's new "strong man," Deputy Prime Minister-Foreign Minister Hafizullah Amin, who supposedly gave the actual signal that triggered the coup, had studied physics at Columbia University, but also knew how to use the Russian-made, rapid-fire AK-47s that did most of the killing on bloody April 27. Taraki went to Moscow that December to sign a twenty-year Treaty of Friendship with the Soviet Union. Russo-Afghan relations had entered a new phase of more intimate cooperation and "comradeship."

ELEVEN

South Asia Today

For India, Pakistan, and Bangladesh the 1970s proved a decade of rapid change. The honeymoon between New Delhi and Dacca that had started in 1971 ended but a few years later as bickering over shared waters and boundaries drove the newlyweds to the brink of divorce. Pakistan's struggle to recapture its faith in itself as a nation was even more traumatic. By 1980, all three major states of South Asia had suffered political upheavals that cost two of the previous decades' leaders their lives and briefly removed the third from her pinnacle of power.

After losing its East wing, Pakistan was diminished in size to South Asia's third most populous power. But a more important result in terms of geopolitical orientation was its new West Asian rather than Southeast Asian focus and interest. The most important theme of Pakistan's post-1971 renaissance was the growth of its Islamic consciousness and the search for closer ties with other Muslim nations of West Asia and North Africa. Zulfi Bhutto's leadership was, therefore, anomalous in two major respects: as architect of Pakistan's China connection, his foreign policy focus was turned the wrong way; and as a secular Western modernist himself, he was hardly best qualified to lead Pakistan's Islamic revival. Bhutto seemed, however, at least from Washington's perspective, to offer the best hope of holding Pakistan together—much the way the Shah did for Iran. Both were expected by Kissinger and Nixon to "stand by each other" and help "insure peace and security" to the Middle East and Persian Gulf areas.

Bhutto's political astuteness—despite the fact that many blamed him for losing Bangladesh—was considerable, and as Pakistan's president, until 1973 when he became prime minister under the new Constitution, he promised much to the common man through his policy of "Islamic Socialism."[1] Though born to one of Sind's wealthiest families, Bhutto nationalized Pakistan's major industries in 1972 and all of its banks in 1974. He also introduced tough land reforms, and promised food, clothing, and shelter to every Pakistani. His People's party was most popular with the poorest peasants of Sind and the Punjab and with urban intellectuals, especially young students in Karachi and Lahore. He had charismatic qualities and was given the unique title *"Quaid-i-Awam"* ("Leader of the People"). Brilliant, eloquent, and unscrupulous, he was generally either loved or hated. In mid-1972 he met with Indira Gandhi at Simla, and they reached agreement on the repatriation of some 93,000 Pakistani prisoners still held in Bangladesh and India. Final troop withdrawals along the western border were also negotiated, and both leaders promised to continue their dialogue toward restoring normalization to Indo-Pakistani relations.

India suffered her worst drought in decades during the early 1970s, and with the Organization of Petroleum Exporting Countries (OPEC) quadrupling its crude-oil prices in 1973, fires of inflation consumed what little economic surplus Indira's government had saved. A wave of student, labor, peasant, and fixed-income middle class unrest swept across the subcontinent from Gujarat to Bihar and back to Bombay, all but drowning Indira. Jaya Prakash ("JP") Narayan (1902–79), Socialist party patriarch and latter-day disciple of the Mahatma, organized a new coalition *Janata Morcha* ("People's party") that rallied opposition leaders all across the land, including Indira's ex-Deputy Prime Minister Morarji Desai, Nehru's stalwart lieutenant. By 1974, Indira's popularity had plummeted to such lows in polls that it hardly seemed possible for her government to survive the next elections. She contrived, however, to keep her Left-wing coalition afloat, receiving more Russian arms and non-military aid after Leonid Brezhnev's first visit to India in 1973. Their joint declaration at the end of that trip called for making the Indian Ocean a zone of peace, which surprised those who knew that Soviet Admiral Zuyenko's fleet of some twenty-two warships was still steaming around the Bay of Bengal at that time, a year after "helping" Bangladesh to clear its war-littered ports and dredge its harbors.

A more significant long-range result of Brezhnev's 1973 visit was the fifteen-year Indo-Soviet Agreement on Economic and Trade Co-operation it launched. Russian scientists, engineers, and other experts began to pour into India from every Aeroflot jumbo jet that landed in New Delhi and Bombay. Indo-Soviet enterprises and projects sprang up all across the subcontinent in

> iron and steel and non-ferrous metals production, prospecting, production and refining of oil, natural gas, coal and other minerals, power engineering; petrochemical industry, shipping and . . . agriculture . . . in further expansion of iron and steel plants in Bhilai and Bokaro to increase their annual capacity to 7 and 10 million tonnes . . . construction of the oil refinery in Mathura with the annual capacity of 6 million tonnes . . . of the copper mining complex in Malanjkhand, of the Calcutta underground railway . . . in the field of atomic energy for peaceful uses, space, electronics, as well as to the development of economic relations.[2]

In May 1974 India shook the subcontinent, touching off its first atomic explosion under the desert sands of Rajasthan. A decade earlier, after China had exploded its first nuclear device, India had condemned that "retrograde step," calling upon all "civilized nations" to ban such behavior. But India subsequently refused to sign the UN's Test Ban Resolution. Had the arrival of the USS *Enterprise* off India's coast accelerated India's nuclear explosion? "India has not ever been an easy country to understand," Prime Minister Gandhi reflected, shortly after that 1974 plutonium blast. Pakistan, which had felt the tremors, believed, however, that it understood its neighbor too well. Bhutto's government immediately funded a crash nuclear-arms program of its own, whose fallout has yet to be felt. Two nations, the mass of whose populations still had not emerged from poverty, thus embarked upon the most costly and perilous of arms races.

For Bangladesh, 1974 was also an explosive turning point. In the aftermath of independence, Mujib behaved as though his life's work was over. He lay back to enjoy the fruits of his personal power and freedom from Pakistani oppression far more than he worried about trying to bring similar pleasures to most of his penurious population. He failed, moreover, to disarm and control thousands of young "Freedom Fighters," who used their weapons to terrorize many of the villagers they were supposed to have liberated. Black marketeering, smuggling, corruption, profiteering, inflation, and hunger became as common to daily life in Dacca as they were in neighboring Calcutta. Many Bangladeshis said that the same Hindu Marwari merchants, bankers, and Calcutta moneylenders were to blame for the wretched plight of both Bengali capitals. Fortunes were, indeed, made overnight in currency manipulation, by businessmen who rushed back and forth between those two cities, but the economic problems created by Bangladesh's vast population and the pressures it imposed on the limited land and food resources went deeper than mere Marwari greed.

Mujib felt he could control the deteriorating situation only by suspending the Constitution, which he did in December 1974. Early the following year, he inaugurated a new system of government, one based on total presidential power, which he took upon himself. By abandoning his faith in the political system that had brought him to power, Mujib succeeded only in signing his own death warrant. He had always been a man of the people, after all, a politician not a general. A gang of officers from his own army assassinated this father of his nation, every member of his family they could find, and all of his loyal followers in Dacca in mid-August 1975.

Indira had by then declared her own "Emergency," virtually discarding India's Constitution in the wake of her unexpected High Court conviction for campaign malpractice in June 1975. The Allahabad suit had been filed against her after the last general election by the opponent she had easily defeated. As a result of conviction, Indira's mandatory punishment required her resignation and banned her from any elective office for six years. But instead of resigning, Mrs. Gandhi got India's president to declare an Emergency on June 25, 1975, had all leaders of the opposition Janata Morcha arrested, and suspended civil liberties. Then she announced a twenty-point program of economic reforms aimed at reducing inflation, getting people to "Talk Less and Work More," making India's hitherto slack and demoralized railway system move all its trains out on time, and frightening office clerks and higher bureaucrats enough to get them to put in a full day's work for a day's wages. Overnight her picture appeared on pillars and posts, concrete walls and mud huts all across the subcontinent, proclaiming in Hindi and English as well as India's other regional languages, "She Stood Between Chaos and Order" and "She Saved India." The press was totally censored, and many posters were slapped up around major cities, warning against "Rumor-mongering," urging "Work Is Worship," seeking to inculcate greater discipline among India's population and ideologically to unify the nation behind Indira Gandhi, battered but unbowed, assaulted by enemies—foreign as well as domestic—yet enduring, like Mother India herself.

Even nature seemed to be on Indira's side. The 1975 monsoon was the best in four years, and in the fall India reaped her biggest harvest of food grains, over 114 million tons, several million of which could actually be stored as bumper surplus. Prices stabilized and for some important food products dropped. Prisons were crowded, but offices were busier than ever, as were factories. The wave of wildcat strikes that had disrupted much of North India's economy during previous years ended. So did smuggling, black marketeering, and political agitation. The Emergency Raj, with its police crackdown spearheaded by elite Central Reserve units directly responsible to the prime minister's office, appeared to work wonders. A timid parliamentary rump remained in special session to rubber-stamp new constitutional amendments that legalized everything the prime minister did, including the past offenses for which she had been convicted and the suspension of future elections. Many an old head, long retired from the British Raj, nodded approval. It was a proper dose of salts that "Madam" had administered, salubrious medicine for India's ailing body politic. But with men like JP and Morarji and thousands of others from George Fernandes to Piloo Mody behind bars, spirits unbroken and firm, the nation was deeply troubled, sorely divided. Even those who most approved of the good things accomplished through Emergency action kept asking, "But why did she have to wait till her own conviction to do all this?" Indira charged that JP and Morarji were planning a revolution, which she had nipped in the bud. They called it *Satyagraha,* reminding her that was how Mahatma Gandhi had taught all of them to fight for freedom.

The Emergency Raj lasted nineteen months. In January 1977 Indira announced release of opposition prisoners and called nationwide elections for that March. Did she believe her own press, which was convinced that her popularity was, indeed, unique, and could pass the test of free elections? Or was her ambitious younger son Sanjay (1947–80) eager to win his first seat in Parliament, hoping then to succeed his mother as leader of her party and the nation? Or was she, like Hamlet, driven to that act by her father's ghost, haunted by the memory of his liberty-loving legacy? Perhaps she feared a martial coup if she waited much longer, for the Army was always there, stronger than her Central Reserve Police, and the memory of Mujib's bloody fall remained fresh.

The Janata coalition ran a vigorous whirlwind campaign, JP coining its slogan promise, "Freedom and Bread." Defections from Indira's own Cabinet on the eve of elections farther eroded her narrowed base of political support, as did several unpopular programs launched the previous year. Enforced sterilization of males, primarily in regions of North India that were heavily Muslim, was the single most abhorred measure, contributing substantially to the defeat both of Indira and Sanjay and of their Congress party.

Octogenarian Morarji Desai emerged as India's fourth prime minister. A devout Hindu Brahman, politically and economically conservative, pro-Western rather than Russian, Morarji tried to steer India from its Moscow course toward one closer to Washington. He personally exchanged many letters with President Jimmy Carter, welcoming him and Miss Lillian to New Delhi. Both deeply religious men, Desai and Carter shared pious hopes and aspirations for humanity's salvation and did their best to help restore some of the warmth of the Truman and Kennedy years to Indo-American relations. Morarji also hoped to improve relations with Pakistan, but soon after he came to power, Islamabad was rocked by violent political upheaval.

Opposition to Bhutto's Pakistan People's party was initially centered in the North-West Frontier and in Baluchistan, where Wali Khan's National Awami party (NAP) was most popular. In addition to the Pashtunistan movement, a "Greater Baluchistan" separatist movement had started along the southern half of the frontier. Bhutto launched virtual war against these tribal guerrillas. Using the old British techniques of "butcher and bolt" as well as air attacks, the government killed thousands of its own Baluchi and Pathan tribals between 1973 and 1976. The planes and bombs used in this most recent and dreadful pacification of Pakistan's southwest border were transferred to Bhutto from the shah of Iran, who had received them from Washington. The desolate frontier zone was left even more inhospitable, its sad but hardy populace even more disaffected following Pindi's worst raids than they had been before. In addition to such martial terror, Bhutto's government relied more upon the ever-expanding secret police force with which he surrounded himself. Rampant inflation and growing political corruption further undermined his base of popular support.

By 1975, the opposition NAP had become so vigorous and vocal that its leaders were arrested and the party itself banned. A new Pakistan National Alliance (PNA) was forged, however, uniting most of the other parties, religious and secular, opposed to "Chairman Bhutto's" regime. Maulana Mufti Mahmud, a bearded orthodox *alim,* was elected president of the PNA in January 1977. Violence was by then so widespread in Pakistan that Bhutto had declared a state of emergency during the elections of February-March 1977, although opposition leaders charged that most of the murders had been initiated by Bhutto's own police. Reports of voter intimidation and shameless ballot-box stuffing by People's Party workers were widespread during the actual elections.

When Pakistan's radio and press reported that 155 of the 200 seats in the all-powerful National Assembly had been won by Bhutto's party, riots of protest spread through most of Pakistan's cities. Bhutto tried to ignore charges of election corruption, suggesting that CIA involvement was the cause of Pakistan's post-election riots. Thousands of protesters were arrested and hundreds killed before martial law was proclaimed in Pakistan's major cities in April. Riots and floods brought Pakistan's economy to virtual paralysis, with inflation rates racing above 25 percent, foreign exchange reserves almost wiped out, food and cotton crops at all-time lows. Bhutto's relations with Washington reached their lowest point at this time when, following his refusal to abandon his government's nuclear-arms program, the Carter administration stopped shipment of 110 A-7 fighters. In June 1977, Bhutto tried to negotiate a settlement with PNA leaders, but he had waited too long. The following month, on July 5, Bhutto's own appointed army commander-in-chief, General Muhammad Zia ul-Haq, led the coup that toppled Zulfi Bhutto and his party. National and provincial assemblies were dissolved, but Zia promised new elections "soon." In September, he arrested Bhutto on charges of ordering the murder of political opponents. Then he suspended elections, indefinitely.

General Zia appointed himself president of Pakistan and soon brought some of the PNA leaders into his Cabinet, especially those who belonged to the fundamentalist *Jamaat-i-Islami*. Born in the Punjab's Jullundur, Zia had been reared in the martial atmosphere of its cantonment as an orthodox Muslim. He was commissioned in the Royal Indian Army in 1945, fought in the 1965 Kashmir War, and had been a divisional commander in the 1971 war. Bhutto personally had picked Zia for his commander-in-chief, promoting him over many senior officers, because he no doubt trusted that Zia would remain grateful and loyal. The year before his coup, General Zia had visited the U.S. for advanced military training. Bhutto went on trial in Lahore early in 1978 and was sentenced to death by the Punjab's High Court. Millions in Pakistan and throughout the world were shocked by the sentence, which was appealed in Pakistan's Supreme Court. The verdict was sustained, but by the narrowest margin, 4–3.

President Zia promised to hold new elections by October 1979.

Insisting he had taken power merely to restore order, he denied any personal interest in politics and said he wanted to return to his military job. He did, nonetheless, embark on a number of foreign visits, first to Saudi Arabia, where he met with the royal family and received vital support for his Islamic state. He also reached agreement with President Daoud of Afghanistan on improving relations between their nations by increased trade and mutual good will and cooperation. Shortly after concluding agreement with Daoud, however, the latter was assassinated. Afghan-Pakistani relations remained friendly for some time after Taraki's coup, however.

Zia visited Kabul briefly in September 1978 on his way to Teheran, met with Taraki, and reported upon his return home: "I made it clear to the Afghan leaders that we have no differences with them, but if they think that they have a difference or two with us then we are ready to talk with them and sort these out in a cordial and brotherly manner."[3] Both Zia and Taraki expressed their confidence that there would be "peace across the border," which was then open to transit trade from Karachi to Kabul. By mid-October, however, more than 100 Afghan soldiers were reported killed in clashes with Pathan guerrillas in the eastern part of the Hermit "Republic," and Taraki took personal command of his armed forces as Afghan civil war intensified. Pathan guerrillas started crossing the border, seeking refuge in Pakistan, and orthodox mullahs and tribal chiefs looked to Peshawar and Islamabad for ideological as well as material support in their struggle against "atheistic Marxist tyranny."

Pakistan's revived interest in and commitment to the Islamic legal code was formalized by Zia on February 10, 1979, the anniversary of the Prophet's birth. Punishment for theft was thereafter to be chopping off the hand or hands of convicted criminals, as in Saudi Arabia. All alcoholic beverages were banned, and any Pakistani caught consuming, selling serving, manufacturing, importing, or exporting liquor of any kind was subject to as much as five years of rigorous imprisonment and 30 lashes. Gambling was similarly prohibited and punished. For those convicted of adultery or rape, the traditional punishment of public stoning was to be enforced, while anyone found guilty of the false imputation of adultery or rape could receive up to 80 lashes in public. An important part of the new Islamic order was to ban any payment of interest on savings, which led to considerable flight of capital from Pakistani banks. President Zia was determined to collect the traditional *zakat* tax from all Muslims, at the rate of 2.5 percent of all wealth or savings, on an annual basis. An agricultural tax (*ushr*) of 10 percent on all crops was also instituted. International appeals to commute Bhutto's sentence to life were ignored by the general-president, who allowed the former prime minister to be hanged before dawn on April 4, 1979. No riots nor widespread protests ensued, but a chill of silent alienation and terror seemed to spread over much of Pakistan, especially in Sind and cities like Lahore and Karachi, where Bhutto's popularity had been greatest.

Much like Pakistan, Bangladesh came under the orthodox grip of a general-president of its own, also named *Zia* ("Light")—Zia-ur Rahman (1936–81), who seized power over Dacca in November 1975.[4] Several martial after-coups had followed swift on the heels of Mujib's assassination, but Major-General Zia's was so successful that he also styled himself "President." Zia put his regime to a minimal test of referendum approval in 1977, and not surprisingly won almost 99 percent affirmation (it was simply a *Yes* or *No* ballot) from the some 30 million Bangladeshis who voted. The following year he restyled Bangladesh an Islamic state, discarding its former close ties with India and Russia with its "People's Republic" title. An aborted coup in 1977, believed to have been instigated either by Moscow, New Delhi, or both, left Zia more strongly entrenched in Dacca.[5] He developed closer ties with China, attended the Islamic Conference and met with Pakistan's Zia, promising to normalize trade and diplomatic relations with Bangladesh's former nemesis, and got substantial support from the World Bank. By denationalizing Bangladesh industry and encouraging foreign private enterprise, Zia attracted U.S. investment, especially in oil exploration and development. With the discovery of considerable oil reserves in Bangladesh, the country's economic future appeared a bit brighter under Zia's "controlled democracy." On May 30, 1981, Zia was assassinated in Chittagong by Major General Manzur Ahmed, who was killed two days later. The aborted coup was apparently triggered by personal jealousy. Vice President Abdus Sattar (b. 1905) became acting president of Bangladesh, but Army Chief of Staff Lieutenant General H. M. Ershad was generally looked to as the new "strong man" in Dacca.

For India's "Wounded Civilization"[6] with its distress-plagued population hovering on the edge of starvation and its growing army of unemployed, the Janata government's restoration of freedom brought little more than a return to the pre-Emergency functional anarchy of the Old Congress years. Inflation, corruption, smuggling, strikes, black marketeering, and bureaucratic bungling all reared their heads as soon as Indira canceled her Emergency ordinances. The political pendulum swung back to the no-controls extreme with alacrity. Prices soared, work slowdowns and industrial strikes spread with contagious speed, and economic growth fell behind schedule as fast as most trains, planes, and buses did. With Morarji at the helm, India's center of power seemed like the eye of a hurricane. Nothing stirred. Prohibition seemed the most urgent matter on the new prime minister's mind.

JP took no active role in government, his fragile health failing him entirely after the 1977 campaign. Morarji's leading Janata lieutenants, both of whom became his deputy prime ministers, Charan Singh (b. 1913) and Jagjivan Ram (b. 1908), appeared able to agree on nothing but their impatient desire to take his place. The "Three Old Men," as they were soon generally called, bickered as India's economy deteriorated, its population alone growing by some 15 million more mouths to feed every year. Birth control, thanks to the gross mishandling of Emergency sterilization, was, moreover, anathema to all shades of Indian political opinion. While Desai, Singh, and Ram battled one another to unrelenting inaction, Indira's popularity and attractiveness increased among India's general electorate, especially in the south. Many still disagreed with her methods, but all admired her energy and determination to *do* something.

The Janata coalition fell apart by mid-1979, its socialist Left wing defecting as Morarji defended his Right-wing *Jan Sangh* ("People's party'') faction against charges of having started bloody communal riots that left over 100 Hindus and Muslims dead in the spring. Stubbornly refusing to step down before mid-July, Morarji only resigned on the eve of a no-confidence motion he knew his party lacked the parliamentary power to win. Charan Singh, a Jat peasant, whose "fondest ambition" in life was to be prime minister, briefly enjoyed that pyrrhic climax to his career before his patchwork government also collapsed less than a month after he was sworn in as India's prime minister.

Rather than ask Jagjivan Ram, who was born an "Untouchable" and was head of India's once-pariah community of 100 million still at the bottom of the socioeconomic ladder, to try to form yet another Janata government, India's Brahman president, N. S. Reddy, dissolved Parliament and set new elections for early January 1980. Indira's Congress (I)—*I* for "Indira"—Party ran on the slogan "Elect a Government that Works!" Twenty-eight months of Janata ineptitude sufficed to restore Mrs. Gandhi to power. Her party won a stunning victory, commanding a two-thirds majority (351 out of 542 seats) in New Delhi's *Lok Sabha* ("House of the People"), to which she and Sanjay Gandhi were both easily elected.

Throughout early 1979, opposition to Taraki's government continued to mount increasingly violent resistance in all parts of Afghanistan. Kabul and other cities remained under curfew every night. Armed soldiers and roadblocks appeared everywhere. Resistance, initially centered north of Jalalabad in the Kunar province of Nuristan near the Durand Line, quickly spread to other valleys, west and south. From 5000 to 6000 Russian advisers were based in Kabul to help Taraki run his government and army. When U.S. Ambassador Adolph Dubs was kidnapped in February 1979, however, by Muslim terrorists, the Soviet-trained and directed Afghan police failed to secure his release, rushing the kidnappers, finding Ambassador Dubs dead when the smoke had cleared. Carter cut back U.S. AID sharply, though several Export-Import Bank projects continued unaffected. Little more than two years before his assassination, Dubs, as deputy assistant secretary of state for Near Eastern and South Asian Affairs, had told

Congress: "In the South Asian region, our primary concerns have been the promotion of regional stability. . . . In keeping with American concerns for the developing world, we had a long-standing interest in the economic progress of the countries of South Asia."[7]

Soon after Dubs's assassination, Vice Premier-Foreign Minister Amin said "the Soviets will protect the Afghan revolution." Amin was generally considered a stronger man than Taraki, much younger at 51 and somewhat more ruthless. He was credited with having recruited the military officers who carried out the assassination of Daoud and his family. He was also believed to have convinced Taraki of the wisdom of sending Babrak Karmal and other leaders of his Parcham party abroad, as ambassadors to Soviet-bloc nations. Recently recalled, however, those ambassadors had refused to return to Kabul.

In March, Afghanistan's government charged Iran with sending armed soldiers across its border to attack Herat, western anchor of the Afghan nation. Russian military advisers were flown to that beleaguered city. Meanwhile, in Kunar, the orthodox guerrillas, who were reportedly being trained and supplied from Pakistani bases over the border, kept expanding their hold over that province, despite increasing air and ground attacks from Kabul forces. Growing numbers of regular Afghan troops thrown into the battle defected with their Kalashnikov rifles and ammunition, swelling and strengthening anti-government ranks. Officially, Islamabad denied providing either money or arms to Afghan refugees within its domain, insisting that "Pakistan's policy toward Afghanistan remains one of good neighborliness and respect for the principle of noninterference into its internal affairs."[8]

The Afghan Army at the time consisted of 100,000 regular troops, three armored divisions, ten infantry divisions, and 144 combat aircraft with 10,000 men in the air force. By September, the army was down to 75,000 troops, and entire units had begun to defect whenever they were hurled into battle. Taraki then resigned reportedly because of "bad health and nervous weakness," and Amin stepped up to the top of Kabul's slippery pyramid of power. Taraki's death was officially reported a month later, when the story of Kabul palace's shootout of September 14, in which Taraki and his guards were gunned down by Amin's new team, finally surfaced. Soviet rocket-armed gunships, heavy tanks, MIG-21s, and MIG-23s as well as SU-20 bombers were now committed to Afghanistan's civil war. Russian generals, including the leader of the 1968 Czechoslovakia invasion, General Alexsei Yepishev, were by this time calling the shots in Kabul. Amin, like Taraki before him, charged the U.S. CIA with directing guerrilla operations, viewing the Islamic revolt within their own nation as a foreign aggression from Iran and Pakistan against their "People's Revolution."

By early December 1979, guerrilla forces were in almost complete control of Afghanistan's countryside. Amin's government secured most of the cities, but only during daylight hours and with armed forces on continuous alert. Even then, repeated urban attacks and troop defections indicated deep and growing disaffection with the Soviet-supported regime among Afghanistan's mostly orthodox, tradition-bound population. The estimated number of Afghan refugees who sought shelter in Pakistan by year's end was close to half a million.

In Iran, the shah's collapse and the return of Khomeini from Paris gave birth to a new revolutionary Islamic republic early in 1979 that was soon followed by the storming of the U.S. Embassy in Teheran on February 14. Ambassador William Sullivan and his staff were rescued at the time. Many Americans left the country when the ambassador was recalled to Washington in April, but 60 others remained. On November 4, Iranian armed revolutionaries stormed the U.S. Embassy compound a second time and took all the Americans hostage, retaining 52 of them until January 20, 1981. A few weeks later, on November 21, 1979, the U.S. Embassy compound in Islamabad was stormed and burned by "students" from the neighboring university. Two American guards and several Pakistani employees were killed, though the rest of the staff managed to escape from the Embassy's roof, after five agonizing hours in the fireproof security vault.

With Washington's attention focused primarily on Iran, and secondarily on Pakistan, Moscow decided early in December to move its armed forces directly into Afghanistan, flying Babrak Karmal and his

Parcham comrades back to Kabul with some 50,000 Soviet troops to help secure his position. The Russians initially claimed to have been invited into the country by Amin and his government, for by Christmas week it seemed quite possible that without massive Soviet support "the rebel tribesmen would have toppled the pro-Soviet government." [9] On the day after Christmas, Amin was gunned down in his palace, apparently by his Russian guards. Babrak Karmal took his place, wiring his "profound and heartfelt gratitude" to Brezhnev. Then turning to his Kabul public, Karmal announced that Amin had suddenly been discovered to be nothing but "a puppet of the CIA." Russian troops kept pouring over the border and flying in to secure every major Afghan airport until by January 1980 more than 80,000 regular soldiers of the Red Army were in full occupation of Afghanistan.

The exodus of Afghan refugees into Pakistan more than doubled in the early months of 1980 alone. Escalating costs of feeding and housing over a million refugees were almost as burdensome to Zia's government as the potential military, health, and political hazards posed by their presence within Pakistan. For the Russian invasion no more ended Afghanistan's civil war than U.S. forces in Vietnam had ended the civil war there. Although for Russia the lines of communication and supply were shorter, more easily sustained and thoroughly secured, Soviet troops were as distinctly foreign and bitterly hated by the average Afghan as British Indian soldiers had been. By 1981, the Russian Army in Afghanistan was mighty enough to secure the cities and keep major highways and airports open during the day, while Karmal and his government remained alive. Afghan guerrilla forces remained active throughout the countryside, however, and were most vigorous in the more remote valleys and rugged mountains of the northeast, taking their steady toll of Russian gunships as well as armored personnel carriers and tanks. More and more of the former regular Afghan Army joined rebel ranks, moreover, leaving fewer than 40,000 of Kabul's troops to support the Russian main force in what soon evolved into a stalemate civil war of attrition.

With Indira Gandhi's return to power in Delhi, India refrained from joining most UN powers in denouncing the Russian invasion of Afghanistan and calling for "immediate, unconditional and total withdrawal" of all foreign troops from that sorely troubled land. Mrs. Gandhi's alliance with Moscow and increasing dependence on Soviet arms and other assistance made her understandably, if not admirably, cautious in expressing any position on the Afghan situation. Her private sympathies were said to be with the Afghans and their traditional longing for total independence, but publicly she said nothing critical of the Soviet Union. After Brezhnev's December 1980 visit to New Delhi, Mrs. Gandhi joined him in demanding dismantling of the U.S. base on Diego Garcia island, but Afghanistan went unmentioned in their joint communiqué.

Pakistan was more outspoken. As one of the movers of the UN Resolution denouncing the Russian invasion, which initially mustered 104 votes, and host of the Islamic Conference which also unanimously called for withdrawal of all foreign troops from its neighboring Muslim state, Pakistan was in the vanguard of international diplomatic opposition to Russia's aggressive drive, as it was on the front line now facing Soviet troops. An extraordinary conference of Islamic foreign ministers was convened in Islamabad shortly after the Russian invasion to demand "the immediate and unconditional vacation" of the Soviet military occupation of Afghanistan. Bangladesh joined her Islamic neighbor in this resolution, abhorring the "presence of Soviet troops in Afghanistan" and upholding "the sovereign and inalienable rights of our Afghan brothers to determine freely their own form of government and choose their own political, economic and social system without external interference or military intervention."[10]

The military stalemate in Afghanistan and the heavy drain it imposed upon Russian resources, combined with the almost unanimous denunciation of the Soviet invasion by world opinion, may have had sufficient impact on the Kremlin to pave the way for a UN-negotiated, long-range diplomatic settlement for Afghanistan and South Asia as a whole. To achieve and sustain any such agreement, however India, Pakistan, and Bangladesh, as well as Afghanistan and the Soviet Union, must first be willing to recognize its potential value to each of their cherished national interests and to the overriding interest of helping to ensure world peace. The role of the United States in furthering such a settlement will be of critical importance, commensurate with America's unique wealth and power. How can Washington's future South Asian policy steer most effectively toward that elusive goal?

TWELVE

Toward a More Rational South Asian Policy

On January 4, 1980, President Carter addressed the nation, declaring the Soviet invasion of Afghanistan "a callous violation of international law and the United Nations Charter." He saw this "deliberate effort of a powerful atheistic government to subjugate an independent Islamic people" as a threat to "the stable, strategic and peaceful balance of the entire world." Carter announced that until the "withdrawal of all Soviet troops from Afghanistan," the United States could not continue to "do business as usual with the Soviet Union." He asked the U.S. Senate to defer further consideration of Strategic Arms Limitation Talks, froze all sales of "high technology" or "other strategic items," severely curtailed Russian "fishing privileges" in U.S. waters, halted delivery of some 17 million tons of grain to the Soviet Union, and called for the boycott of the Summer Olympics to be held in Moscow. "History teaches perhaps very few clear lessons," Jimmy Carter added. "But surely one such lesson learned by the world at great cost is that aggression unopposed becomes a contagious disease." [1]

Several days later, 104 member-states of the United Nations, gravely concerned over recent developments in Afghanistan and their implications for international peace and security, reaffirmed

> The right of all peoples to determine their own future free from outside interference . . . . Mindful of the obligations of Mem-

185

ber States to refrain in their international relations from the threat or use of force against the territorial integrity or political independence of any State. . . . [the UN Resolution] *Deeply deplores* the recent armed intervention in Afghanistan . . . *Affirms* that the sovereignty, territorial integrity, political independence and non-aligned status of Afghanistan must be fully respected: *Calls* for the immediate and unconditional withdrawal of all foreign troops from Afghanistan in order to enable its people to determine their own form of government and choose their economic, political and social systems free from outside intervention.[2]

Carter sent Deputy Secretary of State Warren Christopher, accompanied by National Security Adviser Zbigniew Brzezinski, to Pakistan early in February 1980 for two days of intensive talks with Zia's Foreign Affairs Adviser Agha Shahi to explore Pakistan's security needs. Brzezinski flew to the Khyber and almost killed himself and those accompanying him there when an automatic weapon he clumsily wielded went off with a dangerous, undirected blast that seemed to symbolize America's ineffectual South Asia policy. When Washington's offer of $400 million in aid over the following eighteen-month period, half of it military, was announced, Zia characterized it as "peanuts." Agha Shahi was more diplomatic, explaining in March at Islamabad's Local Bodies Convention: "It was felt on our side that the acceptance of the U.S. offer, unless substantially modified, would have detracted from rather than enhanced, our security."[3] Still smarting from bitter memories of the U.S. embargo on all arms to Pakistan as well as India in 1965, Pakistan found neither security nor comfort in Washington's reaffirmation of their 1959 bilateral mutual-security agreement. Pakistan had long since withdrawn from both CENTO and SEATO, so there was no formal U.S.-Pakistan treaty in force at the time, and most Pakistanis feared that Carter's South Asian policy, thanks in part to Miss Lillian's Peace Corps experience, tilted toward India.

U.S. policy on the eve of the Russian invasion did, indeed, "recognize as a fact of life that no matter what measuring stick one uses," as State Department South Asian expert Howard Schaffer put it, "In-

dia is the most important power in the region.'' The major principle
underlying Washington's policy at the time was *laissez faire,* ''to see
a South Asia that is free of great power involvement and competition,
a South Asia that is able to work out its own problems without fear of
external manipulation or exploitation.''[4] Although India's primacy of
power naturally gave it primary importance, Washington sought
''equally good relations with all the nations'' of the area. By the end
of December, however, the Russian invasion of Afghanistan had reduced India to a distant second place in the overall power configura-
tion, dramatically changing overnight the security situation in South
Asia as well as U.S. policy.

"The country most directly affected, of course, is Pakistan,'' Deputy Assistant Secretary of State for Near Eastern and South Asian Affairs Jane Coon explained to Congress in February 1980.

> In the immediate period ahead, both we and the Pakistanis in-
> tend to continue discussions with those governments to which
> we are looking to provide additional assistance. . . . Saudi
> Arabia is keenly aware of the importance of strengthening Pak-
> istan. . . . In the meantime, our military team has had detailed
> discussions in Pakistan in an effort to determine the scope of
> Pakistan's existing military deficiencies and to identify specific
> types of equipment which the United States might provide to
> strengthen Pakistan's defensive capabilities on the western
> frontier. . . . We are prepared to process certain cash military
> sales even in the absence of agreement on our assistance levels.
> . . . We are confident that a U.S. military sales relationship
> will help Pakistan improve its ability to defend itself against
> the increased threat from the northwest.[5]

While Pakistan thus became the principal focus of U.S. attention
and Pentagon hardware started flowing again toward Karachi and
Pindi, special Washington overtures were directed toward New Delhi
as well. Former U.S. Defense Secretary Clark Clifford was sent as
Carter's special envoy to brief Mrs. Gandhi in late January, urging her
to talk with at least one or both Zias to try to evolve a regional approach to South Asia's security needs. India was also now offered the
most advanced U.S. military supplies, and Clifford may have con-

veyed Carter's assurance of another shipment of atomic fuel, well before Bombay's plant used up its fast-diminishing precious stock. Indira was, moreover, assured that Pakistan's Zia had been plainly told that a Pakistani nuclear test in so unsettled an environment as South Asia would be even more dangerous and unwise than before and would drastically alter U.S.-Pakistan relations, putting at serious risk further cooperation.

The UN General Assembly met again in November 1980 to reconsider "The Situation in Afghanistan and Its Implications for International Peace and Security."[6] Agha Shahi moved another resolution, calling for "the immediate, unconditional and total withdrawal of all foreign troops," noting that "More than 10 months have passed since . . . 104 States Members of the United Nations gave their verdict in clear and emphatic terms on the violations of the independence of nonaligned Afghanistan." Not only had that "unequivocal call representing the will of the overwhelming majority of the peoples of the world" gone unheeded, but Pakistan's foreign minister said, "In recent months we have witnessed an alarming intensification of the conflict . . . and tens of thousands of refugees are forced to seek shelter in Pakistan every month." Not since the birth of Bangladesh had there been so alarming an exodus from any nation. Pakistan, with U.S. and UN aid, was feeding and offering shelter to more than a million Afghan refugees. Many wealthy Muslims also contributed individually, visiting Pakistani refugee camps outside Peshawar as acts of pilgrimage, generously donating alms to their religious brethren before returning home or going on to Mecca.

Since May 1980, the 35 members of the Islamic Conference had established a three-member standing committee, led by their secretary-general and including the foreign ministers of Iran and Pakistan, to explore ways of promoting "a peaceful and honourable political solution" to the Afghan problem. The Committee of Three tried to arrange a meeting with leaders of the majority Khalq and ruling Parcham factions of the Afghanistan People's Democratic party at Mont Pelerin, Switzerland, in June 1980. Karmal, however, refused to allow any Afghan representatives to meet with a group that persisted in refusing to grant diplomatic recognition to his government. The Islamic Conference had voted to suspend Afghanistan from membership and urged its members to withhold recognition of Karmal's regime at its January 1980 meeting in Islamabad. Karmal insisted on full recognition as a prerequisite to any talks.

"Pakistan's non-recognition of the present regime in Kabul stems from its opposition, on principle, to foreign military intervention," Agha Shahi told the General Assembly, insisting that "the Afghan resistance is an entirely indigenous phenomenon." Pakistan would "welcome" the "stationing of international, Islamic or non-aligned observers on the Afghan side of the border to monitor any trans-border movement." Islamabad was also prepared to provide "appropriate guarantees of non-interference to Afghanistan on a reciprocal basis." Agha Shahi had met with Secretary Edmund Muskie in Washington on July 23, 1980, to report on meetings he had held with *"Mujaheedin"* leaders and others seeking formulas for a political settlement. Zia had been in touch with Soviet leaders, who also seemed receptive to the idea of ending the stalemate civil war.

The official Afghan and Russian positions, as expressed in the General Assembly debate in November, remained unchanged from those broadcast immediately after the Soviet invasion. Kabul's Foreign Minister Muhammad Dost said that "What has happened in Afghanistan . . . is totally and exclusively an internal matter." The only foreign intervention came from U.S. "imperialists" and Chinese "chauvinists," who armed and supplied "30 major training camps and 50 military bases for Afghan counter-revolutionaries in Pakistan." Dost accused the CIA and Pakistani authorities and army command of being directly involved and taking an active part in training "counter-revolutionary Afghan bands and dispatching them." Afghanistan's government, Dost insisted, had "asked the Soviet Union to send a *limited contingent* of Soviet troops to . . . help the Afghan army and the people to rebuff the aggression" (italics added). Russia's "positive response," as Dost called it, was merely "in full conformity" with the Afghan-Soviet Treaty of Friendship.

That remarkable revelation must have given Mrs. Gandhi much to

ponder, but it did not swing India's UN vote behind the Pakistan resolution. India's delegate, Mr. Mishra, expressed his nation's "deep
concern and anxiety" at the "virtual return to the polemics and para-
noia of the cold war" caused by the "flashpoint" of Afghanistan,
adding that "a political solution is of the utmost urgency." The suggested basis for such a solution would be "the complete cessation of
all interference or intervention in the internal affairs of States, firm
opposition to the presence of foreign troops in any country, the withdrawal of existing foreign forces and the reaffirming of complete and
reliable guarantees against all forms of interference."

Brezhnev returned to New Delhi in December 1980, reasserting
that "The U.S.S.R. will fulfill to the end its duty to Afghanistan."
He also proposed a five-point plan for peace in the Persian Gulf and
Indian Ocean. That scheme, which Muskie would characterize as a
"fox-in-the-chicken-coop" approach, urged creating a nuclear-free
"Zone of Peace" in the Indian Ocean and Persian Gulf. A new five-
year trade agreement was concluded between Moscow and New Delhi,
and India was promised more Russian crude oil to make up for the
drop in its supplies from Iraq since that nation had launched its war
against Iran in September 1980. As secretary-general of the Islamic
Conference, Pakistan's President Zia attempted, unsuccessfully, to
mediate an end to the Iraq-Iran war, concluding his mission with a trip
to the UN, where he spoke before the General Assembly, and to
Washington, where he met with Jimmy Carter. "Our commitment to
consult very closely with Pakistan was expressed in an agreement
signed in 1959," President Carter informed President Zia, adding, "If
Pakistan should be in danger, that commitment stands today as it did
in 1959."[7]

The superpowers were thus poised, at the start of 1981, nuclear
warhead to warhead at the gates of South Asia and on the high seas of
the Indian Ocean. Three-quarters of a century after the Anglo-Russian
Great Game had almost run its course, a new and potentially far more
disastrous U.S.-U.S.S.R. Game had begun in the same, no longer
remote region. The stakes were much higher. So were the risks. Will
U.S. and Soviet policy toward South Asia have the flexibility as well

as firmness, the wisdom as well as strength, to navigate those troubled waters into the twenty-first century without the sort of collision that might ignite World War III? Nineteenth-century Forward School solutions were no more rational in a nuclear age of total war than an Imperial 1907-model "spheres of influence" agreement will be in an era of jealously independent nation-states. Neither a new arms race nor Washington-Moscow detente will, indeed, solve the complex puzzle of many problems posed by South Asia's current realities.

An international Geneva-type conference on Afghanistan is most urgently required to relieve some of the pressure from South Asia as a whole, in addition to diminishing the costs in human and material terms of the Afghan civil war. The Committee of Three of the Islamic Conference would be an ideal sponsor for such an Afghan summit, and U.S. policy should be designed to do whatever it can to facilitate and support such a meeting. Undiminished economic, diplomatic, and moral pressure of every possible variety should have been maintained against the Soviet Union until its troops withdrew from Afghanistan. Quickly succumbing, however, to vocal pressures from its own Midwestern wheat lobby, the Reagan administration resumed business as usual in vital farm exports to the Soviet Union. U.S. oil drillers also urged resumption of high-technology rig sales, especially since the Russians announced "a $118 million deal with the French for offshore oil drilling rigs to be used in the Caspian Sea."[8] While thus resuming the full flow of trade to the Soviets, Washington's new administration also opted to raise the U.S. offer of martial support of Pakistan from $200 million to over $2 billion.

"If the Reagan Administration can help us consolidate our independence with economic and military aid," Foreign Minister Agha Shahi remarked in response to that new offer, "it would help stabilize the entire region."[9] Pakistan's beefed-up martial shopping list included the Pentagon's latest export fighter-bomber F-16/79, helicopter gunships armed with tank-destroying capability, anti-tank guided missiles, night vision equipment, the most modern tanks and self-propelled guns, and an integrated air defense system for the Durand Line.[10] Fears that Pakistan was about to become the "Finland of the

East"[11] dissolved in the sunshine of the resurrected U.S.-Pakistan military alliance, redolent of the good old CENTO-SEATO days of the 1950s. India's anxious response sounded equally familiar. "It is regretted that India's obsession with a non-existent military threat from Pakistan verges on the surreal," Agha Shahi replied. "The Government of India has ascribed imaginary motives and purposes to the discussions between Pakistan and the United States. . . . A military procurement relationship would in no way affect the course of Pakistan's foreign policy as it has evolved during the last few years. India, which has itself acquired a vast arsenal on concessional terms from a super power, should not adopt double standards."[12]

The wheel of Washington's South Asian policy thus spun itself, with a hefty assist from Moscow, full circle in little more than one quarter-century. Once again Pakistan was to become our martial surrogate, while India's armed forces and military systems would be driven to deeper dependence upon and into closer confirmity with the Red Army. Pakistan's newly supplied army would not only be in better shape to ward off any potential threat to its border from Afghanistan, but could serve in part as Saudi Arabia's martial shield as well. In 1980, Zia reportedly committed two full armored divisions to Mecca's monarchy, ready for rapid deployment to Riyadh (two and a half hours flying time from Karachi) should they be called, in return for $800 million in hard currency.

For South Asia a new arms race had only just begun. How many of those arms would be passed along to Pathan refugee *Mujaheedin?* And how long would it take those more effective freedom fighters, whose mission was to harass Russian troops in occupation of their homeland, to lure the additional 30,000 Soviet soldiers based north of the Oxus onto Afghan soil? Or to invite Russian air retaliation across the Durand Line, much the way our own bombers had been "obliged" to hit Cambodia during the Vietnam War? Then what? U.S. or Pakistani raids on Kabul perhaps? That would be one way of reducing Russian forces, but would it diminish Moscow's influence in Afghanistan? Would it augment our own? And who but the Afghan peoples themselves, and the Pakistanis, and ultimately all of South Asia would be the losers? The ripples of war move out more rapidly today than they did centuries ago.

We cannot hope to succeed in shaming Russia's black pot white, if our own Pentagon kettle stays as black itself. For us to demand or expect an end to foreign aggression while sending every caliber of deadly weapon into Pakistan to arm Afghan guerrillas, who use Pakistani soil as a haven from which to raid their own countryside and kill their own people as well as Russian troops, is not only duplicitous but ultimately self-defeating. We fool no one but our own people. Should the Pakistan Army be used to invade Afghanistan in retaliation for Russian raids on its soil, it is hard to imagine any more favorable scenario that that achieved by the British Indian Army in either the first or second Afghan War. By reversing roles from the old Vietnam War days with the Russians we can, admittedly, bleed them and make Moscow pay a heavier price for its invasion and stubborn determination to stay in Kabul than the Comintern expected. But who will ultimately bear the cost?

What should our policy toward South Asia be? How can we realistically implement what should be our primary goal of helping its people have a healthier existence, free of disease and dirt, the dark walls of illiteracy, and the hollow hurt of hunger? The worst possible policy for us to pursue today and tomorrow and throughout the next century in South Asia is to ally ourselves with any single state of that region—for then, inevitably, we are ranged against one or more of the others. Nor should we align ourselves with a single party, military clique, or religious group. We must break out of the Nabob Game British mentality of the eighteenth century and escape the Anglo-Russian Great Game trap of the nineteenth century as well if ever we are going to encourage stability and at least the prospect of prosperity to the peoples of South Asia. We might begin by committing one-half, or even one-tenth, of the money we are so willing to spend on arms to building fertilizer plants and irrigation canals, hospitals, sanitation systems, schools and libraries throughout South Asia.

What, after all, has been gained from all the billions of dollars in guns and arms we have poured into South Asia since 1954, when that policy first became the keystone of Washington-Karachi relations? Is Pakistan stronger today? Do the people of Pakistan, or its martial leaders, feel closer, friendlier, more grateful to America for all the tanks, planes, and deadly weapons we have shipped to them? And are the Indians closer to us? The Bangladeshis? What makes us think that the Afghans will be different? Will the *Mujaheedin* government that guns down Karmal be the sort of ally we will want to welcome at home? And will Kabul's streets then be safer for Americans? Or Afghans? Our commitment must be to freedom and the first article of our political faith, self-determination.

From all we have seen and heard of the Afghan Civil War, we assume that Karmal and his comrades in power will fall overnight when Russian troops are withdrawn from his palace grounds. But if, indeed, he proves stronger, more popular, than we currently imagine him to be, we should have no objection to recognizing his government and take no action to subvert it. Belated recognition of China and Bangladesh have proved the wisdom of pursuing a pragmatic recognition policy rather than one of wishful diplomacy. If ever we hope to develop a more rational South Asian policy, one that will survive— with the rest of the world—into the twenty-first century, we must stop deceiving ourselves. We must learn the limits of our power in this region and remember that Kabul today is not just Russian-dominated, communist-governed, Soviet-armed, but remains the most remote, in many ways still medieval, modern capital on earth—uniquely Afghan. Just as we hope the Russians must learn that the benefits they may have derived from their invasion of Afghanistan are far outweighed by the resultant loss in international support. To help convince them of the latter, we must do everything in our power to wean New Delhi from Moscow's side and bring India back to a truly non-aligned posture in the world, urging Indira to speak out against the shameless aggression of Soviet force. By halting shipments of U.S. arms, to South Asia, we could gain enough moral leverage in New Delhi to convince Mrs. Gandhi of the truth of our commitment to peace and the disinterested nature of our policy toward the subcontinent. As Nehru's daughter and as self-proclaimed disciple of Mahatma Gandhi, for whom Truth was God, she might then rely upon the ancient national motto of modern India, "Truth Alone Conquers" (*Satyameva Jayate*), openly telling Brezhnev that the Khyber is too close for New Delhi's comfort to be a staging ground for Russian tanks and planes. To help convince India, Pakistan, and Bangladesh of the reality as well as sincerity of our national commitment to the peaceful and free development of their region, we should allocate, as quickly as Congress will allow, a substantial fund for the peaceful development and economic growth of South Asia as a whole.

Though national sovereignty and its delusions have by now made it impossible for South Asia to return to the British Cabinet Mission Plan of 1946, Western Europe's economic Common Market integration has certainly set the precedent of much older, more deeply entrenched rival nation-states working together in what have proved to be their own best national interests. Could not India, Pakistan, and Bangladesh launch the same sort of regional program of economic cooperation? Their natural endowments of resources and economies are, in fact, even better suited to precisely that sort of reintegration—for partition, after all, had artificially, politically, undone what nature and economic forces designed to be interdependent. Punjabi surplus wheat and Bangladeshi surplus jute were both most profitably exchanged for desperately needed Indian manufactured goods. The real standard of living of all three nations would benefit greatly from the removal of all international barriers to trade and artificial currency controls. Additional secondary benefits, sociopolitical and ultimately strategic, would be derived from the feelings of mutual dependence, trust, and support that would grow with increased trade and shared projects for the control of such natural resources as rivers and rains and the development of energy sources such as hydroelectric, coal, oil, perhaps even atomic.

Most importantly, this sense of mutual support, trust, and need could pave the way toward resolution of thornier political problems that continue to undermine each of these nations. Residual communalism, internal and external, is the most malignant of these problems. Hindu-Muslim riots in India have gained momentum in the last decade, taking more lives than they did during the 1930s. The 10 million refugees who fled from East Pakistan prior to the birth of Bangladesh were mostly Hindu. Kashmir has been the cause of two South Asian wars, and should Pakistan touch off a thermonuclear explosion in its environs at any time in the next decade or two, it might well become the center of a third.

What might be called the Economic Commonwealth of South Asia, jointly chaired by India and Pakistan, with Bangladesh, Sri Lanka, Nepal, Bhutan, and possibly Afghanistan, as member states, would receive the total sum of U.S. aid annually allotted to this region for autonomously agreed upon priority projects anywhere in the subcontinent. South Asians alone would determine their economic destiny, though they could certainly call upon experts from any international source, whether it be the World Bank, International Monetary Fund, Ford Foundation, a Polish labor Union, Russian commune, or Chinese university. Our commitment of financial aid must truly have no strings attached to prove most effective. We must, moreover, understand that such a policy is neither wasteful nor altruistic, but as selfish and nationally profitable to us as it would be to South Asia as a whole.

Once again, motivation is the key. If, in fact, our primary motives are freedom and self-determination for all, what better way could we find to help attain all of these goals simultaneously? All of our AID to date has been designed to "save" India or Pakistan or Bangladesh from communism or "subversion" of whatever sort. Much the way nineteenth-century Christian missionaries felt "called" to "save heathen souls," our secular, Western, free-enterprise missionaries have felt compelled to turn each of these states into miniature economic models of America.

We must stop deceiving ourselves about the impact of our economic assistance, whatever its magnitude may be. The Asian country that received the most U.S. AID since World War II, after all, was South Vietnam. We have to learn to accept the limits of what can be accomplished with money, even as we learn the limited utility of pushing arms. Our billions will not remove religious prejudice from South Asian soil. They will not teach all Muslims to love their Hindu neighbors, nor the reverse. Money will not heal festering historic wounds, such as those that remain in the national mind of Pakistan over Kashmir, nor will it silence cries for a "Greater Baluchistan," or a "Dravidistan," or "Assam for the Assamese." Education that leads to better jobs, more land—or more water and better fertilizers for the land—healthier water, cleaner cities, larger, better living quarters all ease the frustration that sparks most irrational violence, whether committed by individuals or by groups within states.

Practical steps can be taken to defuse the more extreme aspects of such passion, and wherever possible those should be supported and facilitated by Washington as an impartial mediator or arbitrator. Kashmir remains the single most bitter historic memory in the national consciousness of Pakistan and stands in the way of full Indo-Pakistani reconciliation and future cooperation based on mutual trust and friendship. Mrs. Gandhi may consider the matter a "dead issue," one that India's government refuses to reopen, but until a plebiscite is held under international auspices in that state with representatives of Pakistan as well as India observing its arrangements or counting the votes, Islamabad will persist in believing—rightly or wrongly—that it was "cheated" out of an integral limb of its body politic at birth.

If, in fact, India's government is correct in arguing that Kashmiris have in several state elections reaffirmed their satisfaction with remaining as they are, an integral part of the Indian Union, then an impartial plebiscite poses no threat to India and should be welcomed as the simplest way of defusing residual Pakistani suspicions. Should a plebiscite favor Kashmiri integration into Pakistan, however, India might find that the advantages to be gained by losing Kashmir would outweigh, or at least balance, those derived from holding it against popular will. Diminished heavy military and administrative costs, for example, might add to New Delhi's overall resources.

The gains in international good will and Pakistani cooperation, moreover, would be enormously enriching and rewarding in many ways and could open the door to a true Indo-Pakistani partnership in defense of the subcontinent, especially with respect to China. Internally, the "surrender" of Kashmir could serve as a major stimulus toward the more rapid secularization and true modernization of India, for it has long been argued by Delhi's "pundits" in power that were India's government ever forced to give up Kashmir, orthodox Hindu extremists would slaughter every Indian Muslim they found. Succumbing to such vainglorious threats, reflecting base and cowardly feelings, only weakens a nation and the ultimate authority of its government. The larger crimes we call wars are far more difficult to control, since they are usually stimulated by power lust of one sort or another. Yet nations preoccupied with solving common problems associated with joint ventures of development should be better able to prevent, or at least minimize, the impact of those as well.

None of this will happen overnight. Our policy toward this vital region of the globe and our commitment to its people and their progress must be long-range. "If we would love our fellow men," John Morley was fond of saying, "we must not expect too much of them." As individuals, we can all champion and strongly advocate human freedoms as the finest ultimate goals of humankind. None of us could tolerate life without them. We must realize, however, that most people do, especially in South Asia. Though Pakistan and Bangladesh both call themselves "Republics" and their leaders are titled "President," both states are, in fact, martial dictatorships. Most Islamic nations the world over have much the same type of rule, in keeping with the laws and tenets of Islam. India, of course, calls itself a "secular, democratic republic," but it too is a traditionally religious, predominantly authoritarian state, which has virtually been ruled by the same single family since independence.

The bureaucratic elites of all three of these major nations of South Asia were, by historic accident, trained to speak English, imbibing a patina of Western traditions, values, aspirations, and habits of thought that have long made us assume—incorrectly—that these are the common coin of their nations and the mass of their peasant populations. In fact, most of the close to one billion people who live in that quarter of the globe inhabit world systems as remote from our own as the Indian Ocean. We must learn to accept cultural distance, respecting their fears and feelings, unobtrusively ready to help them if called upon, wisely refraining from throwing unwanted weight around in their fragile homes. The era of our post-World War II "missionary" attack on "underdeveloped" nations, which gave birth to AID, the Peace Corps, ICA, and a hundred other zealous agencies, organizations, foundations, and corporations may well have run its historic course.

South Asians have learned that there is, in fact, no such thing as foreign aid by individual countries without strings attached. The most benevolent foundation vitally affects and changes the course of any society it "helps" as soon as it injects outside resources into any facet of the "backward" system, whether through individuals, local governments, or national agencies. "All our troubles come from your AID," a professor at a major Pakistani university recently argued. "Rostow and his Harvard School and your World Bank have turned Pakistan into an economic cripple!"[13] Many Indian scholars and government officials feel much the same way, as do some of the brightest leaders of Bangladesh. No good deed goes unpunished, which is perhaps why virtue is said to be its own reward.

Perhaps when we have proved the genuinely disinterested nature of our impartial commitment to this region and its peoples, we may be sufficiently trusted and respected by its governments to host a continuing South Asian peace forum at the UN in New York or in Geneva, which could tackle problems such as Kashmir, Pashtunistan, North-East Frontier agitation, and nuclear-arms control. In all probability, both India and Pakistan will have their own nuclear weapons and short-range delivery systems within a decade. By then, if current tensions remain unresolved, undissipated, it may be too late for anyone to do more than monitor the intensity of the blasts and track the path of the deadly clouds they leave behind to poison the globe.

It has always seemed odd and wasteful to convene peace conferences only after wars are over, instead of holding them before the fighting starts. India and Pakistan could, once again, jointly chair a peace forum, and the U.S. and U.S.S.R. might attend meetings as non-aligned observers. Granted, the forum might prove no more effective at defusing potential explosions or resolving crises than the UN has been, or the Islamic Conference. But if shared information, good will, selfish interest, fear, hope, and rationality have anything to do with averting or mitigating international disasters, surely the time, effort, and money invested in that sort of forum would be worth it. Such diplomatic risks seem far less hazardous than bellicose confrontation or apathetic inertia.

Notes

CHAPTER 1: INTRODUCTION

1. Louis Dupree, *Afghanistan* (Princeton: Princeton University Press, 1973); Vartan Gregorian, *The Emergence of Modern Afghanistan: Politics of Reform and Modernization, 1880–1946* (Stanford: Stanford University Press, 1969); Richard S. Newell, *The Politics of Afghanistan* (Ithaca: Cornell University Press, 1972); Ludwig W. Adamec, *Afghanistan, 1900–1923* (Berkeley and Los Angeles: University of California Press, 1967).
2. Olaf Caroe, *The Pathans, 550 B.C.–A.D. 1957* (Karachi: Oxford University Press, 1976).
3. Astrid von Borcke, "Die Intervention in Afghanistan—das Ende der sowjetischen Koexistenzpolitic?," *Berichte des Bundesinstituts fur ostwissenshaftliche und internationale Studien* (June 1980).
4. Charles A. Rudd, "Soviet Interest and Policy in the Middle East," *Middle East Focus* 3, No. 3 (Sept. 1980), p. 15.
5. Francis Fukuyama, "The Future of the Soviet Role in Afghanistan: A Trip Report," *A Rand Note* (Santa Monica: The Rand Corporation, 1980), p. 4.
6. Thomas J. Abercrombie, "Islam's Heartland Up in Arms," *National Geographic* 158, No. 3 (Sept. 1980), p. 338.
7. Stanley Wolpert, *A New History of India* (New York: Oxford University Press, 1977).

CHAPTER 2: INDIA'S CULTURAL ROOTS

1. George Woodcock, *The Greeks in India* (London: Faber and Faber, 1966), p. 34.

CHAPTER 3: ISLAM'S UNIVERSAL BROTHERHOOD

1. Quoted in S. M. Ikram, *Muslim Civilization in India*, ed. Ainslie T. Embree (New York: Columbia University Press, 1964), p. 28.

2. *Memoirs of Zehir-ed-Din Muhammed Babur*, trans. J. Leyden and W. Erskine, rev. L. King (London: Oxford University Press, 1921).

CHAPTER 4: SOUTH ASIA'S CONQUEST AND TRANSFORMATION BY THE WEST

1. Quoted in Philip Mason (Woodruff), *The Men Who Ruled India* (New York: St. Martin's Press, 1954), I, p. 34.
2. Quoted in William Wilson Hunter, *A History of British India*, new impression (London: Longmans, Green, 1912), II, pp. 272–73.
3. Jadunath Sarkar, *Fall of the Mughal Empire*, 2nd ed. (Calcutta: M. C. Sarkar, 1949), I, p. 3.
4. *The History of the Trial of Warren Hastings, Esq. . . . on an Impeachment by the Commons of Great-Britain for High Crimes and Misdemeanours. Containing the Whole of the Proceedings and Debates in Both Houses of Parliament from February 7, 1786 until his Acquittal, April 23, 1795* (London: J. Debrett and Vernor and Hood, 1796).

CHAPTER 5: THE GREAT GAME

1. See Edward Ingram, *The Beginning of the Great Game in Asia, 1828–1834,* (Oxford: Clarendon Press, 1979).
2. W. Baring Pemberton, *Lord Palmerston* (London: Batchworth Press, 1954), p. 95.
3. Quoted in Vartan Gregorian, *The Emergence of Modern Afghanistan: Politics of Reform and Modernization, 1880–1946* (Stanford: Stanford University Press, 1969), p. 99.
4. Quoted in Asghar H. Bilgrami, *Afghanistan and British India, 1793–1907* (New Delhi: Sterling Publishers, 1972), Appendix XI, pp. 298–306.
5. Patrick Macrory, *Signal Catastrophe: Story of the Disastrous Retreat from Kabul, 1842* (London: Hodder and Stoughton, 1966).
6. Bilgrami, *Afghanistan and British India,* Appendix XVI(b), p. 315.
7. Christopher Hibbert, *The Great Mutiny: India 1857* (London: Allen Lane, 1978).
8. Lawrence's *Minute* of November 25, 1868, quoted in Bisheshwar Prasad, *The Foundations of India's Foreign Policy, 1860–1882* (Delhi: Ranjit Printers & Publishers, 1978), p. 41.
9. Rawlinson's "Memorandum," in C. H. Philips, ed., *The Evolution of India and Pakistan, 1858 to 1947: Select Documents* (London: Oxford University Press, 1962), pp. 443–44.
10. Prince Gorchakov's "Memorandum," in W. K. Fraser-Tytler, *Afghanistan: A Study of Political Developments in Central Asia* (London: Oxford University Press, 1950), Appendix II, pp. 305–9.
11. Lytton to Salisbury, May 29, 1876, in S. Gopal, *British Policy in India, 1858–1905* (Boston: Cambridge University Press, 1965), p. 78. The following Lytton quotes are from pp. 79–91.

12. Quoted in Gregorian, *The Emergence of Modern Afghanistan,* p. 109.
13. Olaf Caroe, *The Pathans, 550 B.C.–A.D. 1957* (Karachi: Oxford University Press, 1976), p. 374.
14. Louis Dupree, *Afghanistan* (Princeton: Princeton University Press, 1973), p. 428.
15. P. E. Roberts, *History of British India under the Company and the Crown,* 3rd ed. (London: Oxford University Press, 1952), pp. 492–93.
16. Quoted from Abdur Rahman's *Autobiography,* II, p. 158, in C. C. Davies, "The North-West Frontier, 1843–1918," in *The Cambridge History of India,* Vol. VI, *The Indian Empire,* ed. H. H. Dodwell (reprint Delhi: S. Chand, 1964), p. 462.
17. Sir George Robertson, *Chitral* (London: Methuen, 1898).
18. Gregorian, *The Emergence of Modern Afghanistan,* p. 154.
19. Minto to Morley, January 16, 1907, in Lady Mary Minto, *India, Minto and Morley, 1905–1910* (London: Macmillan and Co., 1934), p. 81.
20. Ludwig W. Adamec, *Afghanistan's Foreign Affairs to the Mid-twentieth Century* (Tucson: University of Arizona Press, 1974), p. 13.
21. Nikki Keddie, *Sayyid Jamāl ad-Dīn 'al-Afghānī': A Political Biography* (Berkeley and Los Angeles: University of California Press, 1972).
22. Adamec, *Afghanistan's Foreign Affairs,* p. 33.
23. *Ibid.,* p. 34.
24. Rhea Talley Stewart, *Fire in Afghanistan, 1914–1929* (Garden City, N.Y.: Doubleday & Co., 1973), p. 32.
25. *Ibid.,* p. 37.
26. Ludwig W. Adamec, "Translation of Proclamation by Amir Amanulla Khan," in *Afghanistan, 1900–1923* (Berkeley and Los Angeles: University of California Press, 1967), Appendix II, 10, p. 212.
27. General Staff, Army Headquarters, India, *Operations in Waziristan, 1919–1920* (Calcutta: Superintendent Government Printing, 1921), p. 79.

CHAPTER 6: THE IMPACT OF NATIONALISMS

1. V. D. Savarkar, *The Indian War of Independence (National Rising of 1857)* ("Underground Fourth Edition," London, 1909).
2. Victoria's *Proclamation,* Nov. 1, 1858, in C. H. Philips, ed., *The Evolution of India and Pakistan, 1858 to 1947: Select Documents* (London: Oxford University Press, 1962), p. 11.
3. Quoted in J. H. Broomfield, *Elite Conflict in a Plural Society: Twentieth-Century Bengal* (Berkeley and Los Angeles: University of California Press, 1968), p. 66.
4. Banerjea's Presidential Address, Poona, 1895, in *The Indian National Congress,* 2nd ed. (Madras: G. A. Natesan, 1917), p. 221 (hereafter *INC*).
5. *Ibid.,* pp. 795–96.
6. Stanley A. Wolpert, *Tilak and Gokhale* (Berkeley and Los Angeles: University of California Press, Library Reprint Series, 1979), p. 196.
7. *Ibid.,* p. 197.

8. Stanley Wolpert, *Morley and India, 1906–1910* (Berkeley and Los Angeles: University of California Press, 1969).

9. Hafeez Malik, *Sir Sayyid Ahmad Khan and Muslim Modernization in India and Pakistan* (New York: Columbia University Press, 1980).

10. *INC*, p. 25.

11. G. Allana, ed., *Pakistan Movement: Historic Documents* (Lahore: Islamic Book Service, 1977), pp. 6–9.

12. Lady Mary Minto, *India, Minto and Morley, 1905–1910* (London: Macmillan and Co., 1934), p. 47.

13. Syed Sharifuddin Pirzada, ed., *Foundations of Pakistan: All-Indian Muslim League Documents: 1906–1947* (Karachi: National Publishing House, 1969), I, p. 4.

14. DeWitt C. Ellinwood and S. D. Pradhan, eds., *India and World War I* (New Delhi: Manohar, 1978).

15. Philips, ed., *The Evolution of India and Pakistan,* p. 264.

16. Stanley Wolpert, *An Error of Judgment* (Boston: Little, Brown, 1972).

17. Pirzada, ed., *Foundations of Pakistan,* I, pp. 542–43.

18. Jawaharlal Nehru, *Toward Freedom* (New York: John Day, 1941), p. 69.

19. Presidential Address, All-India Muslim League, 1919, in *Evolution of Muslim Political Thought in India,* ed. A. M. Zaidi (New Delhi: Michiko & Panjathan, 1975), II, p. 196.

CHAPTER 7: FREEDOM AND FRAGMENTATION

1. Syed Sharifuddin Pirzada, ed., *Foundations of Pakistan, All-India Muslim League Documents: 1906–1947,* (Karachi: National Publishing House, 1969), I, p. 577.

2. E. M. Forster, *A Passage to India* (New York: Harvest, 1952), p. 50.

3. C. H. Philips, ed., *The Evolution of India and Pakistan, 1858 to 1947: Select Documents* (London: Oxford University Press, 1962), p. 496.

4. Jawaharlal Nehru, *Toward Freedom* (New York: John Day, 1941), pp. 113–14.

5. Pirzada, ed., *Foundations of Pakistan,* (Karachi: National Publishing House, 1970), II, pp. 156–59.

6. G. Allana, ed., *Pakistan Movement: Historic Documents* (Lahore: Islamic Book Service, 1977), p. 116.

7. Pirzada, ed., *Foundations of Pakistan,* II, p. 267.

8. Philips, ed., *Evolution of India and Pakistan,* p. 379.

9. *Ibid.,* p. 380.

10. A. B. Rajput, *The Cabinet Mission, 1946* (Lahore: Lion Press, 1946), p. 141.

11. Pirzada, ed., *Foundations of Pakistan,* II, p. 507.

12. Dorothy Norman, ed., *Nehru: The First Sixty Years* (London: The Bodley Head, 1965), II, pp. 364–65.

13. *Ibid.*, p. 336.

14. *Quaid-i-Azam Mohammad Ali Jinnah, Speeches, As Governor-General of Pakistan, 1947–1948* (Karachi: n.p., 1960), pp. 14–15.

CHAPTER 8: SOUTH ASIA AT WAR WITH ITSELF

1. This story was recounted to the author by Lord Mountbatten in London, June 1979.

2. Alan Campbell-Johnson, *Mission with Mountbatten* (New York: E. P. Dutton, 1953), p. 226.

3. Russell Brines, *The Indo-Pakistani Conflict* (London: Pall Mall Press, 1968), pp. 298–303.

4. Mujtaba Razvi, *The Frontiers of Pakistan* (Karachi: National Publishing House, 1971), pp. 145ff.

5. J. Russell Andrus and Azizali F. Mohammed, *Trade, Finance and Development in Pakistan* (Karachi: Oxford University Press, 1966), pp. 26ff.

6. Mohammad Ayub Khan, *Friends Not Masters* (London: Oxford University Press, 1967), p. 57.

7. Gustav F. Papanek, *Pakistan's Development: Social Goals and Private Incentives* (Cambridge, Mass.: Harvard University Press, 1967).

8. Ayub Khan, *Friends Not Masters,* p. 110.

9. *Pakistan Observer* (Karachi), Oct. 19, 1961, p. 1.

10. Ayub Khan, *Friends Not Masters,* p. 217.

11. *Dawn* (Karachi), Apr. 18, 1962, p. 1.

12. *Pakistan Affairs* 17, No. 3 (March 1, 1964), p. 4.

13. *Pakistan News Digest* 14, No. 13 (July 1, 1966), p. 1.

14. Z. A. Bhutto, *The Myth of Independence* (London: Oxford University Press, 1969), pp. 182–83.

15. *Pakistan News Digest* 14, No. 14 (July 15, 1966), p. CIII.

16. *Ibid.* 17, No. 7 (Apr. 1, 1969), p. 3.

17. *Ibid.* 18, No. 7 (Apr. 1, 1970), p. 11.

18. *Ibid.* 19, No. 7 (Apr. 1, 1971), p. 8.

19. U.S. Senate, *Congressional Record,* May 18, 1971, pp. S7128–29.

20. *New York Times,* Dec. 15, 1971, p. 1.

21. *Pakistan Affairs* 24, No. 38 (Dec. 28, 1971), p. 1.

CHAPTER 9: WASHINGTON'S SOUTH ASIAN POLICY

1. See his *Ambassador's Report* (New York: Harper & Brothers, 1954).

2. Nehru's speech of June 22, 1955, Moscow, in R. K. Jain, ed., *Soviet South Asian Relations, 1947–1978* (New Delhi: Radiant, 1978), I, p. 223.

3. *Jawaharlal Nehru's Speeches* (New Delhi: Government of India, 1964), IV, pp. 276–77.

4. "Policy for Security and Peace," Department of State Bulletin (March 29, 1954), reprinted in *American Foreign Policy,* ed. Harold Karan Jacobson (New York: Random House, 1960), p. 372.

5. *Dawn* (Karachi), Nov. 23, 1962, quoted in Syed A. Husain, "Politics

of Alliance and Aid: A Case Study of Pakistan, 1954–1966," M. Masood, ed., *Pakistan Horizon* 32, Nos. 1, 2 (1979), p. 12.

6. Ayub Khan, *Friends Not Masters* (London: Oxford University Press, 1967), p. 101.

7. *Ibid.*, p. 171.

8. J. K. Galbraith, *Ambassador's Journal* (Boston: Houghton Mifflin, 1969), p. 36.

9. Ayub Khan, *Friends Not Masters,* p. 135.

10. Galbraith, *Ambassador's Journal,* p. 411.

11. Dean Rusk, "Policy, Persistence, and Patience," Department of State Publication 7809, General Foreign Policy Series 199 (Washington, D.C.: Government Printing Office, 1965), p. 3.

12. Appendix IX in Sangat Singh, *Pakistan's Foreign Policy* (London: Asia Publishing House, 1970), pp. 225ff.

13. Jain, ed., *Soviet South Asian Relations,* II, p. 50.

14. President Giri's statement on this matter in his opening address to Parliament reflects Indira's position precisely. Nagendra Singh, *President Speaks* (Delhi: S. Chand, 1970), p. 95.

15. *United States Foreign Policy, 1971,* Department of State Publication 8634 (Washington, D.C.: Superintendent of Documents, 1972), pp. 448ff.

16. "Why We Must Stop Sending Arms to Pakistan," U.S. Senate, *Congressional Record,* May 18, 1971, pp. S7128–29.

17. Jain, ed., *Soviet South Asian Relations,* I, p. 123.

18. Kennedy delivered this speech before the National Press Club in Washington, D.C.

19. *India: The Speeches and Reminiscences of Indira Gandhi* (London: Hodder and Soughton, 1975), pp. 171–74.

CHAPTER 10: EMERGENCE OF MODERN AFGHANISTAN
AND ITS RELATIONS WITH RUSSIA

1. Rhea Talley Stewart, *Fire in Afghanistan, 1914–1929* (Garden City, N.Y.: Doubleday & Co., 1973), p. 76.

2. Ludwig W. Adamec, *Afghanistan, 1900–1923* (Berkeley and Los Angeles: University of California Press, 1967), p. 202.

3. W. K. Fraser-Tytler, *Afghanistan: A Study of Political Developments in Central Asia* (London: Oxford University Press, 1950), pp. 254–55.

4. Vartan Gregorian, *The Emergence of Modern Afghanistan: Politics of Reform and Modernization, 1880–1946* (Stanford: Stanford University Press, 1969), pp. 462–63.

5. Louis Dupree, *Afghanistan* (Princeton: Princeton University Press, 1973), pp. 592–93.

6. *Ibid.,* p. 608.

7. Richard S. Newell, *The Politics of Afghanistan* (Ithaca: Cornell University Press, 1972), Table 4, p. 144.

8. Oct. 30, 1978, reprinted in translation in Afghanistan Council *Newsletter* 7, No. 1 (Jan. 1979), Asia Society, New York.

CHAPTER 11: SOUTH ASIA TODAY

1. See Anwar H. Syed, "The Pakistan People's Party," in *Pakistan: The Long View,* eds. Lawrence Ziring, Ralph Braibanti, and W. Howard Wriggins (Durham: Duke University Press, 1977), pp. 73–76.

2. R. K. Jain, ed., *Soviet South Asian Relations* (New Delhi: Radiant, 1978), I, pp. 410–11.

3. *Dawn* (Karachi), Sept. 16, 1978, reprinted in Afghanistan Council *Newsletter* 7, No. 1 (Jan. 1979), Asia Society, New York, p. 26.

4. Lawrence Ziring, "South Asian Tangles and Triangles," in Lawrence Ziring, ed., *The Subcontinent in World Politics* (New York: Praeger, 1978), pp. 7ff.

5. M. Rashiduzzaman, "Bangladesh in 1977: Dilemmas of the Military Rulers," *Asian Survey* 18, No. 2 (Feb. 1978), 130ff.

6. V. S. Naipaul, *India: A Wounded Civilization* (New York: Alfred A. Knopf, 1977).

7. Norman D. Palmer, "The Carter Administration and South Asia," in Ziring, *Subcontinent in World Politics,* p. 196.

8. "Jung," *Washington Post,* Feb. 2, 1979, reprinted in Afghan Council *Newsletter,* p. 15.

9. Charles A. Rudd, "Soviet Interest and Policy in the Middle East," *Middle East Focus* 3, No. 3 (Sept. 1980), p. 15.

10. *Bangladesh* 3, Nos. 21, 22 (Dacca, June 1, 1980), p. 4.

CHAPTER 12: TOWARD A MORE RATIONAL SOUTH ASIAN POLICY

1. Department of State *Bulletin* 80, No. 2034 (Jan. 1980), p. A.

2. Security Council Resolution, Jan. 7, 1980, in *ibid.,* p. D.

3. *Pakistan Affairs,* 33, No. 6 (March 16, 1980).

4. Howard B. Schaffer, country director for South Asia, address on Foreign Policy, Dec. 1, 1979, in Department of State *Bulletin* 80, No. 2037 (Apr. 1980), pp. 61–62.

5. Ms. Coon's statement of Feb. 11, 1980, reprinted in *ibid.*

6. All quotes from this debate are from the UN's verbatim transcript of that meeting, Nov. 17–19, 1980, Agenda Item 116, A/35/PV.65.

7. Department of State *Bulletin* 80, No. 2045 (Dec. 1980), p. 72.

8. Hafeez Malik, "The Failure of Three-Track Negotiations on Afghanistan," *Journal of South Asia and Middle Eastern Studies* 4, No. 3 (Spring 1981), p. 3.

9. *Los Angeles Times,* Mar. 2, 1981, Part I, p. 1.

10. Francis Fukuyama, "The Security of Pakistan: A Trip Report," *A Rand Note,* (Santa Monica: The Rand Corporation, 1980), p. 28.

11. Malik, "Failure of Three-Track Negotiations," p. 4.

12. *Pakistan Affairs* 34, No. 9 (May 1, 1981), p. 1.

13. In seminar discussion with the author in Islamabad, late Feb. 1980.

Select Bibliography

Adamec, Ludwig W. *Afghanistan, 1900–1923: A Diplomatic History.* Berkeley and Los Angeles: University of California Press, 1967.
———. *Afghanistan's Foreign Affairs to the Mid-twentieth Century.* Tucson: University of Arizona Press, 1974.
Afghanistan Council. *Newsletter.* Vol. 7. New York: Asia Society, 1979.
Ahmad, Ziauddin, ed. *Liaquat Ali Khan: Leader and Statesman.* Karachi: The Oriental Academy, 1970.
Akhtar, Jamna Das. *Political Conspiracies in Pakistan.* Delhi: Punjabi Pustak Bhandar, 1969.
Ali, Chaudhri Muhammad. *The Emergence of Pakistan.* New York: Columbia University Press, 1967.

Bangladesh: The Birth of a Nation. Comp. by Marta Nicholas and Philip Oldenburg. Madras: M. Seshachalam, 1972.
Bilgrami, Asghar H. *Afghanistan and British India, 1793–1907.* New Delhi: Sterling, 1972.
Boulger, D. C. *England and Russia in Central Asia.* Vol. 1. London: W. H. Allen, 1879.
Braibanti, Ralph. *Research on the Bureaucracy of Pakistan.* Durham: Duke University Press, 1966.
Brines, Russell. *The Indo-Pakistani Conflict.* London: Pall Mall Press, 1968.
Brown, W. Norman. *The United States and India, Pakistan, Bangladesh.* Cambridge, Mass.: Harvard University Press, 1972.
Brussels, University Libre, ed. *The Politics of the Great Powers in the Indian Ocean.* Bruxelles: Centre d'Etude du Sud-East Asiatique et de l'Extreme-Orient, 1971.
Budhraj, Vijay Sen. *Soviet Russia and the Hindustan Subcontinent.* Bombay: Somaiya Publications, 1973.

210 SELECT BIBLIOGRAPHY

Caroe, Olaf. *The Pathans, 550 B.C.–A.D. 1957*. Karachi: Oxford University Press, 1976.
Chaudhri, Mohammed A. *Pakistan and the Regional Pacts*. Karachi: East Publications, 1958.
Chawla, Sudershan, and D. R. SarDesai, eds. *Changing Patterns of Security and Stability in Asia*. New York: Praeger Special Studies, 1980.
Choudhury, G. W. *The Last Days of United Pakistan*. Bloomington: Indiana University Press, 1974.
———. *India, Pakistan, Bangladesh, and the Major Powers: Politics of a Divided Subcontinent*. New York: The Free Press, 1975.
Cottrell, Alvin J., and R. M. Burrell, eds. *The Indian Ocean: Its Political, Economic, and Military Importance*. New York: Praeger, 1972.

Das Gupta, Jyoti. *Jammu and Kashmir*. The Hague: Martinus Nijhoff, 1968.
Douie, Sir James. *The Panjab, North-West Frontier Province and Kashmir*. Delhi: Seema Publications, 1974.
Dupree, Louis. *Afghanistan*. Princeton: Princeton University Press, 1973.

Embree, Ainslie T., ed. *Pakistan's Western Borderlands*. Durham: Carolina Academic Press, 1977.

Ferrier, J. P. *Caravan Journeys and Wanderings in Persia, Afghanistan, Turkistan, and Beloochistan*. Karachi: Oxford University Press, 1976.
Fraser-Tytler, W. K. *Afghanistan: A Study of Political Developments in Central Asia*. London: Oxford University Press, 1950.
Fukuyama, Francis. "The Security of Pakistan: A Trip Report." *A Rand Note*. Santa Monica: The Rand Corporation, 1980.
———. "The Future of the Soviet Role in Afghanistan: A Trip Report." *A Rand Note*. Santa Monica: The Rand Corporation, 1980.

Ghose, Dilip Kumar. *England and Afghanistan: A Phase in Their Relations*. Calcutta: The World Press, 1960.
Gregorian, Vartan. *The Emergence of Modern Afghanistan: Politics of Reform and Modernization, 1880–1946*. Stanford: Stanford University Press, 1969.
Gupta, Sisir. *Kashmir: A Study in India-Pakistan Relations*. Bombay: Asia Publishing House, 1966.

Hasan, Masuma, ed. *Pakistan in a Changing World: Essays in Honour of K. Sarwar Hasan*. Karachi: Pakistan Institute of International Affairs, 1978.

Ikram, S. M. *Muslim Civilization in India*. Ed. by Ainslie T. Embree. New York: Columbia University Press, 1964.

Imam, Zafar. *World Powers in South and South-East Asia: The Politics of Super-Nationalism*. New Delhi: Sterling, 1972.

Ingram, Edward. *The Beginning of the Great Game in Asia, 1828–1834*. Oxford: Clarendon Press, 1979.

Jackson, Robert. *South Asian Crisis*. London: Chatto & Windus, 1975.

Jacobson, Harold Karan, ed. *America's Foreign Policy*. New York: Random House, 1960.

Jafri, Hasan Ali Shah. *Indo-Afghan Relations (1947–67)*. New Delhi: Sterling, 1976.

Jain, R. K., ed. *Soviet South Asian Relations, 1947–1978*. 2 Vols. New Delhi: Radiant, 1978.

Khalilzad, Zalmay. *The Return of the Great Game*. Santa Monica: California Seminar on International Security and Foreign Policy, 1980.

Khan, Mohammad Ayub. *Friends Not Masters*. London: Oxford University Press, 1967.

King, Peter. *Afghanistan: Cockpit in High Asia*. London: Geoffrey Bles, 1966.

Lawrence, Walter Roper. *The India We Served*. London: Cassell and Co., 1928.

Marvin, Charles. *The Russian Advance Towards India*. London: Sampson Low, Marston, Searle & Rivington, 1882.

Mason, Philip (Woodruff). *The Men Who Ruled India*. 2 Vols. New York: St. Martin's Press, 1954.

Mishra, P. K. *India, Pakistan, Nepal and Bangladesh*. Delhi: Sundeep Prakashan, 1979.

Myrdal, Gunnar. *Asian Drama: An Inquiry into the Poverty of Nations*. 3 Vols. New York: Pantheon, 1968.

Nadvi, Rais Ahmad Jafri, ed. *Selections from Mohammad Ali's Comrade*. Lahore: Mohammad Ali Academy, 1965.

Naik, J. A. *India, Russia, China and Bangladesh*. New Delhi: S. Chand, 1972.

Newell, Richard S. *The Politics of Afghanistan*. Ithaca: Cornell University Press, 1972.

Palmer, Norman D. *The Indian Political System*. Boston: Houghton Mifflin, 1971.
Phibbs, Isabelle Mary. *A Visit to the Russians in Central Asia*. London: Kegan, Paul, Trench, Trubner & Co., 1899.
Philips, C. H., ed. *The Evolution of India and Pakistan, 1858 to 1947: Select Documents*. London: Oxford University Press, 1962.
Pirzada, Syed Sharifuddin, ed. *Foundations of Pakistan, All-India Muslim League Documents: 1906–1947*. Vol. I. *1906–1924*. Karachi: National Publishing House, 1969. Vol. II. *1924–1947*. Karachi: National Publishing House, 1970.
Prasad, Bisheshwar. *The Foundations of India's Foreign Policy, 1860–1882*. Delhi: Ranjit Printers & Publishers, 1978.

Razvi, Mujtaba. *The Frontiers of Pakistan*. Karachi: National Publishing House, 1971.
Rizvi, Hasan Askari. *The Soviet Union & the Indo-Pakistan Sub-continent*. Lahore: Progressive Publishers, 1974.
Robertson, Sir George. *Chitral*. London: Methuen, 1898.
Rushbrook Williams, L.F. *Pakistan Under Challenge*. London: Stacey International, 1975.
Russia's March Towards India "by An Indian Officer." 2 Vols. London: Sampson Low, Marston, 1894.

Samra, Chattar Singh. *India and Anglo-Soviet Relations (1917–1947)*. London: Asia Publishing House, 1959.
Sayeed, Khalid B. *The Political System of Pakistan*. Boston: Houghton Mifflin, 1967.
Shah, A. B., ed. *India's Defense and Foreign Policies*. Bombay: Manaktalas, 1966.
Sharma, Shri Ram. *Indian Foreign Policy: Annual Survey: 1972*. New Delhi: Sterling Publishers, 1972.
Singh, Sangat. *Pakistan's Foreign Policy*. London: Asia Publishing House, 1970.
Singhal, D. P. *India and Afghanistan, 1876–1907*. Queensland: University Press, 1963.
Spain, James W. *The People of the Khyber: The Pathans of Pakistan*. New York: Praeger, 1962.
Stein, Arthur. *India and the Soviet Union: The Nehru Era*. Chicago: University of Chicago Press, 1969.
Stephens, Ian. *Horned Moon*. London: Chatto & Windus, 1954.
Stewart, Rhea Talley. *Fire in Afghanistan, 1914–1929*. Garden City, N.Y.: Doubleday & Co., 1973.

Tansky, Leo. *U.S. and U.S.S.R. Aid to Developing Countries*. New York: Praeger, 1967.
Tendulkar, D. G. *Abdul Ghaffar Khan: Faith Is a Battle*. Bombay: Popular Prakashan, 1967.
Tripathi, G. P. *Indo-Afghan Relations, 1882–1907*. New Delhi: Kumar Brothers, 1973.

Vali, Ferenc A. *Politics of the Indian Ocean Region*. New York: The Free Press, 1976.

Wall, Patrick, ed. *The Indian Ocean and the Threat to the West*. London: Stacey International, 1975.
Wheeler, Richard S. *The Politics of Pakistan*. Ithaca: Cornell University Press, 1970.
Wilcox, Wayne A. *Asia and United States Policy*. Englewood Cliffs, N.J.: Prentice-Hall, 1967.
Wolpert, Stanley. *A New History of India*. 2nd Ed. New York: Oxford University Press, 1981.

Ziring, Lawrence, ed. *The Subcontinent in World Politics*. New York: Praeger, 1978.
Ziring, Lawrence, Ralph Braibanti, and W. Howard Wriggins, eds. *Pakistan: The Long View*. Durham: Duke University Press, 1977.
Zutshi, G. L. *Frontier Gandhi*. Delhi: National, 1970.

Index

215